The Politics of Racism in France

The Politics of Racism in France

Peter Fysh

Senior Lecturer in French,
Nottingham Trent University, UK

and

Jim Wolfreys

Lecturer in French Politics,
King's College London, UK

First published 2003 by
PALGRAVE MACMILLAN
Houndmills, Basingstoke, Hampshire RG21 6XS and
175 Fifth Avenue, New York, N.Y. 10010
Companies and representatives throughout the world

PALGRAVE MACMILLAN is the global academic imprint of the Palgrave Macmillan division of St Martin's Press LLC and of Palgrave Macmillan Ltd.
Macmillan® is a registered trademark in the United States, United Kingdom and other countries. Palgrave is a registered trademark in the European Union and other countries.

ISBN 1 4039 0515 0

This book is printed on paper suitable for recycling and made from fully managed and sustained forest sources.

A catalogue record for this book is available from the British Library.

Library of Congress Cataloging-in-Publication Data

10   9   8   7   6   5   4   3   2   1
12   11   10   09   08   07   06   05   04   03

Printed and bound in Great Britain by
Antony Rowe Ltd, Chippenham and Eastbourne

For Peter Morris who helped us both more than we can say and who was tragically taken from us as we were completing this book.

Contents

Acknowledgements

In planning, research and writing this book we incurred debts: to the members of Socialisme International, especially Dard, Hassan, Marie, Nick, Ross and Yveline, for their insights and analyses offered in innumerable discussions extending over many years; to our respective employers, the Nottingham Trent University and King's College London for financial support and valuable relief from teaching; to the staff of the Bibliothèque Nationale, the Bibliothèque de la Fondation Nationale des Sciences Politiques and the Bibliothèque de Documentation Internationale et Contemporaine in Paris; to Martin O'Shaughnessy, for reading and commenting on part of the manuscript, and to Jacques Lambalais and Michel Soudais, for taking the time to share their knowledge and experience with us; and to our friends, Cécile, Christine, David, Dot, Jean-Marc, Megan, Monique, Stéphanie and Yuri, for helping in ways too diverse to detail here.

A list of those people who gave us formal interviews and whose comments form part of the subject matter of the text can be found in the bibliography at the back of the book.

It goes without saying that none of the above are responsible for anything we have written; opinions and the inevitable mistakes are ours alone.

Peter Fysh
Jim Wolfreys
October 1997
November 2002

List of Tables

* Reproduced by permission.

List of abbreviations

AF	Action Française
ANPE	Agence Nationale pour l'Emploi
ATTAC	Association pour une Taxation des Transactions financières pour l'Aide aux Citoyens
CF	Croix de Feu
CFDT	Confédération Française Démocratique du Travail
CFTC	Confédération Française des Travailleurs Chrétiens
CGT	Confédération Générale du Travail
CGT-U	Confédération Générale du Travail-Unitaire
CNC	Cercle National des Combattants
CNCDH	Commission Nationale Consultative des Droits de l'Homme
CNGA	Cercle National des Gens d'Armes
CNIP	Centre National des Indépendants et Paysans
CNPF	Conseil National du Patronat Française
CODAC	Commission d'Accès à la Citoyenneté
DPS	Direction Protection Sécurité
ENA	Etoile Nord-Africaine
FANE	Fédération Nationale d'Action Nationale et Européenne
FASTI	Fédération des Associations de Soutien aux Travailleurs Immigrés
FEN	Fédération des Etudiants Nationalistes
FLN	Front de Libération Nationale
FN	Front National
FNJ	Front National de la Jeunesse
GISTI	Groupe d'Information et de Soutien aux Travailleurs Immigrés
GNR	Groupes Nationalistes Révolutionnaires
GRECE	Groupement de Recherche et d'Etudes pour la Civilisation Européenne
HCI	Haut Conseil à l'Intégration
HLM	Habitation à Loyer Modéré
JALB	Jeunes Arabes de Lyon et sa Banlieue
LCR	Ligue Communiste Révolutionnaire
LICRA	Ligue Internationale Contre le Racisme et l'Antisémitisme

LVF	Légion des Volontaires Français Contre le Bolchévisme
MDC	Mouvement des Citoyens
MJR	Mouvement Jeune Révolution
MNA	Mouvement National Algérien
MNP	Mouvement Nationaliste du Progrès
MNR	Mouvement National Républicain
MOI	Main d'Oeuvre Immigrée
MRAP	Mouvement Contre le Racisme et pour l'Amitié entre les Peuples
MSE	Mouvement Social Européen
MSF	Mouvement Social Français
OAS	Organisation Armée Secrète
ON	Ordre Nouveau
ONI	Office Nationale de l'Immigration
PCF	Parti Communiste Français
PFN	Parti des Forces Nouvelles
PPA	Parti du Peuple Algérien
PPF	Parti Populaire Français
PS	Parti Socialiste
PSF	Parti Social Français
RMI	Revenu Minimum d'Insertion
RNP	Rassemblement National Populaire
RPR	Rassemblement pour la République
SF	Solidarité Française
SFIO	Section Française de l'Internationale Ouvrière
SGI	Société Générale de l'Immigration
SONACOTRA	Société Nationale de Construction pour le logement des Travailleurs
SUD	Solidaire, Unitaire, Démocratique
UDC	Union du Centre
UDCA	Union pour la Défense des Commerçants et Artisans
UDF	Union pour la Démocratie Française
UMP	Union pour la Majorité Présidentielle

1
Introduction

In June 1981, cheering crowds watched the newly elected French President, François Mitterrand, stride into the Pantheon to place red roses on the tombs of Jean Jaurès, the historic leader of French socialism, and Jean Moulin, the Resistance hero. After 23 years of unbroken right-wing rule the left was back, pledging to nationalise industry, create jobs, cut the working week and end discrimination against immigrant workers. While Gaullist and Giscardian conservatives prepared themselves for opposition after their narrow defeat, on the fringes the National Front's motley band of a few hundred fascists, racists and ex-collaborators had failed even to get a presidential campaign off the ground, their leader, a verbose former paratrooper with an eye-patch, unable to find 500 councillors or parliamentarians to sign his nomination. During Mitterrand's first term of office, however, all of France's established political parties were rudely upstaged as the Front won millions of votes in election after election against a backdrop of rising unemployment, poverty and political corruption. After a 40-year career spent defending the Third Reich and its French collaborators, hounding Jews, Communists and trade unionists and fighting to prolong French rule in Vietnam and Algeria, Jean-Marie Le Pen appeared to have abandoned the eye-patch, swapped his combat fatigues for a suit and tie and taken to the parliamentary road.

In the 1980s and 1990s the National Front (NF) became a major player in French politics, helping to split the right-wing vote in presidential and parliamentary elections, sending deputies to the national and European Parliaments and winning control of city governments. The party sunk profound roots into the French political landscape, its thousands of candidates in grassroots local elections attracting a hard core of support in every region. The more insidious social effects of the Front's activities are incalculable; the party took the lead in scapegoating gays for the spread of AIDS, supported attacks on abortion clinics and assaulted opponents on seven occasions during election campaigns between 1986 and 1995, killing three of them (*Le Monde* 24 June 1995). During a decade and a half of relentless progress, although usually confined to the role of isolated and often vilified minority, the Front had a powerful effect on

1

the atmosphere of French politics and the policy process, inducing the mainstream parties to borrow from its racist rhetoric and programme in pursuit of electoral advantage. By the early 1990s the Socialist Edith Cresson and the two main conservative leaders, Jacques Chirac and Valéry Giscard d'Estaing, seemed intent on outbidding each other in demonstrating their 'understanding' of some voters' concerns about what one of them called the immigrant 'invasion'. In government the conservative parties not only amended the asylum law and enacted a battery of new regulations to restrict entry and residence rights, but appeared intent on taking the scapegoating of immigrants to absurd levels prior to being swept out of office in June 1997. The victory of Lionel Jospin's 'plural left' coalition was part of a broader shift to the left among important sections of French society following the development of a grassroots protest movement late in 1995 against conservative plans to reform the social security system. This 'social movement' went on to address a range of issues, not least racism and immigration, during Jospin's term in office, and his record on these questions is assessed in Chapter 8. The new context provided for racists and anti-racists alike after 1995 contributed to a dramatic reversal in fortunes for the Front, so much so that by 1999 the Front had split in two with its chairman, Bruno Mégret, forming a rival party and leaving Le Pen's organisation in some disarray. If this event appeared to confirm, albeit belatedly, analyses which saw the Front as a flash in the pan, such hopes were dashed by the result of the 2002 presidential election when Le Pen won more votes than the Prime Minister, Lionel Jospin, and went on to contest the second round against Chirac.

In view of Le Pen's successes in presidential elections (14.4 per cent of the vote in 1988, 15 per cent in 1995, nearly 17 per cent in 2002), and his alert, resourceful and domineering performances in the television studios, it has sometimes been suggested that the National Front is no more than a one-man band (Charlot 1986; Vaughan 1991), likely to decline in influence were he to leave the scene (Bihr 1992). This dangerous illusion is belied by the fact that National Front supporters always place Le Pen's personality *below* agreement with the party's ideas when ranking the factors which influence their vote, and a higher proportion of survey respondents say they agree with the Front's ideas than are actually prepared to vote for it. What kind of organisation, then, is the National Front?

By the time the first edition of this book appeared in 1998 two books and a number of chapters in English had already given descriptions of the National Front's policies and activities, listing some reasons why its existence is harmful to French democracy. We set ourselves a more rigorously analytic task: to identify what is special about France that could explain why such an organisation should have emerged in the 1980s to occupy such a prominent role in French society. Other countries such as Britain, Germany and Belgium had large Muslim minorities but did not suffer political extremism on a comparable scale, while levels of unemployment comparable to that reached in France existed elsewhere in Europe, along with other indicators of economic crisis, without the same political consequences. We therefore looked beyond the size of the immigrant-origin population in France, or the practice of the Islamic religion to explain the development of the extreme right in France. In any case, as we explain in Chapter 3, contact with immigrants has been shown to be no better indicator of NF voting support than other variables such as poor housing. Despite the obvious relevance of social and economic factors in accounting for the resort to extremism, our explanation of the Front's success in establishing itself as a key political player focuses first and foremost on domestic political causes, which we analyse in terms of two essential variables: the unexpected strength of racism and the failings of anti-racism. We argue that anti-racism in France, when confronted by the rise of the National Front, suffered from two key weaknesses. One was overestimation of the degree to which the principles of political liberty and administrative and cultural uniformity, exalted by the country which has enshrined the 'Rights of Man' in a succession of republican constitutions, would or could guarantee fair and equal treatment of newcomers. The other is an inadequate understanding of the principal racist organisation in France, the National Front.

In Chapter 2, covering the period from the 1880s to the 1970s, we show that the Republic did not even try to offer immigrants the equal treatment implied by its abstract principles; all those who came as workers in response to successive phases of capitalist expansion were offered work permits which kept them tied to specified regions and professions. The Poles were in addition encouraged to maintain the religious and community structures which delayed their full integration into the host society, while the Algerians were officially regarded as 'subjects' with virtually no rights until they conquered their independence in 1962. The bloody nature of the war of liberation and the outbreaks of organised racist violence which were its sequels in turn made a mockery of the frequently repeated official certainty that France was one of the least racist countries on the planet.

Yet the myth of the protective Republic endured. One of the key arguments of our book is that some of the anti-racist movements founded during the 1980s and 1990s and described in Chapter 6, deliberately avoided defending the right to be different (even by so innocuous a practice as covering one's hair), on the grounds that to call into question official uniformity somehow threatened France's democratic institutions. Chapter 6 also illustrates other ways in which anti-racists were handicapped in their efforts either to confront the NF itself, or to fight the incidence of generalised racial discrimination. On the one hand SOS Racisme, which for a while offered the promise of developing into an effective, campaigning, mass-membership youth organisation, was manipulated for short-term gain by its political sponsors. On the other, partly owing to the very success of SOS Racisme, few actors developed a strategy aiming at collaboration between the mainstream left and the grassroots associations of those young citizens of immigrant origin who felt the effects of racism particularly keenly.

The theme of the strength of racism is particularly addressed in Chapters 4 and 5. From the Dreyfus Affair to collaboration with the Third Reich to the Algerian War, French history has thrown up a number of episodes in which a racist extreme right gained imposing strength, threatening indeed to overthrow the Republic. On one level, this historical legacy alone helps account for the strength of contemporary extremism. The question of the nature of a possible affiliation between movements which arose in these quite different historical periods is an important one. While virtually all of the English and some of the French writing on the NF has fought shy of trying to pinpoint its ideological identity and the nature of its political project (Shields 1990; Hainsworth 1992; Birenbaum 1992; Marcus 1995; Soudais 1996), some French writers have been more specific, taking the view that the support for agitators at the end of the nineteenth century, for Marshal Pétain during World War II, and for Jean-Marie Le Pen today, are simply different examples of a recurring French tendency to look for a 'strong leader' at times of crisis, expressed by short-lived movements which combine nationalism, radical anti-parliamentarism and an unhealthy dose of anti-semitism. Broadly speaking, this is what we could call the 'national populist' reading of the National Front (Taguieff 1984, 1986; Milza 1987; Winock 1990).

Although the continued success of Le Pen and his friends into the 1990s led some commentators to question certain aspects of these earlier analyses (Milza 1992; Perrineau 1995a), the influence of the national populist reading on anti-racists in France had two consequences which arguably undermined their efforts to draw others into campaigns against the Front. Firstly, the reduction of the National Front's political success to the fleeting conjunction of passing discontents implied that their neutralisation would quickly see the party disappearing from view. Our analysis of the sources of NF support in Chapter 3 gives reasons for believing that that is not likely to happen. Secondly, a party whose political project is no more than an amalgam of disparate interests is a party without drive or purpose which could be sucked into the parliamentary game, its radicalism blunted by the careerist temptations of its representatives. In the 1980s commentators often based an expectation that this fate awaited the NF on evidence of internal conflict painted as a struggle between 'moderates' and 'hardliners'. A similar argument resurfaced after the 1999 split, with Mégret's new party, the Mouvement National Républicain, thought to be following a more moderate path towards integration into the mainstream establishment than Le Pen's apparently more extremist route, which would eventually take him back to the margins of politics.

In tackling these questions while trying to avoid the vagueness of other writing on the Front, our study of its origins and structure, in Chapters 4 and 5, leads us to reject the premises of the national populist position. Far from being a chance amalgamation of forces with little in common, the Front is the long-planned and carefully nurtured project of a hard core of leaders who identify with a French fascist tradition. Chapter 4 establishes this conclusion by tracing the history of the extreme right in France from the 1940s to the 1970s. But it also covers an earlier period, from the 1880s, in order to illustrate the variety of standpoints from which various groups of counter-revolutionaries have sought to overthrow the Republic. This in turn supports our conclusion, reached at the end of Chapter 4, that, starting from its fascist origins, the Front had by the 1980s achieved an unprecedented organisational fusion of the whole extended family of the French extreme right.

Some commentators, while conceding that this has occurred, have seen internecine rivalry as the primary weakness of the organisation and the reason for its split. In Chapters 5 and 7 we show why this is not so. Chapter 5 examines the structure and ideology of the NF and in Chapter 7 we see how the impact of external pressures, from electoralism to anti-racism, caused these structures to implode. Analysis of a number of doctrinal sources suggests that the spokesmen of the Front's various ideological currents are by no means so dogmatic as might have been expected, and that elements of the sets of ideas which they individually defend are in fact compatible to a degree which allows us to identify a National Front 'doctrine' eclectic enough to keep the currents from falling out yet coherent enough to provide a credible world view and the beginnings of a guide to action. We conclude that the core doctrine of an organisation masquerading as a normal democratic party is anti-egalitarianism, based on the natural selection of racial and social elites, nurtured by 'communities of destiny' in which the individual is seen as no more than a component in a total social whole which satisfies his or her every need. The parallel with the fascist doctrine of the 1930s is inescapable. We also analyse the way in which elements of the Front's doctrine are expressed in the party's propaganda, skilfully adjusted to meet the political conditions of the moment, while some elements are kept hidden, expressed only by means of a 'dual discourse' which allows party spokesmen to maintain the illusion of respectability and yet pass coded messages loaded with elitism and racist venom to their members and supporters.

A crucial part of our argument is that the rallying of different forces to the organisational focus which the Front represents neither blunted the fundamental aims of the fascist core leadership nor blurred their strategic vision of the way in which the Front can be used in pursuit of them. As we wrote in 1992 (Fysh and Wolfreys 1992), the fascist origins of the leadership and their fascist doctrine and strategy, when placed in the context of the crisis afflicting French politics and society together with evidence that the Front's supporters include social categories in economic difficulties with weak links to any existing political tradition, offer so many points of comparison with the organisations which profited from the admittedly much sharper crisis of democracy in the 1930s, that it seems not only legitimate but also necessary to describe the National Front as a fascist organisation. This interpretation is further supported by the fact that, unlike most other parties, it is not only a vote-gathering machine. If its progress down the parliamentary road is visible and recordable, the network of satellite groups and associations binding together its members and sympathisers is less well known. The party's leaders, as they have told us candidly, do not expect to come to power as a result of 'normal' parliamentary competition, but rather thanks to the rallying point which the party would offer during a period of profound social upheaval.

This tension between the party's vision of the road to power and its participation in the electoral process was brought dramatically into focus by the break-up of the organisation in 1999. But the events which led to the split also underlined how the context within which the Front was operating had changed. If the initial emergence and consolidation of the Front can be explained by the particular traditions and circumstances of French history and politics, various developments meant that it became increasingly subject to more general conditions affecting far-right parties across Europe. Of course, as we show in Chapters

7 and 9, these conditions are reflected in specific ways depending on domestic political circumstances, but by the late 1990s a crisis of mainstream politics and institutions was shaping political developments across Europe. The economic impact of neo-liberal globalisation meant that most countries had experienced, to varying degrees, financial deregulation and the privatisation of public services and nationalised industries. While many saw a fall in unemployment, job insecurity and social inequalities remained. Politically, the reconfiguration of relations between nation-states and the global economy intensified debates over European integration, causing divisions to emerge among conservative parties around questions of national sovereignty, while social democratic parties drew the conclusion that the forces of the global market could no longer be arrested by government policy. The gradual emergence of a broad consensus over neo-liberalism contributed to a blurring of the left–right divide, accelerated by the widespread corruption of mainstream parties. Corruption and the apparent lack of clear political alternatives on offer contributed to popular alienation from the electoral process and political institutions. Growing disaffection with the mainstream gave opportunities to the far right in its various guises, from the xenophobic populism of Pim Fortuyn's movement in Holland and the self-styled post-fascism of Gianfranco Fini's National Alliance in Italy to Jörg Haider's Freedom Party in Austria. All of these parties were able to emulate the NF's success in France and gain a foothold in local and, in some cases, national government.

Each of the various organisations of the European far right has adapted to its own national environment. Some, like the late Fortuyn's movement, are closer to right-wing populism than fascism. But as our description of the inter-war extreme right in Chapter 4 illustrates, the divide between conservative nationalism and fascism is not fixed. Populist currents can provide space for fascist groups to flourish while fascist parties can accommodate more conservative elements within their organisation. One major difference between the experience of inter-war fascism and today is that Mussolini and Hitler provided successful examples for other movements to follow. Post-war fascism, as we show in Chapter 4, was forced to adapt this model to a new situation. The parties of the extreme right are now searching for a way of operating under contemporary conditions. Some, like Fini's National Alliance, seized upon the collapse of their domestic party systems in the 1990s to refashion themselves as 'respectable' parties in an attempt to fill the void. Others, like elements of the German and British far right, remain wedded to a less nuanced and more openly racist or violent outlook. Such distinctions reflect the path which the far right is trying to tread between participation in the mainstream via the electoral process and what Le Pen refers to as the building of a 'mass party'. Our account of the Front's 1999 split and its aftermath reveals a party trying to come to terms with the tensions which arise from these conflicting strategic options. In this sense, then, although our starting point is the specific national context of the Front's emergence, the analysis of its origins, structure and strategy can help make sense of other parties in other contexts.

There are elements of our book which take a historical approach. We have turned the clock back sometimes as far as the middle of the nineteenth century in Chapters 2 and 4, in order to delve into elements of French political culture which help to explain present events. Politics is the result, nonetheless, of decisions made and actions undertaken by protagonists of causes in the here and now. We have therefore adopted a very contemporary focus in the rest of the book beginning, in Chapter 3, with a narrative of the period during which racism appeared to infect an entire political class, with little attempt made to stop the epidemic. Political conditions before and after 1988 were quite different. The National Front made its electoral breakthrough in a period dominated by the hopes raised and then dashed by a new Socialist–Communist coalition which briefly held out the hope of a changed world before relapsing into austerity and managerialism. Le Pen and his cohorts were universally regarded as nine-day wonders who could not last. After 1988 we enter a period in which the standing of conventional politicians was brought low by a series of corruption scandals, in which no outgoing government succeeded in winning any of the elections of 1988, 1993 and 1997, and the fortunes of the mainstream parties fluctuated wildly. Successive governments feebly implemented aspects of the National Front's programme while having not the slightest effect on its electoral popularity. As Le Pen himself frequently commented, 'Why vote for the copy, if you can have the real thing?' It took the optimism generated by an unexpected burst of working-class militancy around Christmas 1995, the most powerful since 1968, together with shock at the National Front's ability to win control of city governments, to kindle a series of determined grassroots protests, not only against the Front itself, but also against the xenophobic policies of a conservative government which was swept out of office in June 1997. This backlash against racist scapegoating helped bring the tensions which led to the break-up of the organisation into the open. Therefore, although most of what follows here deals with the disturbing level of success achieved over the past two decades by a modern fascist organisation, grounds for optimism remain. That the Front survived the split and went on to further success, and that its success has been mirrored elsewhere, underlines the importance of understanding such organisations, where they come from and what makes them tick, in order to defeat them. This book aims above all to contribute to that process.

2
The Republic and Her Immigrants

Indisputably, French society has displayed a unique record in the assimilation of foreigners. For roughly 150 years, since the beginning of industrial expansion, hundreds of thousands of those who came originally to escape poverty or persecution in their home countries, have settled down, married and brought forth children and grandchildren who grew up French, so that today between a third and a fifth of all French citizens are thought to be of foreign origin. In this chapter we outline two contrasting explanations of this phenomenal success, suggesting that neither is very useful as an interpretation of the past. This is important because prescriptions for present action continue to be deduced from both of them. According to the conservative Senator, Alain Griotteray,

> The Italians, the Spanish, the Belgians or the Portuguese who have crossed or are still crossing our frontiers have never been completely disoriented: they are European and they are still in Europe: they find the Catholic churches of their own religion, and the men and women who welcome them are after all quite close to their cultures of origin. (Griotteray 1984, pp.103–4)

This hymn to the supposed natural affinity and good relations between the French and their European 'cousins', contrasted with the impact of would-be immigrants belonging to a different 'Islamic world in the throes of a demographic, political and religious revival' (Griotteray 1984, p.115), is echoed by Jean-Marie Le Pen, who wants to distinguish

> ... those foreigners of European origin, who are easy to integrate, and those who come from the third world who are difficult to assimilate both because of their large numbers and because of their specific cultural-religious characteristics which incite them to refuse assimilation ... (Le Pen 1985a, p.112)

For Le Pen and Griotteray, shared culture and history are the keys to successful integration. Their vision of French identity is an ethno-cultural one. They believe that foreigners who come into France should be as much like the French as possible; those who cannot achieve that should be rejected. As we show in Chapters 4 and 5 of this book, this ethno-cultural conception of French identity is part of the doctrine of a powerful anti-democratic current which, when it briefly achieved power in the 1940s, participated in a policy of racial extermination.

A rival and more widely supported version of French identity attributes the success of mass immigration not to the cultural affinity of the people involved but to shared *values* expressed by allegiance to a republic which offers citizenship to anyone who would accept the principles of fraternity, equality and political liberty. First thrown up in the revolutionary upheaval of 1789–99, this principle was powerfully reasserted in the 1880s by political and intellectual elites who needed to find a justification for demanding the return of Alsace-Lorraine, annexed by Prussia in 1871 and attached on ethno-cultural grounds to the German empire (Noiriel 1992, pp.5–43). Followers of this tradition see the elective 'republican' model of voluntarily chosen citizenship as the key to the efficiency of the French melting-pot, commonly conflating France's unique *record* of successful assimilation and her supposed unique *capacity* for it. This orthodoxy has been given an official seal of approval by the High Council for Integration (HCI):

> It must be stressed, that this *French model of integration* [emphasis in the original] is inspired by a system of thought which rejects the determinisms of ethnicity, class and religion and is based on a collective desire to live up to the past, and especially to work together for common aims and ambitions. (Zylberstein 1993, p.8)

Ironically, however, the republican model of integration is no less demanding of cultural conformity than the ethno-cultural model. In order to secure their victory, the revolutionaries of 1789 pursued a policy of stamping out all vestiges of provincial or corporate autonomy, preventing any mediating institutions from filtering the loyalty owed by the citizen directly to the state. In the contemporary context, that means ethnic organisation is out, or again in the words of the HCI:

> ... permanent community structures are not compatible with the deeply rooted character of our country which, inspired by the principles of the Declaration of the Rights of Man, affirms the equality of men over and above their cultural diversity. (Zylberstein 1993, p.9)

Although conceptually distinct, the republican and ethno-cultural approaches do not exclude each other. The republican tradition has been around for so long that ethno-culturalists are able to claim it as part of French 'culture' while paying scant attention to its meaning. Armed with ritual references to the Rights of Man, pundits of right, left and centre have often combined to thrust the duty of conformity fairly and squarely on the shoulders of newly arriving immigrants. Griotteray, Pasqua (1992, pp.25–8) and de Villiers (1994, pp.83–101) are hostile to cultural practices which deviate from their own preferred European 'norm', warning that recognition of ethnically organised interest groups would result in a 'communitarianism' corrosive of national unity. Yet one of the most telling attacks on cultural difference has been made by Badinter, Debray, Finkielkraut and other 'left-wing' intellectuals who in 1989 claimed that a tiny number of schoolgirls wishing to cover their hair in obedience to a precept of their Muslim religion threatened to destroy the role of the education system as an agent of republican socialisation (*Nouvel Observateur* 2 November 1989). Among the supporters of Badinter and her friends were even a number of organisations consciously identifying themselves as anti-racist. One of the central themes of this book will be the counterpoint between the powerful revival of the ethno-culturalist tradition, thanks to Jean-Marie Le Pen's National Front, and the failure of anti-racists to challenge that revival, thanks to a republican uniformism which leads them to refuse to defend the right to ethnic and cultural difference.

This chapter is a record of 130 years of immigration, from about 1850 to about 1980. While it tries to remember that immigrants were also the subjects and not just passive victims of their own history, its framework is a series of political and economic contexts which, we suggest, were much more decisive in structuring the immigrants' reception than the two interpretative traditions outlined. Far from blending smoothly and painlessly with their French cousins, European immigrants were often greeted with indifference, rejection or outright violence. Cultural affinity made little headway against parochialism and the hard facts of competition for jobs in contexts which ranged from the very formation of the industrial working class, through the inter-war depression to war, resistance and the Cold War. The experience of north African migrants, to whom we turn in the second half of the chapter, needs to be linked to decolonisation, the optimism of the post-May '68 period and the ending of the post-war boom.

1850–1918, the formation of the working class and the consolidation of the Third Republic

The take-off of industrial capitalism encountered obstacles in France which were not present in Britain. The French peasants had long limited the size of their families so as to minimise the division of family property when it was passed on from one generation to the next. Population was so static that French agriculture employed at least 100,000 foreign seasonal workers a year for a century until after World War II. Until the railways began to destabilise craft-based micro-economies in the 1890s, by bringing cheaper mass-produced goods to previously remote areas, country-dwellers had little motive or desire to go to the textile centres of Rouen, Lille and Lyons, which were reproducing the desperately long hours of child labour, the promiscuity, the poor sanitation, accidents, disease and mortality familiar in Britain. Even when industrialists responded by siting their enterprises in rural areas, the locals proved an ill-disciplined workforce, prone to absenteeism and ready to leave the workshop in the middle of the day to tend their fields (Noiriel 1990).

The gap was filled by foreigners, whose ability to manage on modest incomes was noted approvingly by the Paris Chamber of Commerce as early as 1847. By the 1851 census they numbered 378,561, concentrated mostly in Paris and the frontier departments, in building, agriculture, textiles and mining. They numbered half a million in 1861, three-quarters of a million in 1872, a million in 1881 – altogether 2.6 per cent of the population in these early years of the Third Republic; of this number half were Belgian and just over a quarter from Italy. At a time when the term 'foreigner' as likely designated someone from another province as from another country, the last thing the pioneer migrants had to worry about was whether their papers were in order. On the other hand, when times were bad, outsiders of whatever origin were instinctively viewed as dangerous rivals for work or an extra bargaining counter on the side of the employers, even if they were not actually strike-breakers. The failed harvest and hardships of 1847/48 set off disturbances amongst the miners of Languedoc and in the Alps, whence the Piedmontese were forced to flee along with their wives and children. Demonstrations to the cry of 'Down with foreigners' took place in Paris and five other departments (Wihtol de Wenden 1988, pp.18–19). The long depression of the 1880s and 1890s saw hundreds of Belgian miners attacked and forced to flee from the Pas-de-Calais, abandoning homes and furniture in their wake, as well as a series of battles between French and Italians in the south. Several hundred Italians fled from Marseilles in June 1881 after being pursued by mobs which tried to force them to shout 'Vive la République!' In 1893 at Aigues-Mortes, in the Gard, a mob broke through a police cordon which was attempting to escort 80 Italians out of the town, beating their victims to death with shovels and improvised clubs (Wihtol de Wenden 1988, p.20; Noiriel 1988, pp.258–61).

In this context, the debate which began in the pages of the *Economiste Français* pitting free-movement liberals against those who would reserve 'French jobs for French workers' led to the piecemeal adoption of a set of legal regulations which was neither rigorously exclusionary nor imbued with republican generosity but a patchwork, reflecting the play of rival interests rather than a rational and uniform master-plan. In 1889 a new nationality law imposed French citizenship on all those born in France with at least one parent also born in France. A century later, some claimed this *droit du sol* as a particularly generous feature of the republican model, but at the time generosity was not an issue; worried by the low French birth rate which left the army being steadily outnumbered by the Prussians who had defeated them in 1870 and were still occupying Alsace and part of Lorraine, the legislators were concerned above all to end the 'abuse' which allowed the children of foreigners raised in France to escape military service. Weil (1996) has pointed out how successive amendments to the nationality law have taken ever more account of length of residence in France, seen as a rough measure of socialisation. In reality, only a tiny fraction of those who have French citizenship voluntarily opted for it in the manner prescribed by the 'republican model'.

In employment, the trade unions – dominated by an 'aristocracy' of craftsmen – persuaded the government to adopt a quota policy in public works projects. Barristers managed to exclude foreigners from their ranks entirely and after an intense lobbying campaign, doctors – soon followed by dentists and midwives – succeeded in barring those who did not hold French qualifications. One by one the private railway companies, ostensibly on 'security' grounds, began a purge of their foreign employees, later established in law when the railways were merged and nationalised and the privilege of state employment was restricted to French citizens only. In recounting these 'victories' of the 1890s, Noiriel (1988, pp.280–3) suggests that the growing atmosphere of exclusionism suited the needs of politicians who, in order to stimulate participation in the national political battles of the gradually stabilising Third Republic, sought to create a sense of the 'national' where previously only the regional or parochial existed. Social legislation likewise reflected the Republic's ambiguous attitude towards those on whom it was coming to depend but could not bring itself to love. French and foreigners were treated identically by the laws of 1892 and 1900 limiting the working week of women and children, as by measures of 1893 and 1906 laying down some elementary safety rules and prescribing a period of weekly rest, but foreigners were barred from positions of responsibility in trade unions, insurance funds and grievance arbitration panels. They were likewise refused free medical assistance, barred from public hospitals and excluded by a 1905 law from assistance offered to the old and infirm. An 1898 law on compensation for accidents at work was interpreted to prevent families living abroad from receiving benefits and to cut off benefits from handicapped workers who themselves returned home. Most of these dis-criminations were not abolished until the 1970s and 1980s. Some, such as the right to sit on industrial tribunals, have never been abolished. The most basic discrimination of all became in time standard practice – the issuing of work permits only for specified regions or industries (Noiriel 1988, pp.111–16).

Escaping oppression: Jewish workers of the *belle epoque*

The foreign population was swelled at the turn of the century by the arrival in France of 100,000 of the three and a half million Jews fleeing the pogroms of Russia and central Europe. Ironically, they did not get a much warmer welcome from their co-religionists than did the Italians or Belgians. Some of the half-million-strong indigenous Jewish population, enjoying political and religious liberties since the Revolution and with a socio-occupational profile matching that of the French population as a whole, could not help referring to the poor, often unhealthy, working-class, yiddish-speaking refugees as 'parasites' (Green 1985, pp.84–107). To the French, the newcomers were not only outlandish figures from another world but also dangerous subversives, who continued in exile their combat against Tsarist despotism mainly via the famous *Bund*, the General Union of Jewish workers of Russia and Poland. Their arrival, coinciding with a period of political and social crisis in which the Republic itself was momentarily threatened, swelled the current of existing anti-semitism to a flood which burst out during the Dreyfus Affair into a series of mob attacks which had all the characteristics of a pogrom (see Chapter 4). The Jews responded like all immigrants by forming a series of self-help societies, mainly insurance funds and employment agencies, as well as developing an active cultural life with a number of yiddish theatres and newspapers, and organising their religious life in a decentralised network of prayer-rooms independent of the established consistory of French

Jews. The Parisian clothing industry, in which the immigrants were largely employed, offered plenty of challenges to their collaboration with their French fellow workers: the continual arrival of new refugees who were always at first potential strike-breakers, the difficulty of understanding each others' languages, the pattern of subcontracting which exerted a permanent pressure on sweat-shop owners to cut piece-rates as low as possible, the close-season which threw thousands out of work for a few months every year. Bundist autonomist ideology and their own strong community ties led Jewish workers to organise their own newspaper, the *Idisher Arbayter*, and independent trade sections which affiliated to the Confédération Générale du Travail (CGT). Their struggles radicalised by echoes from the Russian revolution of 1905, the Jewish rank and file were often criticised by the French leadership of the confederation for being too militant and for producing political programmes which clashed with the CGT's strictly syndicalist ideology. But the French movement also gave much practical support, such as turning over the Bourse du Travail for meetings, paying for leaflets and contributing articles to the *Idisher Arbayter* (Green 1985, pp.190–240).

These poor Jewish immigrants, whose chaotic, polyglot struggles belong to a vanished era, may have contributed as much to republican values as they profited by them, by helping to neutralise the anti-semitism then still habitual among the French left. While indigenous Jews remained silent they organised a meeting of solidarity with the imprisoned Captain Dreyfus, wrongly accused of spying for the Germans, and despatched an open letter to French Socialists criticising their failure to take up a case which some of them dismissed as a mere squabble between factions of the bourgeoisie. It was partly as a result of these initiatives that the great Socialist leader Jaurès abandoned his neutrality, condemned anti-semitism and began to draw attention to its prevalence in French-occupied north Africa. A decade later, in 1911, nearly 2000 Jewish workers held a meeting of protest at the Bourse du Travail after an electricians' union leader used the word 'Jew' in a derogatory fashion during a strike of railway workers in a company largely owned by the Rothschilds. It was the ensuing sharp polemic which led French trade unionists gradually to abandon their practice of routinely using 'Jew' as an insulting synonym for finance capital (Green 1985, pp.229–34).

The 1920s, demographic crisis and industrial expansion

The carnage of the Great War and the rapid expansion of industry led French employers in 1924 to set up the Société Générale de l'Immigration

(SGI), a company which organised medical screening and doled out work contracts in no less than twelve European countries, allegedly making 80 francs on every one of the 500,000 workers it brought into the country between 1924 and 1930, a cool 40 million franc profit all told (Schor 1985, pp.213–20). Even so, the SGI is thought only to have issued contracts to 35 per cent of the foreigners who came to France in the 1920s, the rest either coming of their own accord or being the victims of various scams which deposited them in France with false papers and imaginary work contracts. Most, in any case, were 'regularised' when they found work (Weil 1995, p.32). Between 1911 and 1931 the number of Italians doubled to peak at 800,000, 28 per cent of the foreign population; during the 1920s nearly half a million Poles arrived, becoming the second largest group with 17.5 per cent of the total, with the Spanish taking third place and the Belgians relegated from second to fourth (Noiriel 1992, p.70). The total number of foreigners in France was now over 4 million, a record 6.59 per cent of the population. More of them worked in agriculture than in any other industry, yet they represented only 3.2 per cent of the agricultural workforce, for France was still a country in which nearly half the population worked on the land. In contrast, on the eve of the depression, in construction (29 per cent of the workforce), heavy metals (38 per cent) and mining (42 per cent), the foreigners appeared indispensable (Noiriel 1990, p.121).

From the beginning, the overcrowding in the industrial districts exposed the newcomers to charges that they spread disease. In 1905 the Professor of Law at Nancy University stigmatised the thousands of Italians crowded into cellars, attics and makeshift wooden sheds lining the roads in the Lorraine valleys as a danger to the French 'race', vagabonds living on the margins of health and morality, and endowed with extraordinary sexual powers. In the same year the local newspaper targeted the Italians' 'strange concoctions', 'deplorable way of life' and 'chronic filth' (Noiriel 1984, pp.173–85; 1988, pp.158–70). An outbreak of smallpox in Toul in 1922, certainly due to the unspeakable conditions in which incoming Poles were subjected to rudimentary medical examinations, was blamed by the local mayor on 'these nomads, of various degrees of cleanliness' who were repugnant to French people. After disease, the immigrants were blamed for crime and terrorism. The activities of a gang of thieves operating in northern France, finally brought to justice in 1927, fuelled regular newspaper columns devoted to the 'foreign bandits' (Schor 1985, pp.420–2), as did the assassinations of the President of the Republic by a mad Russian in 1932 and of the Foreign Secretary, blown up in the company of the King of Yugoslavia, in 1934. While the most imaginative stereotyping was the work of the extreme right, led by Georges Gaudy of the Action Française – who in 1933 confessed himself unable to distinguish between '... a degenerate Italian, a Semite, a cross-bred Argentine ... These creatures, viscous as an octopus, soft as a sponge, would, if you squeezed them, discharge nothing but pus' (cited in Schor 1985, p.181) – an exhaustive study of the press by an extremely attentive observer left him hard put to discern 'any difference of tone or vocabulary' (Schor 1985, p.433) between these sheets and others such as the mainstream Radical *L'Oeuvre* which, in 1925, attacked the 'thousands' of Spaniards, '... who vegetate with their priests, their customs, their jumping, climbing and clinging insects, their naïve and innocent ignorance of the most elementary precepts of hygiene' (cited in Schor 1985, p.424).

Distinctive regional contexts allowed some groups to escape such insults. Police reported that a 50,000-strong Italian farming community in the hitherto depopulated south-west enjoyed the 'confidence' and 'esteem' of their neighbours, who could only approve of the newcomers' contribution to a revival of the local economy which saw the price of their own holdings rise to four or five times its 1914 level (Schor 1985, pp.437–47). In the Alpes-Maritimes, where the proportion of Italians in the local population grew from a quarter to as much as a third during the inter-war period, neighbouring fascist Italy and its consulate actively dissuaded their subjects from adopting French nationality, language or customs because it suited them to keep alive the notion that Nice and the surrounding area were historically Italian lands. The local French extreme right, for whom Mussolini was a model and a potential ally, appeared curiously unworried by the threat which diseased and criminal aliens posed to French civilisation, proclaiming that their friendship for Italy was so great that they desired only to abolish the frontier between the two nations. Nonetheless, the atmosphere was frequently uneasy since the local Radicals liked to portray the Italians, most of whom were poor, as competitors for scarce jobs or, at moments of international tension, raise a panic by casting them as potential saboteurs in the event of invasion (Schor 1985, pp.377–85).

For those immigrants who needed help to settle into their new way of life, it was not the institutions of the Republic which were the dominant influence, but their employers, in collaboration with the government of their home country. The coal owners' lack of interest in seeing their new miners integrated into French society was underlined by the agreements they signed in 1919 and 1924 with the Polish government and episcopate, allowing native priests and teachers to accompany the recruits, helping sustain their native language and fervent Catholicism, although the latter hardly assisted their assimilation into the local society since the workers of the Nord and Pas-de-Calais were largely dechristianised (Ponty 1995, p.42). The managers of the Longwy steelworks collaborated with the Polish consulate in Strasbourg in setting up a Polish musical society and scout troop and in reserving a section of the local library for Polish books (Noiriel 1984, p.203, n.102). Since they mainly came as whole families, the Poles were lodged in the company housing traditionally provided by the coal and iron bosses in their permanent struggle to recruit and hang on to labour. Thanks to this ready-made concentration, especially in the famous *corons* of the coal districts, Polish families made up as much as 20 per cent of the population of an *arrondissement* like Béthune, often 40–45 per cent of the mining communes and 70–80 per cent of the families in the streets of the *corons*. In these circumstances they developed a richer community life than any other group of immigrants, with some 500 associations covering 100,000 members. They had their own churches, cafés and food shops, their own radio station and two daily newspapers (Ponty 1995, pp.26, 42; Noiriel 1988, pp.180–4). In this reconstituted homeland, republican pressure on the Poles to abandon their ethnic organisation was limited to the sardonic comments on their style of dress offered by the knots of French who used to gather to watch them preparing to go down the pit.

The employers' 'divide and rule' tactics were scarcely challenged by the CGT, which in the early 1920s stigmatised foreign workers in the frontier region of Lorraine as a danger to national security and led demands for a block on foreign recruitment in the building industry. Its 1924 conference accepted a motion calling for a halt to immigration but added rather lamely that this should be achieved by fraternally persuading would-be immigrants not to leave their own countries. In the Communist-led CGT-Unitaire (CGT-U), which had split from its reformist rival just after the war, pressure from building trades delegates in Paris and Marseilles – the latter boasting of dealing with competition from 'colonial' labour by throwing the 'wogs' into the dock – forced their leaders to concede in 1926 that xenophobia was rising rapidly 'even in CGT-U ranks'. Nonetheless, they stuck to their revolutionary positions, demanding open borders and the free movement of labour instead of organised recruitment, which allowed the employers to eliminate known militants and choose only those who seemed the most docile (Schor 1985, pp.449–61; Gallissot *et al.* 1994, pp.43–6). A CGT-U network of special 'language groups' with their own newspapers seeking to draw foreign workers into struggle, met with only modest success, recruiting an estimated 12,000 Italians and 2500 Poles at best during the 1920s (Schor 1985, pp.59–61) and failing to build permanent bridges with indigenous workers. Militancy was liveliest in the iron mines of Lorraine, where the border with Luxembourg, the chaotic physical environment and the permanent construction sites provided a fall-back to those sacked from the mines or the steelworks. Even here, however, every outburst of militancy was followed by a wave of sackings and expulsions, with the Lorraine branches of the CGT-U sometimes reduced to rumps consisting almost entirely of foreign workers. The most ardent of the anti-fascist exiles, furthermore, often preferred to organise on their own in sections of the Italian Communist or Socialist parties (Noiriel 1984, pp.234–9).

The depression, the rise of Nazism and the Popular Front

The coincidence of the depression with the arrival of Jewish refugees from Nazi Germany triggered a massive rise in the number of press articles debating the place of foreign workers in French society. The extreme right's simple and oft-repeated demonstration that it was necessary to expel, from among the 1.2 million foreign workers (in 1933), a number equivalent to the 400,000 unemployed, found the left divided. While some objected on moral grounds to tossing away human beings as if they were commodities or, more pragmatically, highlighted the non-substitutability of different types of labour and the likely effect on the demand for goods and services, others were seduced by the idea of voluntary repatriation, paid for by the state. The Communists and the CGT-U maintained their 'open border' position until 1936, arguing that the way to tackle unemployment was by banning overtime, cutting the working week and bringing forward retirements (Schor 1985, pp.581–7). But throughout the period from 1922 to 1935 the divided workers' movement was on the defensive. Building workers complained that the foreigners engaged to help build the Maginot line were possible spies; French musicians went up and down the Paris boulevards invading concert halls where foreign orchestras were playing. In 1931 there were repeated battles in the northern textile districts between French strikers and Belgian scabs (Schor 1985, pp.559–62).

The employers in the heavy industrial regions, who had a stranglehold over local utilities, were able to insulate their workers from the influence of agitators by putting uniformed guards on the company housing estates and threatening to cut off electricity and water not only from the houses of those of their own workers who did not give satisfaction, but even from cafés which offered rooms for Communist meetings (Noiriel 1984, p.196).

Everywhere, the price to be paid for militancy was the sack, with a good chance of it being followed by expulsion. In the five years after the great depression began to bite in 1931, 23,000 (one-third of the workforce) were laid off and deported from the Longwy mines and steelworks alone, following a procedure worked out by the employers and the prefecture: single foreign men first, then married foreigners, followed by single Frenchmen, and then the rest (Noiriel 1984, pp.234, 267–70). In the coal districts of the Nord and Pas-de-Calais, the disastrous consequences of conflict between the CGT and the CGT-U were demonstrated at Leforest in 1934, where the CGT denounced a pit occupation organised by the rival confederation as an attempt to exploit the workers' misery for political ends, claiming that a number of French workers were being held against their will by more militant Poles. The defeat of this action accelerated the flight or repatriation by the trainload of over 120,000 Poles, amid the indifference of their former neighbours and colleagues, republican egalitarianism ensuring only that no account was taken of the length of stay in France and that every victim was limited to a maximum 30 kilos of luggage (Schor 1985, pp.574–5; Ponty 1990, pp.304–14). The policy of expelling redundant labour became official from the end of 1934 when a right-wing government signalled its arrival in office by imposing quotas in 533 occupations before routinely denying the renewal of permits to those who had been in France less than ten years if they worked in a sector affected by unemployment. Altogether it is estimated that as many as one-third of all adult male immigrants were repatriated during the 1930s (Magraw 1992, p.254).

Once again the middle classes were at the heart of the battle. A series of strikes and demonstrations by medical students – during one of which a Jewish student was lynched – targeted the nearly 4000 foreigners in their midst who, it was feared, might apply for naturalisation given a relaxation of the law in 1927 and the shadow which Nazi rule in Germany cast over central Europe. In 1933 exercise of the medical profession was limited to those of French nationality, after a long campaign to convince the public of the dangerous incompetence of foreign doctors, and soon all newly naturalised citizens were barred from applying for a job in the public sector for at least five years after their acquisition of French nationality – a restriction also obtained by the barristers and aimed against the 300 Germans finishing their law studies in 1935 (Noiriel 1988, pp.284–7).

But the Nazis' threat to the European balance of power gave the French Republic another chance to demonstrate its commitment to the human rights of the foreigners who found their way for whatever reasons on to its territory. Abandoning his suicidal policy of treating Social Democrats and Nazis indistinguishably as enemies of Communism, Stalin opened the way for the Communists to go to the polls in alliance with Socialists and Radicals on a modest programme for 'bread, freedom and peace', resulting in the election of the 'Popular Front' government in June 1936 amid the biggest general strike yet seen in France. Pinning their hopes on a government headed by a Jewish Socialist, Léon Blum, foreign workers joined in strikes and demonstrations in greater numbers than ever before, turning *en masse* to the reunified CGT, in which their numbers rose from 50,000 (1 in 15) in March 1936 to between 350,000 and 400,000 (1 in 8) in the autumn of 1938 (Schor 1985, p.639; Gallissot *et al.* 1994, pp.47–8). Extreme-right pamphleteers lost no time in venting with masochistic delight their outrage at the alleged collaboration of three of their traditional hate figures, the Jews, the Socialists and the foreign workers. While one 'revealed' that the strikes were fomented by agents specially sent from Spain, Germany and Russia, and another lambasted Blum, 'come from a wandering race, ... head of a people foreign to his flesh' (cited in Schor 1985, p.647; pp.639–40), a third accused the government of helping its friends and supporters by 'systematic naturalisation of the dregs of the cosmopolitan underworld', fabricating French citizens from 'Italian dregs, Russian mould and German dung, which results in a strange species, neither man nor beast' (cited in Schor 1985, pp.649–50).

Indeed, an amendment to the naturalisation law in 1927 had reduced the residence qualification from ten years to three. But expanding the number of candidatures did not necessarily mean that acceptances would rise in proportion. The high cost, the poverty of many potential applicants, the lengthy procedure and the prejudice of the officials in charge combined to ensure that, after a spurt from an average 5000 a year before 1927 to about 25,000 afterwards, the annual number of naturalisations fell back to 15,000 by the mid-1930s and was unaffected by the year-long tenure of the Popular Front government (Schor 1985, pp.534–43; Gallissot *et al.* 1994, pp.38–9). Spurred by the League for the Rights of Man and the Socialist left wing, Blum's government did relax the general surveillance of foreign workers, doing its best to welcome German refugees from Hitler (Livian 1982), but in other respects it fell short of the hopes which friends of the foreign workers had placed in it. No move was made to repeal the quota system activated in 1934, while employers who took on foreign workers were subjected to a special tax. The Minister of Agriculture, Georges Monnet, a close friend of Blum, set about reducing the number of foreign land-workers, while demands that a junior minister be made responsible for implementing the CGT's idea for a common legal 'status' went unanswered. Succeeding ministers of the interior insisted that foreign workers should not get involved in politics or industrial disputes (a group were expelled in August 1936 for just that) and did everything they could to prevent refugees from the Spanish Civil War crossing the frontier.

War, resistance and the Cold War

On the eve of war an opportunistic policy of mass naturalisations was launched at last, with 73,000, mainly Italians, obtaining citizenship in 1939 and another 43,000 in the first half of 1940 (Weil 1995, pp.52–3). But the Republic, now led by Daladier, did not drop its guard completely, taking powers to reverse the naturalisation of anyone whose actions, committed 'at whatever date', were 'disapproved of by the government', and promptly interning the 200,000 or so Spanish Republican militiamen who eventually did enter France in the last days of January 1939. The men were held for several months in 15 concentration camps, some of them no more than barbed-wire enclosures of parts of the Atlantic beach, where many died of typhus and were buried in the sand. Meanwhile, the women, children and old people were reduced to burning the furniture to keep warm in a collection of barracks, convents and disused châteaux. The impression caused by this reception doubtless contributed to the reputation gained by the Spaniards in later years of being those foreigners most concerned with home-country affairs and indifferent to what was happening in France (Schor 1985, pp.673–94).

When war was declared 80,000 Poles and 12,000 Czechs and Slovaks formed their own army units in co-operation with the French authorities, while Jews and Hungarians called for enrolment in the French army. Germans, Italians and Spanish, rejected by the regular army, were allowed into the Foreign Legion. In the event, following the stunning Nazi *Blitzkrieg* and the beginning of the occupation, many foreign demobbed soldiers or escaped prisoners found their way into armed resistance, the Communists among them structured by the pre-war 'language groups' known collectively as the Main d'Oeuvre Immigré (MOI), and soon reinforced by Jewish youths left orphaned by the Vichy militia's swoops on their family members (Vichy collaboration in the Holocaust is discussed in Chapter 4). In the steel districts of Lorraine, the collaboration between the Vichy authorities, the Italian consulate and the French employers in banning the unions, persecuting and deporting militants and restarting production for the Nazi war machine left only the Communists seeming to defend 'France'. The war achieved what the struggles of the inter-war years could not – the creation of an enduring solidarity between French and Italian workers; for the first time the Italians felt no contradiction in declaring themselves Communist *and* French and many threw themselves into acts of sabotage all over France. For several months in 1943, when the French Communists' own armed groups had been immobilised by captures, the MOI formed the only effective combat units in the capital, carrying out one attack every two days. Captured, imprisoned, tortured and ultimately executed, many left in their letters moving testimonies of their attachment to France and their faith in the ultimate triumph of the republican values of democracy and freedom (Courtois *et al.* 1989; Noiriel 1984, pp.312–16). At the Liberation, with foreign resistants posthumously honoured by de Gaulle's provisional government and their exploits told and re-told by the Communist press, the Republic seemed to live again for three short years the universalist ideals of 1793.

Then came the Cold War and accusations that the Communists were fomenting industrial disputes for the benefit of a foreign power. During six years of strikes in the steel industry, starting in 1948, mostly in pursuit of higher pay and shorter hours, workers of foreign origin took the brunt of the repression. Naturalised Italians now appearing regularly in each group of CGT officials were dismissed, recent service in the cause of the Rights of Man counting for nothing in their defence (Noiriel 1984, pp.323–4). In 1948 the Italian immigrants' organisation, Italia Libera, was banned for supporting a long and bitter miners' strike and its leaders again plunged into clandestinity. The police of the Fourth Republic spent three years tracking Carlo Fabra, holder of the Croix de Guerre and Médaille de la Résistance, finally deporting him to his home country in 1951 (Courtois *et al.* 1989, pp.415–16). Most tragically of all for these workers who had given their all for an internationalist ideal, their own side deliberately omitted for many years to honour their sacrifice. In the poisonous Cold War atmosphere which enveloped French political and intellectual life in the 1950s and 1960s, the French Communist Party, desperate to prove its patriotic credentials, recalled its contribution to the resistance via regular editions of a book of 'Letters of Executed Communists' – from whose ranks all foreigners were rigorously excluded until the mid-1980s (Courtois *et al.* 1989). Fraternity, one of the Republic's highest ideals, had become a source of shame.

What does this all too brief survey of a century of European migration tell us about the processes of immigration and integration in French society? Firstly, it is clear that there is no such thing as integration into the abstract category of 'Frenchman'; immigrants are not integrated into 'high' French culture but into a subculture defined by class and region, so that many Italian steelworkers became 'Lorrainers' while thousands of Poles became part of the 'extended family of miners'. Indeed in 1954, 30 years after they first began to arrive, 80 per cent of Poles in France were still workers, compared to no more than 40 per cent of the population as a whole (Tripier 1990, pp.42–55). Secondly, integration, such as it was, was achieved in the teeth of economic and social discrimination which the abstract political rights of the Republic did little to alleviate, governments even collaborating in the expulsion of those who had become surplus to requirements. Thirdly, ethnic community organisation, like that enjoyed by the Poles in the Nord and Pas-de-Calais, was neither a threat to the Republic nor a barrier to the acquisition of French culture by the descendants of the primo-migrants. The Poles provide a perfect example of the way in which individuals can acquire and function adequately in two or more cultures simultaneously. Finally, for those who won and clung to some sort of acceptance, the key republican institutions of army and school were hardly decisive factors in their success, for both primo-migrants and many of their children avoided naturalisation and army service if they could; compulsory primary education was not applied to foreigners until 1936 and a strategy of progression through the network of *écoles normales* to become teachers, the classic route of social progress for workers and peasants, was barred to them until they had obtained French nationality. In short neither the 'ethno-cultural' nor the 'republican' models of integration seem to apply to the experience of European immigrants in France. Their welcome, like that of the thousands of Italians who became 'French' through activism in the Communist Party and the trade unions, depended on the shifting conjuncture of successive economic and political contexts. As we see next, more or less the same thing applied to those who came from further afield.

North Africans in France: unwilling 'subjects' of the Republic

When the Ministry of Munitions made up the labour shortage in the armaments factories during World War I by importing tens of thousands of workers from north Africa and Indochina, it introduced a new category of migrant which fitted ill with the republican model of elective citizenship. Neither foreigners nor citizens, France's Algerian 'subjects' had no vote, were not allowed to hold meetings, edit newspapers or contest the colonial power. Nor could they move to metropolitan France without a special permit, often refused by the colonial authorities for fear that local labour would become scarcer and dearer (Ageron 1964). Nonetheless, the pioneers of the war years formed the nuclei around which later arriving friends and family members would gather. On the eve of World War II, there were around 120,000 north African workers in France, 70,000 of them in the Paris region. The appalling conditions endured by some mirrored those experienced by the Italians at the turn of the century; by 1937 they formed 10 per cent of the workforce in the steelworks and iron mines of Lorraine, many preferring to live in the woods rather than the filthy sheds or disused wine-cellars offered for rent (Noiriel 1984, pp.306–7). That some of those called up in 1914–18, among them the future nationalist leader Messali Hadj, were touched by the respect and generosity shown to them by the people of metropolitan France said a lot about the style of the colonial regime back home. In the 1920s, as workers in the building industry or the factories of the burgeoning Parisian industrial belt, Messali and his comrades discovered the art of trade union organisation, journalism and political debate and it was no accident, given their doubly discriminated status, that their first autonomous organisation, the Etoile Nord-Africaine (ENA), founded in 1924 with the help of the Communist Party, adopted a combined programme of workers' action and revolutionary nationalism. Banned in 1929, the ENA was re-founded in 1933 independently of the Communists and from then on concerned itself primarily with the national question, exploiting the network of Arab-owned cafés to sell its newspaper and other propaganda, which it also endeavoured to post to likely sympathisers back home (Stora 1992a).

The republican authorities were uncertain how to deal with this new variety of migrant. A student hostel functioned briefly in the capital but closed in 1935 when its inmates proved too political. A Muslim hospital was eventually opened in 1935 in Bobigny, after a number of communes refused to have it on their territory, the first Muslim cemetery following a year later. From the mid-1920s Paris and a number of provincial cities created offices for 'north African native affairs' with the task of helping migrants to find work and lodgings and deal with paperwork, but charged also with surveillance and expulsion of undesirables, provoking the Socialist Magdeleine Paz to query the merits of a paternalist policy aiming at the 'protection' of a subject population by means of 'spying, corruption, crude police methods, the whole lot associated with the most abominable racial prejudice ...' (Schor 1985, pp.520–2). Meanwhile the ENA campaigned against the construction of the 'official' Paris mosque, completed in 1926 with the help of a special tax on the 'natives' which it dismissed as a 'showcase' for tourists from which poor immigrant workers would be largely excluded (Stora 1992a, p.35).

Messali was to pay a heavy price personally for the radical nationalism which won his movement few allies. While supporting social advancement and equal citizenship, the CGT refused to defend Algerian political or even cultural autonomy, calling for 'assimilation in the framework of French culture and habits' (Schor 1985, p.521). As for the Communist Party, its turn towards an anti-fascist alliance with bourgeois parties ruled out support for movements of national liberation. During the general strike in 1936 Messali was carried shoulder high through Algiers by crowds of workers, his radical demands far outrunning the cautious reformism of the Islamic Ouléma movement, the newly created Communist Party of Algeria and especially the Popular Front government, whose timid plan to offer citizenship to a tiny part of the Algerian population was rapidly abandoned in the face of colonialist resistance. Banned again in January 1937 the ENA's re-foundation within three months as the Algerian People's Party (PPA) provoked the arrest of half a dozen leaders, promptly condemned by the Communist *L'Humanité* as 'Trotskyists' serving the interests of fascism. On the contrary, Messali's spurning of an offer of release by the Vichy authorities in 1940 in exchange for his endorsement, all the more valuable to them because of the strategic military importance of the north African territories, ensured that he remained in jail or in exile throughout World War II (Stora 1992a, pp.45, 81).

Once the world conflict was over, uncomfortably aware of what the restoration of the Republic owed to help from their allies, French leaders were in no mood to accept the affront to their prestige represented by the loss of French overseas territories. In May 1945 de Gaulle's provisional government crudely and bloodily suppressed, at the cost of thousands of lives, a premature explosion of popular frustration in eastern Algeria (Droz and Lever 1982, p.32). The Fourth Republic, created in 1946, was no less myopic and scarcely more generous. Its 'Algerian statute' of 1947 granted the three Algerian departments 30 deputies in the National Assembly, to be chosen by two electoral colleges in which the votes of the just under 1 million *pieds noirs* of European origin were equal in weight to those of the nearly 8 million Algerians (among whom women had no vote at all). A new Algerian assembly with virtually no independent powers was elected on the same basis. Among the absurdities engendered by this 'reform' were that the full civic rights available to Algerians living in France – to which they were now able to move freely – would allow them to debate the affairs of the Republic on an equal footing with their fellow workers, while they were disqualified from affecting the fate of their home territory. Within a few years, this collapsing house of cards would pull the Republic down with it.

Algerians at war

The war to keep Algeria French, when it came in 1954, never had the unanimous support of the French public. Units of conscripts resisted mobilisation in incidents such as occurred in Rouen in October 1955 when airmen barricaded themselves into their barracks, attracting a show of solidarity by local Communists which escalated into three days of fighting with riot police. Artists, writers, academics and teachers formed committees of intellectuals against the war. News magazines (*France-Observateur, L'Express*) were periodically raided or confiscated for denouncing the use of torture or reporting on desertions from the army. A network of students and intellectuals helped the nationalists transport the huge sums of money they collected from the mass of immigrant workers in France (Hamon and Rotman 1979). But there was no political mechanism which could translate such reservations into decisive collective action. The right-wing parties were largely in favour of keeping Algeria 'French'. The hidebound and bureaucratic Socialist Party, the SFIO, in office for two years during 1956–57, stepped up the war in a bid to prove its credentials as a party of government which led only to the splitting off of its own left wing. The French Communist Party, by far the largest in France, was experienced in clandestine methods, with considerable resources derived from its bastions in municipal government, a solid core of 20 per cent of the electorate, control – since a new split in 1947 – of the biggest industrial union confederation, the CGT, and in consequence ready access to its 37,000 Algerian members. It was the one organisation which could have defied the government, organised acts of solidarity with the rebellion and brought the war to a close much sooner.

Yet the Communist leaders were determined to avoid any action which might jeopardise the party's hard-won material assets or challenge its influence over the mass of industrial workers. Accordingly they condemned those of their own members who deserted from the armed forces, helped to block the emergence and recognition of an independent union confederation for Algeria and were reluctant to back nationalist strikes and demonstrations in support of Messali Hadj who had been arrested again in 1952 (Stora 1992a, pp.111–16). When thousands of Messalists – now renamed the Algerian National Movement (MNA) – attended a Communist May Day rally in 1955 with banners carrying slogans such as 'French workers, the Algerian emigration is with you!', they were refused permission to address the crowd, to the incredulity of many of those present. A year later the Communists joined other parties in granting the Socialist-led government virtually unlimited 'special powers' to restore the colonial order in Algeria. On 9 March 1956 the Messalists were left to march on Parliament alone, meeting a bloody repression which left them counting hundreds of arrested, injured and missing, some of them drowned in the Seine. It was their last public demonstration of the war (Stora 1992a, pp.182–3).

Divisions in Algerian ranks further damaged the chances of Franco-Algerian solidarity. During 1954 Messali had fallen out with officials of his own movement who wanted to abandon its traditional references to Islam and its revolutionary programme and organisational focus on the propertyless workers and farmers in favour of a more inclusive appeal acceptable to the tiny Algerian elite. At one of two rival congresses Messali unwisely had himself elected 'President for life', thus adding the cause of internal democracy to the other heads of dissent. In the midst of these wranglings, on 1 November, a secret group not closely linked to either side launched the co-ordinated attacks on military outposts and police stations in different parts of Algeria which marked the beginning of the armed struggle. Ageing, cut off from the home territory by house arrest in provincial Niort in western France, Messali was reluctant to believe that the war had begun without him. Ironically, his supporters in Algeria had their minds made up for them by a wave of repression unleashed by the colonial authorities in the weeks after 1 November 1954, which forced many of them to leave the towns and take to the hills. Messali's opponents, taking the name National Liberation Front (FLN), began a series of physical battles for the assets of the movement which in France grew into a fight for control of the immigrants whose weekly contributions financed the rival organisations and kept the liberation army in the field. Hit squads from each side shot up the other's hotels and cafés and assassinated their cadres in a fratricidal struggle which cost 4000 lives in France and 6000 in Algeria, an irreparable loss for the nation struggling to be born (Stora 1992a, pp.203–21). The FLN gained the upper hand, thanks to its fusion with organisations representative of the urban Algerian elite and its capture of the nationalist students' union. But it was the campaign of economic sabotage and attacks on military targets in France itself, launched by the FLN in August 1958, which tipped the balance decisively in its favour, inducing a stream of former MNA activists to cross over to the organisation which seemed to be most actively prosecuting the war (Haroun 1986, pp.85–113, 265–6).

The August campaign also had the effect of sealing the isolation of Algerian immigrant workers in France, who were subjected to night-time curfews in the major cities, random arrests, interrogation, beatings, imprisonment and internment without trial, as the police tried to discover and disarm the FLN commandos. By the end of 1959, over 11,000 were in prison or concentration camps. Many others were deported back to Algeria, where they suffered summary military justice. It is estimated that 44,282 arrests were made during the course of the war, affecting a tenth of the entire Algerian immigrant community (Stora 1992a, pp.290, 316). In these circumstances, migrant workers had every reason to seek security in isolation, while the FLN abandoned the strategy of class solidarity, giving absolute priority to the armed struggle and couching its appeals in vague terms to 'the French people' (Stora 1992a, p.177; Haroun 1986, p.108). By the end of the war the 36,000 members of the FLN French Federation had turned the immigrant community into an almost self-sufficient counter-society. They levied an 'income tax' to finance the war effort and imposed fines for breaches of discipline or anti-social behaviour; health and social welfare committees inspected lodgings, handled claims for unemployment, accident or sickness benefit and did not hesitate to issue recommendations about relations between the sexes and regular observance of the Muslim religion (Stora 1992a, pp.343–51). There was education and training for those who wanted to join the struggle, support for prisoners and their dependants, a press and propaganda department, garages, workshops for the production of false papers and an extensive network of links with sympathisers in Europe and the Middle East. On two occasions the Federation sustained punishing hunger strikes by its prisoners, the second involving all 18,000 of the movement's detainees, which it claimed as the largest co-ordinated hunger strike ever undertaken in prison conditions (Haroun 1986). One of the last public displays of disciplined solidarity occurred on 17 October 1961, in defiance of the Arabs-only curfew imposed by the Paris chief of police, when peace negotiations were already under way and the armies in the field marking time. Some 20,000 Algerians, women and children included, were savagely attacked by police and paramilitaries, chased, thrown into the Seine, or corralled in barracks and sports centres, to be strangled, shot or beaten to death with clubs. Upwards of 10,000 were arrested, 200 were murdered, an unknown number were missing. Medical teams working round the clock tended the injured, who were ferried to the hospitals by Parisians using their own cars. Jews under the occupation, in the words of Jean-Paul Sartre, had suffered less savagery from the Gestapo than the Algerians at the hands of the police of the Republic, while its politicians vainly lied about the consequences (Haroun 1986, pp.361–77; Einaudi 1991).

Unsupported by any major French political force, the café owners, factory workers and building labourers of the French Federation bore eight years of war with great courage and endurance. Their sacrifices were immense, but so was their contribution; in some years, they supplied 80 per cent of the entire budget of the provisional government (Haroun 1986, p.307). Yet their victory left those who wished to remain and raise their children in France facing the future in difficult psychological circumstances. Anyone born in Algeria before 1962 had the right to French citizenship, but had to ask for it. Few among the survivors of the war would have been moved to do so by the thought that they shared the values and aspirations of the French Republic, now in its fifth edition. And what of their children? Would not their unreserved identification with France in some sense render pointless the cause for which half a million were thought to have laid down their lives? These were humble dilemmas when set beside the fate of the losers. About 200,000 Algerians, some little believing in the possibility of French defeat, others in continuation of a family tradition, called *harkis* from the name of their military units, had fought on the French side. Abandoned to their fate in the chaotic last days of the war, up to 150,000 of them were massacred as traitors by the victors, the rest managing to escape to France. Kept from contact with the existing immigrants, for whom they were traitors, and from the French, for whom they were an embarrassing reminder of defeat and disavowal, they were parked in disused army camps and given work – when they could get it – in remote forestry projects dubbed 'Indian Reservations' by their children who, when they grew up, suffered worse educational and employment prospects than any other group in France (Méliani 1993; Hamoumou 1993). Today numbering half a million, their economic and social exclusion has little to do with 'culture', still less to do with their status as citizens of the Republic; it has everything to do with the politics of decolonisation.

Immigrants and the long boom, 1945–80

The post-1945 era at first seemed to bring with it slightly more generous official attitudes to the in-migration of foreigners. The inauguration in 1945 of a National Immigration Office (ONI) to co-ordinate selection, medical screening and the rationing of permits according to the predicted needs of each sector of activity, obliged employers to share control of the recruitment process with representatives of the trade unions and the state. In 1952 France ratified the Geneva Convention on the protection of refugees, installing a more rigorous judicial procedure for the granting of asylum. Furthermore, de Gaulle's call for 12 million 'beautiful babies' to make good a century of demographic decline, chimed with the belief of a new generation of pro-natalist civil servants that future immigrants should not be regarded simply as disposable labour but as a valuable long-term addition to the French population. Some of them, however, like Georges Mauco, secretary of the government's advisory committee on population from 1945 until 1970, had strong views about what sort of foreigners France required. A proposal to give priority to 'Nordics' followed in order by 'Mediterraneans' and 'Slavs', with workers of 'other origins' relegated to the bottom of the list, was only narrowly prevented from being officially adopted in 1945 by the intervention of the Council of State, which pointed out its scant compatibility with republican values (Weil 1995, pp.80–9).

The procedures of the ONI proving rather cumbersome, no more than 160,000 new European immigrants arrived in the period 1949–55, more than balanced by 180,000 Algerians, despite the deliberate siting of ONI offices in preferred European countries (Weil 1995, p.94). Outlawed in principle, there were increasing signs that ethnic selection had been adopted in practice. From 1956 onwards, both administration and employers turned a blind eye to the quota system and the requirement that recruits should obtain a permit before leaving their home country. Young Portuguese fleeing the prospect of military service in colonial wars were the objects of particular favour, some even allegedly being allowed to cross the frontier without their passports (Weil 1995, p.100). Between 1960 and 1970, 65 per cent of all newcomers are thought to have been 'regularised' after entry by the issue of work and residence permits once a job had been found, a procedure which effectively granted free entry to Europeans on the same terms on which it was enjoyed by Algerians. These 'measures' helped ensure that more Europeans than Maghrebis were sucked in by explosive economic growth during the rest of the 1950s and the 1960s, their numbers increasing by 479,000 during 1954–68 (277,000 of them Portuguese), while the number of Algerians resident in France rose from 211,000 to 474,000, Moroccans and Tunisians together totalling 120,000 by the later date (Tripier 1990, p.66). The proportion of Europeans in the total foreign population was still 60 per cent in 1975, declining to 47.6 per cent only in 1982 as European children of the third generation were born French, while family members steadily joined the African men who had gone ahead of them.

By the mid-1960s, demographic considerations were taking second place to enthusiastic recognition of the economic value of immigrant labour, from whatever origin and by whatever route it arrived. While the Prime Minister welcomed the resulting downward pressure on wages (Wihtol de Wenden 1988, p.87), his Minister of Labour told the press in 1966 that

... clandestine immigration in itself is not without benefit, for if we stuck to a strict interpretation of the rules and international agreements, we would perhaps be short of labour. (cited in Gaspard and Servan-Schreiber 1985, pp.28–9)

The employers joined in, savouring the flexibility offered by foreign workers who were 'ready to move from one region or workplace to another and, if necessary accept a period of unemployment', not to mention the savings the country could make on the costs of education, healthcare and pensions, the newcomers being generally adult, young and healthy (*L'Usine Nouvelle* 26 March 1970, also cited in Gaspard and Servan-Schreiber 1985, pp.29–30). Even the trade unions gave up worrying about migrants as competitors in the job market and began to talk about immigration as a permanent structural feature of capitalism (Gallissot *et al.* 1994, pp.85–7). Foreigners' status at work was still, however, a precarious and discriminated one. Some of those who became unemployed could be refused renewal of their permit and ordered to leave the country on the grounds that they were a public charge (Miller and Martin 1982, p.64). Until 1968, many were employed only on renewable three-month contracts (Tripier 1990, pp.165, 175). In the mid-1960s the foreigners' share of industrial accidents matched their concentration in the most dangerous industries and tasks: 40 per cent in building (where they comprised 18.2 per cent of the workforce); 21 per cent in chemicals (7.9 per cent of the workforce); 20 per cent in engineering (10 per cent of the workforce) (Tripier 1990, p.77).

The events of May 1968 signalled, as for the working class as a whole, the beginning of a change of atmosphere rather than a transformation of their condition. Workers were given a hefty pay rise, allowed to organise union branches at work, and found their employers more willing to negotiate deals on wages, unemployment insurance and pensions; but not much else changed, while the specific grievances of foreign workers were drowned in the din of revolutionary rhetoric. The main trade union confederations had already in 1967 begun to demand equality for immigrants on an unprecedented range of issues including not only wages but social benefits, the right to change jobs and the right to union activity, yet they were unable to prevent the expulsion of 250 foreign workers for their parts in the May–June events (Gallissot *et al.* 1994, pp.87–8; Tripier 1990, pp.173–4; Miller 1981, p.84). In the five years immediately following 1968 the combativity of the working class amid continued rapid growth gave foreign workers the confidence to stage strikes which put an end to some of the more scandalous cases of arbitrary and racist management behaviour and illegally unsafe and unhealthy working conditions. The strike by 100 mainly north African workers at the Penarroya auto-components plant in St Denis at the end of 1971 heralded 'a veritable wave of foreign workers' strikes that swept France in 1972' (Miller 1981, p.93). In 1973 the long strike of Paris dustbin men and a three-week strike of 400 unskilled Algerians, Spaniards and Portuguese in Renault-Billancourt, laying off 7000, alerted public opinion to the demand for 'dignity', which appeared as a constant refrain in the strikers' articulation of their grievances (Tripier 1990, pp.188–9; Weil 1995, pp.105–6). This wave of militancy, coinciding with pressure from the EEC, the International Labour Organisation and the unions, keen to open a channel of communication with the rank and file, had by 1975 persuaded Parliament to dismantle the legal barriers to foreigners becoming workshop delegates or works committee members (Gallissot *et al.* 1994, pp.100–1; Tripier 1990, pp.175–6).

Yet little progress was made on the key demand of many of the strikes, promotion from the grade of labourer to semi-skilled status which would have brought with it higher and guaranteed pay. In the mid-1970s foreign workers were still victims of a quarter of all fatal industrial accidents, while only 1 per cent of those eligible had benefited from training to upgrade their skills (Miller and Martin 1982, pp.70–1; Tripier 1990, p.185). Barely a decade and a half after 1968 the massive modernisation and shake-out in the steel and automobile industries revealed the way in which the '30 glorious years' of the long post-war boom had been built on a racialised hierarchy of labour, symbolised by Renault's flagship Billancourt works in the Parisian suburbs. In 1984 the 6800 foreigners at Billancourt made up 81 per cent of all the unskilled workers; 60 per cent of the lowest graded foreigners were north Africans, among whom an incredible 90 per cent of the Algerians had worked there for ten years or more without improving their position (Tripier 1990, pp.154, 198–9). With no community networks to favour their advancement, poor French and no recognised skills to begin with, they were the most vulnerable among the foreigners turned away from re-training courses which allowed many French workers to hang on to their jobs during downsizing by moving up the skill hierarchy (Echardour and Maurin 1993, pp.504–11). In this context the growing demand by Muslim workers for special rooms to be set aside near the workshops for daily prayers has been interpreted as evidence of a need for the spiritual satisfaction with which religion or heightened community identification could compensate their second-class status. It would be a mistake, however, to believe that religious leaders became a rival focus of loyalty, subverting that claimed by the employer and the unions. For one thing, even committed Muslims were not unanimously in favour of praying at work. For another, some employers, particularly in the Citroën-Talbot group deliberately fostered the use of *imams* (prayer leaders) for purposes of social control, while the CGT itself, after a three-year hesitation, moved to recruit *imams* and organise its own prayer room at Billancourt. Those politicians of both left and right who tried to portray north African workers as tools of Islamic agitators during the wave of strikes against redundancies in the auto industry in 1982–84 were indulging in a little racist manipulation of their own (Kepel 1991; Mouriaux and Wihtol de Wenden 1988). Meanwhile Maghrebi youngsters' keen awareness of the occupational ghetto to which their parents had been consigned would sharpen their own critical attitude to French society, as we shall see below (Chapter 6).

Outside the workplace, the two decades after the Algerian war saw the strengthening of an array of forces committed to humanitarian and even egalitarian values, creating a fund of sympathy for immigrants unprecedented in French history. The leftist Catholics who had sided with Algerian independence in their journal *Témoignages Chrétiens* were vindicated by the Vatican Council's endorsement of decolonisation and democratic principles, while the Catholic young workers' movement was steadily infected with left-wing ideas through contact with the people it was trying to influence. Among the unions, the small and traditionally class-collaborationist French Confederation of Christian Workers (CFTC) split in 1964 when the majority of its members abandoned the religious connotation and founded a new organisation, the CFDT. Expanding rapidly, the new French Democratic Confederation of Labour became a serious rival for the CGT with a much more open democratic structure and an outlook in which vaguely Christian humanism mixed with third worldism and the advocacy of workers' self-management. Declining to restrict itself to workplace issues only, the new confederation drew attention to migrants' poverty and terrible housing conditions, holding its first conference on immigrant-related issues in 1966.

In the same year, 156 grassroots immigrant support associations came together as a federation, the FASTI. The Movement Against Racism and for Friendship between Peoples (MRAP), closely linked to the Communist Party, was the successor of a pre-war movement against anti-semitism, which in the 1960s began to take an increasing interest in the problems of north African workers. In 1972, social workers and legal experts founded the GISTI, the Group for Information and Support of Immigrant Workers, which began to publish a high-quality journal in which government white papers, decrees and circulars were carefully dissected. Members of all these organisations, and others, like the League for the Rights of Man, the International League against Racism and Anti-semitism (LICRA) and the inter-faith CIMADE provided legal advice and representation, lobbied national and local government in support of individual cases or to seek changes in the law or administrative practice, exposed and prosecuted racist crimes, pursued and publicised the activities of Nazi sects, as well as joining demonstrations in support of actions undertaken by immigrants themselves. Many of the latter concerned housing conditions, particularly those of north African and Portuguese workers.

Until the end of the 1960s, most of the Algerians in France were single men who took it in turns with others from the same village to stay a year or two, sending back money vital to the survival of their rural communities, of which they were regarded as 'delegates'. A high proportion lived together in employers' hostels, Maghreb-owned hotels in the more run-down parts of the city centres or shanty accommodation adjacent to the building sites where they worked. The gradual replacement of this pattern of 'rotation' by strategies of personal advancement, reflected in a slow rise in the proportion of women, from 6.5 per cent in 1954 to 26.7 per cent in 1968 and 32 per cent in 1975, changed the pattern of demand for housing in the Algerian community. This and the arrival of a quarter of a million Portuguese between 1962 and 1968 exhausted the supply of affordable family housing and swelled the numbers living in cardboard and corrugated-iron shanty towns – the *bidonvilles* – thrown up on the outskirts of the major cities. With many more taking refuge in warehouses, cellars, allotment huts and anywhere else that owners were unscrupulous enough to offer beds for rent, an estimated 650,000 were living in *bidonvilles* or slums by the end of the decade (Tripier 1990, pp.72–6; Weil 1995, p.122). It was not until a fire in a slum dormitory killed five Malian workers in 1970, provoking an occupation by leftists of the headquarters of the French employers' organisation, that the government developed a plan to rehouse the shanty dwellers (Weil 1995, pp.106–7). Since its first stage involved shipping the immigrants to pre-fabricated transit camps, usually sandwiched between railway lines and motorway slip-roads, it was not until well into the 1970s that it became common to have Portuguese and north Africans as neighbours. Many of those respondents who told pollsters in the 1950s and 1960s that the newcomers would be unable to adapt to French culture were unlikely to have been speaking from much knowledge of the subject.

The housing issue which achieved the biggest political profile was the four-year rent strike by the residents of hostels run by a part-government, part-employer funded agency, SONACOTRA. Set up in 1958, its mission was not only to provide cheap housing, but also to put Algerian workers beyond the reach of the FLN. The physical inadequacies of the accommodation, the small size and paper-thin walls of the rooms, were therefore compounded by a regime in which meetings were banned and the wardens, often retired military personnel, had the right to go into any room at any time in search of unauthorised visitors. At the end of 1975 SONACOTRA alone ran 275 such hostels with 73,660 beds, 83 per cent occupied by foreigners, of whom in turn 68 per cent were Algerians (Kepel 1991, pp.126–9). An increase in rents at the end of 1975 triggered a strike which had spread to 42 hostels, affecting 30,000 residents by 1978, in which eviction battles with the police alternated with demonstrations up to 10,000 strong supported by a heteroclite coalition of Christians, trade unionists and extreme-left groups. Victory eventually went to the government and the courts, sealed by the deportation of hundreds of strikers (Miller 1981, p.89; Weil 1995, pp.156–7, 163).

The colonial legacy and racial violence

Discrimination in work and housing is part of a wider west European experience in which mass migration responded to bursts of sketchily regulated economic growth. In France it was underpinned by a half-avowed but granite-like belief in racial hierarchy, as the editors of *Le Monde* discovered in the spring of 1970 when they provoked a debate on racism and were surprised by the number and range of those 'even among *Le Monde*'s readers' who openly espoused racial segregation (*Le Monde* 19–20 April 1970). A law forbidding discrimination in recruitment or in the offer of a service was not passed until 1972, after a long campaign by the MRAP and the LICRA. As discriminated individuals plucked up the courage to complain, the MRAP's legal advice service – one among many – dealt with 20 cases a week in the mid-1970s (*L'Humanité* 7 July 1977). One involved a Tunisian worker in Grenoble who came to blows with staff of the ANPE, the state employment agency, over an advertisement for a welder which specified a 'European' only. He was beaten up by the police and given a suspended prison sentence, while the agency staff denied their collusion with racism, arguing that if they did not warn potential recruits of restrictive conditions they would be wasting their time applying (*Libération* 21 July 1977).

A more frightening aspect of the colonial legacy was the undertow of racial violence which surged up from time to time in response to political events, such as Algeria's nationalisation of French oil interests in 1971, after which north African cafés were bombed and machine-gunned and the bodies of murdered foreign labourers 'regularly fished out of the Seine' (Miller 1981, p.98). The murder of a Marseilles bus driver by a deranged north African in August 1973 sparked another wave of reprisal attacks, fanned by a self-styled 'Committee of Public Safety', whose posters called on citizens to 'Stop the Arab aggressors'. By Christmas, the *'Nouvel Obs'* had counted 47 deaths for the whole year (*Nouvel Observateur* 24 December 1973). Often the attacks were relatively spontaneous, the work of isolated individuals or groups of drunks, which all too often went unpunished thanks to the indifference of the police and the courts, whose inadequate training and attitudes 'dating from the Algerian war' were condemned by representatives of four police unions at a joint press conference with the MRAP (*Le Monde* 20 August 1976). Others required more organisation, like the series of 14 incidents near Nice which led to the arrest of six teenagers in December 1975, or those in the same area in June 1979 in which two victims were deliberately run down by cars (*Le Monde* 20 June 1979). Most chilling of all were the attacks carried out in cold blood by politically motivated groups, like the Club Charles Martel which exploded a bomb in the waiting room of the Algerian consulate in Marseilles in December 1973 killing four and wounding 18, or the Nazi sect whose bombing of the synagogue in the Rue Copernic in Paris killed three and wounded 20 in 1980. In the second half of the 1970s there were 30-odd attacks in which cemeteries, synagogues and other Jewish premises were desecrated, machine-gunned, bombed or fired. In most cases the daubing of swastikas and Nazi slogans on targets such as monuments to pre-war politicians or associations of former resistants and deportees identified the outrages as part of a long-running French affair, rather than emanating from the Middle East. They included several attacks on the MRAP, of which one, a bombing by the Nazi sect, the Joachim Peiper Group, wrecked three flats in the apartment block housing the association's headquarters (*L'Humanité* 15 July 1977). But more than 80 of the 120 organised racist attacks recorded between 1975 and the end of 1980 by *Le Monde* concerned non-Jewish targets (*Le Monde* 7 October 1980). Some were the work of ex-OAS (Organisation Armée Secrète) members or groups of *pieds noirs* 'repatriated' from Algeria, who exploded four bombs in the south of France and another at the Algerian consulate in Paris in April 1975 (*Libération* 11 April 1975). Others, such as those who damaged the premises of Algerian community associations in Paris, Roubaix and Lyons in the same weekend (*Quotidien de Paris* 30 July 1975), or the Parisian commandos who attacked a group of immigrant-origin school students with clubs and tear-gas in front of their *lycée* (*L'Humanité* 11 March 1980), and shot at north African residents of a housing estate in the suburb of Bondy (*L'Humanité* 13 June 1980), did not identify themselves.

The Republic's leaders consistently reacted with remarkable insouciance to the efforts of anti-racists to get them to take action to defend target groups. When the Prime Minister Jacques Chaban Delmas reassuringly told readers of the *Tribune Juive* in 1971, 'We are without doubt one of the least racist countries in the world ... it would be counter-productive to campaign against what doesn't exist, in the sense of a systematic tendency or an organised movement' (cited in *Le Monde* 6 February 1971), he was echoing, no doubt unconsciously, Justice Minister Jean Foyer, who in 1963, less than two years after the pogrom of 17 October, told the National Assembly that France had 'reason to congratulate herself for the absence of acts of racial discrimination or segregation on her territory' (*Le Monde* 13 June 1963). Asked what he was doing as Interior Minister to protect persons of north African origin during the wave of terror in September 1973, Raymond Marcellin truculently denounced the 'so-called anti-racist campaign' fomented by 'a number of extremist organisations and politicised trade unions which tend to accredit the idea of a generalised racist attitude in our country, which is manifestly false' (*L'Humanité* 25 September 1973).

Economic crisis and state racism

Such attitudes made conservative ministers during the 1970s part of the problem as far as immigrant workers were concerned. Although there were parallels between the depression of the 1930s and the curtailing of growth in western Europe in the mid-1970s, the political context offered a sharp contrast with that of 40 years previously. While Third Republic governments had been at the mercy of a powerful legislature in which large contingents of doctors and lawyers routinely lobbied and voted for laws protecting their interests, the institutions of de Gaulle's Fifth Republic usually allowed a powerful executive to impose its agenda on a subservient chamber – even if popular consent was less easy to manage. Already before the oil price hike – and against the wishes of both employers and unions – the government had decided to stop the practice of regularising those who bypassed the official ONI procedures, once again exempting only the Portuguese from the new rules enshrined in the so-called Marcellin–Fontanet circulars, effective from 1 January 1973 (Weil 1995, pp.109–10). The 1974 election brought into the presidential palace a self-styled 'liberal', Valéry Giscard d'Estaing, whose immediate blanket suspension of all new immigration, including family reunions, was originally intended to be accompanied by a substantial increase in funding to solve the housing crisis; when this money was not made available as planned, the new under-secretary responsible for immigrant affairs resigned after only a few weeks in office.

His successor, Paul Dijoud, managed to salvage some strands of a liberal policy by abolishing the tying of work permits to particular sectors of activity, so that immigrants could change jobs more easily, by persuading employers to increase their contributions to a special immigrants' housing fund and ensuring that the right to receive a ten-year permit after four years' continuous residence was respected properly for the first time since it was decreed in 1945. In April 1976 he abandoned the block on family reunions, albeit subject to the considerable bureaucratic obstacle that the breadwinner must dispose of a suitable lodging (Weil 1995, pp.142–50). Despite what appeared to be good intentions, Dijoud's efforts were not a political success, partly because the hundreds of regulations governing immigrants' rights were not adequately publicised and left an enormous amount to the discretion of administrative officials – a situation of 'infra-law' stridently denounced by the government's critics (Wihtol de Wenden 1988, pp.200–1). Furthermore, Dijoud was not the only minister foreign workers had to deal with; successive ministers of the interior systematically imposed five years' exclusion from France on those whose papers were not in order. As punishment for those who had overstayed their three-month tourist visa, this seemed harsh; inflicted on teenagers born in France, of foreign parents, who had neglected their duty to obtain residence permits after their 16th birthday, it appeared morally criminal. Culprits were frequently held in detention before being deported, in conditions in which it was difficult for their friends or supporters to discover their fate, like the 'secret prison', discovered at Arenc in the Marseilles area in 1975. The French authorities also collaborated with foreign dictatorships in clamping down on foreign workers' political activity – still illegal in the Republic – thanks to which a hundred or so CFDT and CGT members were arrested while on holiday in Morocco, some tortured and imprisoned, others disappearing from view altogether (Weil 1995, pp.153–5).

With no return to fast growth in sight, history began to repeat itself as Prime Minister Jacques Chirac and Labour Minister Michel Durafour both drew very public attention to the 'paradox' that a country with 2 million immigrant workers had 900,000 unemployed (Wihtol de Wenden 1988, p.206). Lionel Stoléru, who took over responsibility for immigrant workers in March 1977, bombarded his colleagues with papers demonstrating that the money sent home by foreigners represented an annual loss of 7 billion francs to the balance of payments and calculating the rate of repatriation necessary in order to wipe out unemployment. Faced with the failure of his scheme to induce voluntary return by the offer of 10,000 francs per head – only 4000 applications were made, instead of the 50,000 hoped for – he announced a three-year suspension of family reunions. A storm of protest forced him to concede that families would be allowed to settle in France, although barred from working, but this regulation was in turn annulled by judicial review at the end of 1978. Giscard and Stoléru next made determined efforts to find a way to avoid giving new ten-year residence permits to most of the more than 600,000 Algerians who would be due for them in 1979, when their current papers expired. Negotiations initially aimed at jointly organised repatriation of 100,000 per year for four years foundered on the Algerian government's refusal to countenance anything but voluntary returns. A simultaneous attempt to pass a law allowing the government to deny permit renewal to those who had become unemployed – which flew in the face of International Labour Organisation conventions endorsed by the Republic – was ruled out by the Council of State. The best that Stoléru could achieve was the *loi Bonnet*, passed in January 1980, which widened the range of offences punishable by deportation.

As the decade – and the Giscard presidency – drew to a close it became clear that government policy had been largely counter-productive, persuading many to settle permanently in France, for fear that the door might be closed even more tightly in future. The ending of regularisation, the on-off banning of family reunions, the repression of the rent-strikes and the long debates on aided repatriation, during which permits were only renewed temporarily, had all been resisted by lobbying, demonstrations and hunger-strikes. Under the circumstances, it was not surprising that the MRAP in 1980 identified the worst threat to immigrants as a 'state racism' which systematically singled them out as those who should pay the price for economic ills (*Le Matin* 24 March 1980). If state racism there was, added to social disadvantage and the colonial legacy, a meagre consolation was that at least, until now, no major political party had openly campaigned for votes by targeting immigrants. In the 1980s just such a party emerged. In our next chapter, we explain how.

3
The National Front Breakthrough and Consolidation, 1981–92

Breakthrough, 1981–88

On 10 May 1981 François Mitterrand was elected President of the Republic, defeating by a narrow margin the conservative Valéry Giscard d'Estaing, on a programme of sweeping socialist and democratic reforms. Baptised by French political scientists the '*alternance*', this first victory for the left since the foundation of the Fifth Republic in 1958 was the culmination of a decade of polarisation in which voters had given their support in almost equal numbers to two rival coalitions, Socialists and Communists on the one hand, and Gaullists and Giscardians on the other, all four parties at times winning close to a quarter of the popular vote each. Yet unsuspected either by those who took part in the left's victory celebrations, or by their opponents weighing up the chances of a quick return to power, this passing symmetry was about to be destroyed by a new force, all but politically non-existent in 1981, whose scores of 10–15 per cent in election after election reimposed the multiparty pattern which had been a characteristic reflection of French social and cultural divisions for more than a century (see Table 3.1).

In the second part of this chapter we will examine in detail information about the kind of people who vote for the National Front (NF), their situations and motivations. In this first part, we analyse the political context in which the four-party system was broken up. We describe how the left's reform programme rapidly turned to austerity and had run out of steam by 1983/84, as Socialist and Communist leaders helped prepare the ground for the Front by a series of clumsy attacks on immigrants. The mainstream right, lacking a strong and unifying conservative tradition and weakened by partisan rivalries, alternately tried to make deals with the NF and to condemn it, aping its discourse in a futile effort to stem a slippage of voters and members to Le Pen's side. Meanwhile the National Front manoeuvred with great adroitness, exploiting the extraordinary personality of its leader, recruiting gullible fellow-travellers who helped give it a respectable air, then discarding them ruthlessly by moving its agenda to the right. By 1992, the depth and spread of the party's support and its ability to set the issue agenda testified to its consolidation as a seemingly permanent part of the political landscape.

Table 3.1   The National Front vote since 1984 (Mouvement National Républicain vote in brackets)

Election	Number of votes	% of votes cast
1984 European	2,210,334	11.00
1986 Parliamentary	2,705,336	9.70
1988 Presidential	4,375,894	14.40
1988 Parliamentary	2,359,528	9.70
1989 European	2,121,836	11.80
1993 Parliamentary	3,152,113	12.70
1994 European	2,049,634	10.50
1995 Presidential	4,571,138	15.00
1997 Parliamentary	3,824,000	15.10
1999 European	1,005,225	6.69
	(578,774)	(3.28)
2002 Presidential	4,804,713	16.86
	(667,026)	(2.34)
2002 Parliamentary	2,862,960	11.34
	(276,376)	(1.09)

Mitterrand's victory was immediately followed by parliamentary elections in which, thanks to massive abstentions on the right, the Socialists gained a secure majority over all the other parties combined. Although their support was not essential, four of the 44 Communist deputies were taken into the government, a useful pledge against any temptation to use their industrial muscle in the event of future conflict. This combined left government lost no time in implementing some of its key election promises, raising pensions, the minimum wage and family allowances, abolishing the death penalty, setting up a ministry for women's rights and drafting ambitious new laws to devolve power to local government, change the balance of power in the workplace and nationalise a large swathe of manufacturing industry. The situation of immigrant workers and their families was transformed as random identity checks were stopped, special controls on foreigners' right of association abandoned and the government declared itself willing to regularise all those who had come into the country without first finding a job through official channels. Later, the multiplicity of different residence and work permits for different nationalities were replaced with a single renewable ten-year permit.

The 'gang of four' on the defensive

It was easier to reverse the previous government's policies at the stroke of a pen, however, than to affect the global economic climate or change attitudes towards foreigners. As inflation and imports took off, thanks to the public's increased purchasing power, the government's economic policies were blown off course. In June 1982 a wage and price freeze accompanied the first of several devaluations of the franc, while the conservative opposition forced a series of all-night sittings in Parliament in a successful bid to hold up the nationalisation law. A rash of violent incidents pitting the police against largely unemployed immigrant-origin youths in deprived suburbs led the right to harp endlessly on about the government's 'laxity' in regularising 132,000 'illegals'. Immigrant car workers striking to get a better pay-off for the modernisation and restructuring which would see their jobs replaced by robots were attacked by Prime Minister Pierre Mauroy, who claimed they were being 'stirred up by religious and political groups' whose concerns had 'little to do with French social realities' (*Le Monde* 29 January 1983).

The Socialists thus approached the spring local government elections in defensive posture. The veteran mayor of Marseilles, Gaston Defferre, appealed for votes on the basis that he would be tougher on immigrants than the right. The distribution of 2 million copies of an expensively produced pamphlet entitled 'Living together, immigrants in our midst', which offered a series of fairly neutral facts and figures to counter racism, was held up on the orders of the Prime Minister's office (Plenel and Rollat 1984, p.199). Similar silence was maintained on the 1981 pledge to grant foreigners the right to vote in local elections. The Communists were scarcely better placed. Only two years before, in a vain bid to drum up a few extra votes for party leader Georges Marchais in the presidential election, Communist mayors in the Parisian suburbs had led a series of populist stunts against immigrants, most spectacularly in Vitry-sur-Seine, where a protest against the 'dumping' of a group of Malians from a neighbouring conservative municipality involved the partial destruction of the hostel in which they were living. While party members argued that they were courageously tackling questions which everyone should recognise as relevant, their attitude could hardly contribute to building an alliance with the children of immigrants who enjoyed their civic rights and might have been tempted to use them in campaigning against the NF. Instead it merely helped to legitimise the central plank of the NF programme (Plenel and Rollat 1984, pp.159–61; Schain 1987).

But the candidates of the mainstream right also helped to force immigration on to the political agenda. A future Gaullist Prime Minister, Alain Juppé, whose campaign newspaper explicitly evoked a link between 'clandestine immigration, delinquence and criminality', signed a leaflet with other candidates in the neighbouring northern districts of Paris, proclaiming, 'We must stop this invasion.' In the third district, the Giscardian Jacques Dominati's newspaper carried a front-page headline 'The right to law and order', above a picture of Africans, while his party colleague in St Etienne called for an end to '*délinquance bronzée*' (Milza 1988, pp.172–3). In Marseilles, Jean-Claude Gaudin, the local leader of Giscard's party, the Union for French Democracy (UDF), ran against Defferre under a programme with the title 'Marseilles for the *Marseillais*'. In Toulon, the outgoing UDF mayor, Maurice Arreckx, complained to a mainstream weekly, *L'Express*, that France

> ... was never supposed to have a role as refuge for the unemployed of Africa and Europe. Our country has become a dustbin for the collection of revolutionaries, delinquents and anarchists of all types. We should kick them out. (cited in Wihtol de Wenden 1988, p.324)

Socialists who defended immigrants were treated to a vicious type of innuendo, impossible to rebut: the mayor of Dreux, like the mayor of Chambéry, was credited with an Algerian lover, as well as a secret ten-year-old black child and a 16-year-old son from a previous relationship with a Moroccan. Hubert Dubedout, the mayor of Grenoble, refused to contradict the rumour that his mother was a Kabyl, originating from Algeria. As he pointed out, not so long ago people had been cowardly enough to declare publicly that they were not Jewish: 'I'd rather lose an election than give in to such cowardice' (cited in Gaspard and Servan-Schreiber 1985, p.62). Dubedout was indeed defeated, the Socialists losing control of Chambéry, Suresnes, Roubaix and Nantes in similar circumstances. Altogether, the left lost 30 of the 220 towns with more than 30,000 inhabitants, a serious mid-term defeat which reflected the left electorate's disappointment at the slow-down in reforms and the failure to halt the rise of unemployment, as well as the return to the polls of right-wing voters who had abstained in the 1981 parliamentary contest. Nevertheless, on the evening of the results, the defeated Socialist candidate for mayor of Paris, Paul Quilès, chose to criticise the media, whose images of striking workers with 'dark-skinned faces' had, he said, frightened and antagonised the 'domestic' electorate (Bihr 1986, p.68).

The NF had run full lists of candidates only in Nice, Montpellier and ten districts of Paris (where Le Pen's list scored 11 per cent in the 20th), some NF members being invited to join mainstream conservative lists in a further half-dozen towns (Perrineau 1989, p.42). If they did not yet have enough members or enough visibility to turn to their own account a climate of opinion which was set in their favour, all that changed in the autumn, thanks to Dreux, a small town east of Paris with a significant immigrant community and a large working-class population, to whom the recession had given a 10 per cent rate of unemployment (Gaspard 1990). In the spring council elections the NF general secretary, Jean-Pierre Stirbois, who had campaigned in the town for several years, had joined the conservative list but the election was declared invalid on a technicality. In the September re-run Stirbois was able to present his own list, with the slogan 'Two million unemployed are two million immigrants too many', championing the little man in opposition both to the Socialists and to the Gaullist mayoral candidate, a banker. The NF score of 16.72 per cent on the first round presented the conservatives with a major strategic dilemma of a type which would haunt them for more than a decade. Stirbois might run again in the second round and take his chance on getting a small number of councillors under proportional rules. Such a course, however, would more or less guarantee that the Socialists would top the poll and win control of the council.[1] To prevent this, the local conservatives promptly agreed to a fusion, co-opting four NF candidates on to their own list, three of whom were subsequently elected. The affair hit the headlines when Giscard's former Health Minister, Simone Veil, and one or two others, publicly condemned the deal and advised abstention from the poll. Bizarrely, the complaint of her UDF colleague and NF-friendly former Interior Minister Michel Poniatowski, that Veil, an Auschwitz survivor, was swayed by the memory of her own past, seemed to confirm the proposition that Auschwitz and Stirbois were in some way connected. The Gaullist leader, Jacques Chirac, having in the spring declared that an alliance with Le Pen in Paris would have been 'unnatural', now decided that four NF municipal councillors in Dreux were not as 'dangerous' as the four Communists in government (Plenel and Rollat 1984, pp.98–9). Thanks to these various dimensions of self-contradiction, the media spotlight remained fixed on the Front for the rest of the year,

---

1. Recently revised rules had established a semi-proportional system for the larger municipalities. The list which got the most votes on the second round was guaranteed half the council seats, the remainder being shared out on a proportional basis among the lists in contention, including the winning list.

as it polled 9.3 per cent in another re-run council election in the Parisian suburb of Aulnay-sous-Bois and Le Pen himself won 12 per cent in a parliamentary by-election in Morbihan in Brittany, a constituency which fortuitously contained his birthplace.

The difficulties faced by the mainstream right in dealing with the Front were heightened by the fractured nature of the conservative tradition in France. Suspicious of political democracy until well into the twentieth century because of its association with anti-clericalism, conservatives, Christian Democrats and liberals had a history of forming short-lived rival parties, their number reduced to two only during the 1970s under the impact of de Gaulle's exceptional moral authority and electoral rules which stacked the odds against small parties, compelling some kind of amalgamation among friendly forces (Bartolini 1984). In the early 1980s, leaders of the two main parties were not on particularly good terms. Weakened by the death in office in 1974 of de Gaulle's chosen successor, Georges Pompidou, the Gaullists had re-formed in 1976 as the Rally for the Republic, under a young leader, Jacques Chirac, whom they followed uneasily on a deliberate course of confrontation with President Giscard and his supporters. The rival formations stood against each other in every seat in the parliamentary elections of 1978, Chirac going on to contest the presidency in 1981. Although he was eliminated in the first round, about a sixth of his supporters switched to Mitterrand on the second and his campaign was widely regarded as having cost the President the election (Lecomte 1982). As for Giscard's Union for French Democracy, it was not even a party at all, but a federation, formed in 1978 as part of his strategy to build a coalition which would back his campaign for re-election. It was made up of separate groups of Christian Democrats and liberals, supported by tiny factions of Radicals and self-styled Social Democrats (Colliard 1982).

Ejected from power in 1981, the conservatives patched up their quarrels and returned to the practice of conducting protracted negotiations ahead of each election, in order to draw up lists and allocate candidates to constituencies. Parliamentary elections were usually handled at national level, but in local contests a politician had a permanent incentive to try to steal a march on his rivals by concocting in secret a list including prominent local personalities whose contacts would guarantee delivery of a fraction of the vote, a factor which added spice to internal disagreements about the merits of local deals with the NF during the next few years. However, such conflicts also reflected, as pollsters soon demonstrated, the genuine depth of shared values across all three factions of the right in the early 1980s. As Table 3.2 shows, the word 'conservatism', which in the UK for so long automatically conveyed a sense of pragmatic preservation of what already exists, had little resonance in right-wing French political culture. On the other hand the terms 'right', 'Christian Democracy' and 'Gaullism' evoked varying degrees of sympathy in all three camps, the latter perhaps surprisingly endorsed by a healthy minority of those who lean to the NF. Other polls found that, amongst supporters of all three parties, more than 70 per cent favoured sending immigrants back to where they came from and more than 60 per cent favoured the restoration of the death penalty (Plenel and Rollat 1984, p.127). In his campaign in the Morbihan, a constituency where immigrants were less than 1 per cent of the population, Le Pen exploited such crossover and convergence in the value systems of the right by campaigning on unemployment, taxation and moral permissiveness (Plenel and Rollat 1984, pp. 96, 108).

Table 3.2   Shared values among supporters of the French right

In answer to the question, 'Where politics are concerned, tell me if each of the following terms mean something positive for you or negative?', samples of supporters of each party gave a percentage of positive responses as follows:

UDF		RPR		NF	
Right	73	Gaullism	78	Right	56
Gaullism	73	Right	75	Extreme Right	49
Centre	67	Centre	54	Gaullism	39
Chr. Demo'cy	46	Chr. Demo'cy	38	Conservatism	29
Conservatism	24	Conservatism	28	Chr. Demo'cy	27
Extreme Right	12	Extreme Right	10	Centre	24

Source: Poll carried out 18–24 October 1985 (SOFRES 1986, p.61)

The National Front leader took full advantage of the media attention his party was getting to 'say out loud what people think quietly to themselves', as he liked to put it, contrasting his party's down-to-earth style with the elitism of the established parties. These he termed the 'gang of four', an early example of his clever tactic of borrowing catchphrases from contemporary headlines. With typical earthy crudeness he told the weekly news magazine, *L'Express*,

Europe wasn't built over the centuries by accepting invasions, by lying down and opening her legs, she knew how to say no ... Have a look, on a lovely afternoon, at the café terraces on the *grands boulevards*, see all those immigrants! When we approach, they tell us: 'Go on, gentlemen, get to work! We need feeding!' Me, I say: 'What gives them the right?' (*L'Express* 16 September 1983)

A few weeks previously, the government had announced the creation of teams of inspectors to crack down on clandestine workshops and tough new border controls to curb illegal immigration. But these measures served only to lose it friends on the left while failing to wrest the initiative from Le Pen. In February 1984 he was interviewed for the first time on the prestigious prime-time current affairs programme, *L'heure de vérité*. Despatching with ease a panel of specially chosen journalists, he treated a mass audience to a first taste of his peculiarly bombastic and hectoring style, demanding a minute's silence for the victims of 'Communist dictatorship', asserting that the racism he abhorred more than any other was 'anti-French racism' and suggesting that while he did not consider himself an anti-semite, 'this doesn't mean that I ought to feel obliged to like the Veil (abortion) law or admire the paintings of Chagall' (cited in Rollat 1985, p.98). A Front insider later claimed that the party gained a thousand new recruits within three days of the programme's transmission (Durand 1996, p.53).

The Front therefore prepared for the European elections of June 1984 with the wind in its sails. Braving strong counter-demonstrations, 60,000 supporters attended a hundred meetings throughout France to hear speakers expound the ideas in the party programme, *Les Français d'Abord*, published on 15 May. Alongside the principal themes, immigration and law and order, it pandered to the middle and upper classes by attacking the 'Socialo-Communist' nationalisations, calling for the abolition of income tax and the freeing of businesses from bureaucratic regulation. Articulate, 'respectable' figures came to the fore, such as the businessman Jean-Pierre Schénardi, under whose leadership the Val-de-Marne federation grew from four to 350 members in two years. Meanwhile the Socialists' stock was sinking even lower. Another bout of occupation strikes in the car industry coincided with a march on Paris in support of redundant Lorraine steelworkers by thousands of their natural supporters. On the right, a series of monster regional demonstrations against educational reforms intended to deepen Catholic schools' integration into the state system, brought together supporters of the mainstream conservatives and the Front, partly thanks to the activism of a powerful Catholic fundamentalist current, one of whose leaders, Bernard Antony (*aka* Romain Marie) was running in the election on the NF ticket. But the conservatives played into Le Pen's hands by presenting a single list of candidates headed by Simone Veil, despised by the extremist fringe because of her Jewishness, her role in liberalising abortion laws in the 1970s and her forthright condemnation of the NF during the Dreux by-election. The results gave her 43 per cent of the vote, with the Socialists on 20.75 per cent, not only a shattering defeat compared to their 37.5 per cent share of the vote in 1981, but below even their score of 24 per cent in the previous parliamentary contest in 1978. The NF list won 10.95 per cent of the vote and ten seats in the European parliament, a stunning breakthrough signalling to themselves and to the outside world that the by-election successes had been no freak; from now on they were a force to be reckoned with in national politics.

But the greatest shock of the night concerned the Communist Party, for a generation the biggest in France, which from 1945 until 1980 had won between a quarter and a fifth of the vote at practically every election. Their decline to 15–16 per cent in the two elections of 1981 had been partly attributed to the dynamism of the Socialists. Now their humiliating 11.2 per cent of the poll, together with the Socialists' own poor showing, revealed that long-term sociological change, including the rise of the tertiary sector and feminisation of the workforce had eroded the compact battalions of blue-collar workers who were the party's core voters, setting challenges which the ageing and unimaginative party leadership was unable to meet (Howorth 1982; Raymond 1990). Soon the party was to be destabilised even more by the break-up of the Soviet empire and unprecedented outbursts of dissidence within its own ranks (Bell 1993).

The Front enters parliament

After a million-strong demonstration against the education bill had filled the streets of Paris just a week after the election, Mitterrand reacted with a three-fold strategy designed to redress the situation before the general election due in 1986 and the presidential two years later. First, he withdrew the schools bill and dispensed with the services not only of his Education Minister but also his Prime Minister. Although the Communists simultaneously decided to leave the government, judging that they would be better able to rebuild their support from the outside, the replacement of Pierre Mauroy, symbol of a traditional anti-clerical and class-conscious left, by the upper-class and youthful Laurent Fabius, product of France's elite civil service training system, had more to do with decor than with policy, for the turn from state interventionism towards deregulation and from Keynesian reflation towards austerity, had already been made (Holmes 1987). Secondly, aware of the existence of various grassroots campaigns against racism among the French-born children of immigrants, Mitterrand instructed his back-room staff to finance and help run a youth organisation, SOS Racisme, which would ultimately have much greater success in mobilising votes for himself in 1988 than in rolling back the general influence of the National Front (see Chapter 6). Certainly the latter task was seriously set back by the egregious Fabius. Interviewed on television shortly after taking over, the Prime Minister declared that the National Front asked the right questions but gave the wrong answers (*Antenne* 2, 5 September 1984). In fact, the exact opposite was true. If immigrants really were to blame for unemployment and rising crime then deporting them might be a logical option (Bihr 1986, p.69). Since such social problems were the result of quite other causes, as any school student studying for the *baccalauréat* could have told him, it was unlikely that following NF policies would solve them. Nevertheless, Fabius soon announced restrictions on the right to family reunion and a new voluntary repatriation scheme.

Mitterrand's third strategic ploy was to activate one of his 1981 election promises, the introduction of proportional representation for parliamentary elections. In doing so he was thinking ahead to what might happen during the two years between the end of the parliament elected for a five-year term in 1981, and the next presidential election, due in 1988. If the Socialists lost in 1986, as seemed likely, Mitterrand would be faced with the prospect of eking out the last two years of his mandate in an uncomfortable 'cohabitation' with a conservative government. On the other hand, if Fabius' demeanour and Mitterrand's own speeches in favour of the value of 'enterprise' could succeed in reassuring middle-class voters, while the party's natural base returned to the polls for an election in which much more was at stake than had been the case in 1984, then proportional rules ought to narrow even more the likely gap in seats between left and right. At the same time the right would be further weakened by the return of a handful of National Front deputies. On election day, 16 March 1986, the plan worked almost to perfection; the Socialists clawed their way back to 31 per cent of the vote, the Communists and the NF tied on 9.7 per cent, so that the 41 per cent for the RPR–UDF coalition was sufficient only for a majority of two seats over all other parties. Although there was nothing in the rules or the practice of the Fifth Republic that obliged him to do so, Mitterrand chose as Prime Minister the leader who commanded the most votes in Parliament, Jacques Chirac, evidently hoping that the difficulties he would face would disqualify him as a serious presidential challenger in 1988.

The NF's result was a triumph which demonstrated how little account its electors took of left-wing journalists' attempts to discredit Le Pen by

revealing unsavoury episodes from his past, such as the accounts of five
Algerians who accused him of having tortured prisoners while serving
in the French army in Algiers (*Libération* 12 February 1985), or the
allegation that he had hoodwinked an alcoholic cement millionaire,
Hubert Lambert, into leaving him millions of francs in his will in the 1970s,
before hastening his death by plying him with drink (*Le Matin* 1 April
1985). After long years in the political wilderness, Jean-Marie Le Pen had
the satisfaction of seeing elected alongside him, among the ten
Euro-deputies or the 35-strong parliamentary delegation, other founder-
members of his party like Dominique Chaboche, Jacques Bompard and
Martine Lehideux, along with a variety of representatives of the fractured
extreme-right tradition, including the Solidarists Stirbois and Michel
Collinot, the Catholic fundamentalist Bernard Antony, the royalist
Georges-Paul Wagner, as well as former terrorists Pierre Sergent and
Roger Holeindre, veterans, like Pascal Arrighi, of armed resistance to
Algerian decolonisation.

It was a triumph which brought with it, however, a test of the party's
cohesion and autonomy. In successive years, in 1984, then in 1985 when
it fielded 1500 candidates in county council elections, and now in 1986,
not only in the parliamentaries but also in regional elections held on the
same day, the party's accelerated development had obliged it to open its
lists to new members and sympathisers coming from a variety of horizons.
Some were political lightweights offered comfortable sinecures mainly
for their financial support, as was the case with the former Romanian
diplomat Gustave Pordea, whose connection with the international
church of the Reverend Moon, like that of Pierre Ceyrac, was the subject
of much press hilarity. There were representatives from the extreme-right
fringe in higher education, Bruno Gollnisch and Jean-Claude Martinez,
and political opportunists who turned to Le Pen when they were unable
to secure an investiture from one of the mainstream parties. Of these,
Edouard Frédéric-Dupont was one of the few who would leave the NF
group and sit as an independent soon after being elected to the National
Assembly. More significant were converts with important contacts in the
mainstream who conferred on the Front an aura of respectability and
seriousness. These included Jean-Marie Le Chevallier (a former collaborator
of the UDF's Paris boss, Jacques Dominati), Olivier d'Ormesson, member
of a well-known conservative family who had himself been elected to the
European Parliament on the conservative ticket in 1979, Dr François
Bachelot, former chairman of the Chamber of Liberal Professions, and
Michel de Rostalon who arrived via the Centre National des Indépendants
et Paysans (CNIP), a vehicle for the interests of middle-class industrialists

and farmers which had traditionally acted as a bridge between the extreme right and the conservative fringe. Finally, there were those like Jean-Yves Le Gallou and Bruno Mégret, a former RPR parliamentary candidate, authentic members of the extreme right, associated with an exclusive think-tank, the Clock Club, who had their own very definite ideas about the way the party should develop.

This impressive array of 'notables' was joined by a steady trickle of converts from the conservative grassroots. In Alsace, party branches in Mulhouse and Strasbourg were taken over by former members of the UDF and RPR respectively. In the 20th district of Paris, the local UDF president led two-thirds of his section into Le Pen's ranks, as did the former RPR leader in Toulouse. Other transfers occurred in the Loire (St Etienne and Roanne) and especially on the southern littoral (Sète, Draguignan, Avignon, Nîmes, Montpellier, Narbonne, Béziers; Plenel and Rollat 1984, pp.68–71). One journalist estimated that one out of every two new NF members was a former member of the RPR or UDF (*L'Express* 20 January 1984).

Seeing it inject so much fresh blood, there were those who expected the would-be anti-system party rapidly to degenerate into playing the parliamentary game, perhaps supporting Chirac's government in return for limited concessions to its own demands. Some of the 35 new deputies and the 135 new regional councillors might well succumb to the seductive influence of what were for many of them unprecedented material perks, including parliamentary assistants, access to official cars, a handsome salary (of which party HQ was quick to demand a share) and the blandishments of those who wanted their support in order to run for regional presidencies or positions on important committees. Himself a veteran of a previous experiment in parliamentary extremism in the 1950s, Le Pen no doubt already had an idea of his tactics. In 1984 he had made a speech stressing the supremacy of the party organisation. 'Any activist who strays from the discipline of the movement will be cast aside without pity, whatever the shared feelings or memories which may have linked them to us' (cited in *RLP Hebdo* 20 January 1984). On the eve of the 1986 session he led the entire parliamentary group to the grave of François Duprat, to pay homage to the National Front founder member whose career as a Holocaust revisionist and pro-Nazi pamphleteer had been cut short by a car bomb in 1978 (see Chapter 4). In his speech at Duprat's graveside Le Pen declared that he had not died in vain, since 'the combat to which he gave his life continues' (*National-Hebdo* 27 March–3 April 1986). If new deputies who were converts from the mainstream or relatively recent recruits to the NF had any reservations about such an eulogy, they were not made public.

Yet it was not long before the press unearthed evidence of a conflict between Stirbois and two of the party's Euro-deputies, Le Chevallier and d'Ormesson, which it took to be the sign of a battle for control of the organisation between the party's 'old guard' and the Front's more recently recruited 'moderate' elements (*Le Monde* 1 October 1987). Such a line of analysis seemed to be supported by the appointment of Bruno Mégret as Le Pen's campaign manager for the 1988 presidential election. 'We are going to ensure', he announced, 'that what remains of the damaging and caricatural image of Jean-Marie Le Pen disappears. This campaign is going to demonstrate his statesmanlike qualities' (*Le Monde* 2 April 1987). Yet Mégret's approach was entirely consistent with the parliamentary strategy being pursued by Le Pen and Stirbois. It was the NF leader himself who after the 1985 cantonal elections had demanded that the organisation adapt to changing circumstances, telling the party's National Council that three things were essential for the Front to progress: it needed to be organised nationally, to be united and to be respectable (*Article 31* January 1986). Partly in order to fulfil the last requirement, party headquarters forbade branches to draw up their own lists of candidates for the parliamentary elections, Stirbois imposing his choices with little or no regard for the opinions of the membership and expelling those who showed their dissidence too openly. In at least one case an endorsement meeting degenerated into a fight. Ironically, the methods which some of Stirbois' opponents denounced as 'fascist' (*Le Matin* 16 October 1985) were being deployed in order to make the Front more electable.

Once elected, however, it was soon obvious that the NF deputies had no intention of adhering to parliamentary traditions. They played little part in the detailed discussion of laws, instead loudly demanding a referendum on the restoration of the death penalty, something which was procedurally impossible according to the constitution. In October 1987, in protest at poor attendance by the mainstream parties in a debate on drugs, the NF deputies wreaked havoc in the chamber for a full ten hours, standing on the benches, hurling insults and exchanging blows with others (*Nouvel Observateur* 16, 22 October 1987).

Meanwhile Le Pen himself remained the party's unrivalled spokesman, guardian of its 'outsider' status and anti-system image. In February 1987, playing on fears generated by the AIDS epidemic, he declared that homosexuals, drug users, Africans and 'Israelites' were most at risk and demanded the creation of detention centres for those who were HIV-positive. Speaking on prime-time radio on 13 September he asserted that the existence of gas chambers in Nazi death camps were 'a point of detail in the history of the Second World War'. In the face of the predictable universal condemnation which such provocations aroused, Le Pen stubbornly refused to retract them, accusing the 'immigrant lobby' of organising a witch-hunt against him. What became known as the 'detail' remark quashed any hope that he would choose to ally himself with the party 'moderates' against Stirbois, a fact which d'Ormesson acknowledged by resigning from the party and condemning the NF as a revolutionary movement with fascist overtones (*Quotidien de Paris* 28 October 1987). Despite the supposed moderation of certain other deputies, nobody followed d'Ormesson's example. Bruno Mégret took no exception to Le Pen's comments and would soon become fully integrated into the party, taking an important post in the leadership. It is by no means certain, then, that Le Pen was fighting 'on ground which was not of his choosing' in the 'detail' affair, still less that the parliamentary punch-up or the collapse of a pact between RPR and NF councillors in the Paris region were a 'blow' to him, as some have supposed (Hargreaves 1988, p.32). It is true that the NF's standing in the polls plummeted in the following months. But this was ground easily recovered, and in the meantime Le Pen had separated himself from a faintheart like d'Ormesson (who had already served his purpose), driven a wedge between the mainstream and any of his followers tempted to compromise and strengthened the loyalty of his fascist hard-core. We discuss this whole question further in Chapter 5.

Towards the presidential election

The 'detail' affair was in fact an episode in Le Pen's campaign for the presidential election, which he formally announced in April 1987, shortly after a 10,000-strong rally in a Paris concert hall and a march through the streets of Marseilles by 20,000 of his supporters, a full year before the election was due. Party activists spent the summer months touring France's beaches with a caravan, holding meetings and film shows at which they pushed the party's promises to restore the death penalty, abolish income tax 'within five to seven years' and enact a comprehensive system of expulsions and discriminations against foreigners. Mégret used his contacts in the 'establishment' to organise a series of dinner debates to which councillors and opinion formers in each locality were invited, with the aim of raising money from a selection of industrialists and aristocrats. In December, Le Pen himself began a series of meetings all over the country, at which the public paid the equivalent of £3 to see a spectacular performance in which he would make his entry to the strains of 'The March of the Hebrew Slaves' from Verdi's *Nabucco*, mount a stage flanked by Olympic-style flames and roam around alone for up to two hours without a single note, deploying his comic talents via a radio microphone clipped to his tie, mocking the 'gang of four', impersonating his rivals and tirelessly concocting stories in which the triple strands of immigrants, AIDS and crime were all deftly woven. To a meeting of Christians organised by Bernard Antony he declared that governments ought to find their inspiration in the morality of the Ten Commandments; before an audience of *pieds noirs* in Montpellier he exalted the colonising mission of 'greater France', declaring that 'the white man' could not 'completely abandon his burden', and in Strasbourg, in front of an audience of 500 young nationalists from various European countries, he predicted that if Europe was to have a future it must be an 'imperial' one (Servent 1988).

While Le Pen was thus dominating his party's communications strategy, the other candidates manoeuvred to set up their own bids for the presidency. Chirac's acceptance of the premiership in 1986 reflected his judgement that it was better to be in the public eye for two years – albeit at the risk of wearing out the public's patience. But it did leave room for Raymond Barre, who had served as Giscard's Prime Minister from 1976 to 1981, to prepare his own campaign by methodically knitting together a network of contacts in the various fractions of the UDF. There was little difference in programmatic terms between these two, and indeed the RPR and UDF won the 1986 election on a joint programme of government largely inspired by the sort of deregulatory liberalism which had recently enjoyed such signal success in the UK and the USA. There were the traditional disputes about the potential spoils of victory, the Barre camp criticising Chirac for the way in which key blocks of shares from the newly privatised firms ended up in the hands of loyal RPR supporters, while the second-rank figures within each party attached themselves to one of the *presidentiables* in the expectation of getting a high-profile post in the event of victory. But as the campaign neared its end the Chirac and Barre camps were somewhat unexpectedly polarised in the positions they took up – tacitly and without referring to the NF – on the issues raised by Le Pen.

Chirac's priorities on taking office were deregulation of the economy, law and order, and immigration. Balladur, at the Ministry of Finance, abolished the Socialists' wealth tax, put through with tremendous speed a huge programme of privatisations and began to encourage citizens to invest in private pensions, while denying the government had any hostility to the welfare state. Pasqua, at the Ministry of the Interior, tightened controls over entry and residence permits, restored random identity checks and organised an immediate and symbolic deportation by charter flight, amidst carefully staged publicity, of 101 Malians, not all of them illegal, lifted from a workers' hostel. He also announced the government's intention to amend the nationality law in a way which would limit the automatic acquisition of French citizenship at the age of 18 of youngsters born in France of foreign parents. The intention to win back votes from the NF by borrowing from its programme could hardly have been more clearly signalled (Fysh 1987).

Before a year had passed, however, the government was knocked out of its stride when students resisted plans for increased selection in higher education, their demonstrations reaching a peak after one of their number, Malik Oussekine, was killed by police clearing the Latin quarter in the early hours of the morning of 4 December 1986. Public outrage at this crime, committed by members of a special unit of motorcyclists, the *voltigeurs*, in which the pillion rider wields a specially long club, was such that the government not only withdrew the education reform and accepted the resignation of the Minister of Higher Education, but also shelved the planned reform of the Nationality Code by handing it over to a commission. Almost immediately after Christmas, a clumsy attempt to apply deregulatory principles in the public sector by telescoping pay-scales and abolishing seniority increments, provoked strikes in the railways and the public utilities. Meanwhile, the undeclared civil war within conservative ranks over what attitude to take towards Le Pen and his troops rumbled on. In May 1987, Michel Noir (RPR), the Minister of Foreign Trade, whose father had died as a deportee in Germany during the war, had his name hissed at his party congress after writing in a newspaper article that it was better to lose an election than to lose one's soul by allying with Le Pen. In July Hervé de Fontmichel (UDF) secured his re-election as mayor of Grasse by incorporating six NF candidates on to his list and was promptly expelled by the tiny Radical Party. In September, Le Pen's outburst on the gas chambers gave Philippe Séguin, Minister of Social Affairs, the opportunity to pledge on television that he would leave the RPR if it ever made a formal deal with the Front. Chirac, the coalition leader, gave no lead at all, alternately denouncing racism in the abstract and claiming to 'understand' the reasons why people voted for the NF (Fysh 1988; Hargreaves 1988).

While Chirac tied himself in knots trying to be all things to all voters, Raymond Barre, mainly thanks to his backers, who included Simone Veil and leaders of the social Catholic fraction of the UDF, managed to position himself as the man of tolerance, who would not stoop to pick up votes from the gutter (Morris 1988). But it was Mitterrand who had all the best cards in his hands. He did just enough to maintain the outward signs of formal collaboration with the Republic's government, while sharply dissociating himself from policies with which he disagreed by delaying legislation to implement the privatisations, receiving delegations of the student demonstrators at the Elysée palace and chatting with railway and power workers on their picket lines. These carefully staged manoeuvres earned him the affectionate nickname *tonton* (uncle) among the students, allowing him to adopt the pose of 'father of the nation' in the looming presidential contest. Whereas in 1981 he had promised radical change, he now shunned the Socialist label, stressed his role as President of all the French and promised, in a letter distributed to all households, to continue his actions in favour of deliberately non-ideological causes like the construction of Europe, world peace and education, a stance summed up in his campaign slogan, *La France Unie*, a united France.

When the votes were counted on 24 April, they revealed that Barre and Le Pen were eliminated, along with the clutch of minor candidates. Barre's score of 16.54 per cent, the lowest by any UDF candidate until then, was in one sense the result of the parallelism of his and Mitterrand's strategies; 'there was no political space for two senior citizens when one was already President' (Morris 1988, p.30). In another, it revealed that the size of the 'centre' constituency was hardly greater than that of the extreme. Le Pen not only topped the poll in many towns and cities of the south-east, he also came within 2000 votes of outpolling Barre in Paris and did outscore him in the former centrist heartland of Alsace. With good reason he described his 4.4 million votes, 14.4 per cent of the poll, as a 'political earthquake'. Chirac's 19.9 per cent was enough to put him in the second round but was seen by most commentators as a shattering defeat, giving him no chance of making up the ground on Mitterrand, who led with 34.1 per cent. Causing an unprecedented segregation of three right-wing electorates, Le Pen's populist appeal had forced the mainstream into a sociological ghetto, with Barre and Chirac each receiving only 7 per cent of workers' votes. Thanks to his repeated failures to confront Le Pen's racism, Chirac appeared as the champion of a 'hard' right, with 32 per cent of his voters saying they favoured a multiracial society, and 55 per cent favouring electoral pacts with Le Pen, while pluralities of Barre's supporters took the opposite view (Grunberg *et al.* 1988).

In the fortnight between the two rounds, Chirac and his henchmen orchestrated a series of dramatic stunts in a frantic effort to persuade Le Pen's disappointed voters to transfer to him in the second round. Charles Pasqua, the Minister of the Interior, succeeded not only in freeing, thanks to some unrevealed concession, three civilian hostages from captivity in Beirut, but also in bringing home from a lonely atoll to a French prison a Special Boat Squad agent convicted in New Zealand for her part in sinking a Greenpeace campaign ship a few years earlier. Meanwhile Bernard

Pons, Minister for the Overseas Departments, authorised a bloody assault against independence fighters holding hostages in the Pacific territory of New Caledonia which succeeded only in causing the deaths of several of the combatants on either side. In case there was any doubt about whom these messages were aimed at, Pasqua gave an interview to a right-wing magazine in which, conceding that there were surely 'a few extremists' in the NF, he added that, 'on essentials' the Front had the same preoccupations and defended the same values as the mainstream (*Le Monde* 5 May 1988). These gestures turned out to be fruitless; while Barre's voters largely transferred to Chirac and those of the extreme left swung to Mitterrand, it is estimated that up to a million of Le Pen's voters did not bother to go to the polls in the run-off, and of those who did, a quarter voted for Mitterrand (Hargreaves 1988, p.33), seeing him comfortably returned to the Elysée with the largest second-round majority since 1969. A clear majority for candidates of the right on the first round had turned into a victory for the left on the second.

But further evidence of the Front's potential to distort the 'normal' electoral process was soon to be at hand. After a brief and fruitless effort to tempt senior Barrists into the government, Mitterrand again dissolved the chamber, as he had in 1981, in search of a majority more to his liking. In the subsequent elections, the NF candidates found themselves facing a difficult obstacle course. The two-round first-past-the-post system having been restored by the outgoing government, they would first have to make it into the second round by winning the votes of at least 12.5 per cent of the registered electors in their constituency and then persuade any other similarly qualified right-wing candidates to withdraw, leaving them to carry the right's banner against the left. They in fact won an average 9.8 per cent of the first-round vote, down on Le Pen's presidential score but comparable to the 1986 vote. Only 30 of them passed the 12.5 per cent barrier; in some cases they promptly withdrew but in others they were ordered to maintain their candidatures, consequently splitting the right-wing vote and bringing about the defeat of conservative candidates who had earned the NF's enmity. But in the south, where nine NF candidates had actually outscored their mainstream rivals on the first round, two years of amicable tripartite RPR–UDF–NF management in the Provence–Alpes–Côte d'Azur region had prepared the ground for a spectacular deal, brokered by the UDF parliamentary leader, Jean-Claude Gaudin. In Marseilles and its suburbs, five RPR and three UDF candidates stood down in favour of the better-placed NF candidate, while the NF returned the favour in another eight seats. As it happened, six of the RPR–UDF candidates were elected and none of the Front's were, a crucial fraction of the conservative electorate preferring to abstain or vote for the left rather than see a Frontist in Parliament. But a parallel local deal did produce success; near Toulon, in the neighbouring constituency of the Var, Yann Piat, the ninth NF candidate to defeat her mainstream rival on the first round, benefited from his withdrawal in the second and went on to become the Front's sole deputy in the new Parliament.

After five dramatic years, in which its breakthrough had been aided by the frequency of elections conducted under proportional rules, some of them contests with little impact on domestic policy which left open the possibility of a protest vote (Machin 1990), the Front seemed to have come full circle, its parliamentary party wiped out at a stroke. It was tempting to think that, deprived of this platform, the party would dwindle and disappear. On the contrary, during the next four years, in the less prominently publicised arena of local government, it put down sturdy roots and found its crude vociferations against minorities increasingly echoed by politicians who liked to think of themselves as 'mainstream'.

Opportunities, challenges and consolidation, 1988–92

During Mitterrand's second term of office the social conditions which had helped spur the rapid growth of the National Front up to 1988 showed little sign of abating. Between 1985 and 1990 the proportion of firms linking pay rises to individual performance more than doubled, the proportion of the workforce affected rising from 45 per cent to 60 per cent, while the number of temporary contracts tripled, accounting for 37 per cent of all new hirings in 1991 (INSEE 1993; *Le Monde* 30 September 1992). After a brief recovery in 1987–90 unemployment rose to more than 12 per cent of the active population and the early 1990s saw the revival of pitched battles between youths and the police on the council estates of the urban peripheries. On the political front, three Socialist prime ministers, Michel Rocard (1988–91), Edith Cresson (1991–92) and Pierre Bérégovoy (1992–93), headed a series of minority governments which made little attempt to return either to the radical reformism or the statist economic management of the early 1980s, contenting themselves instead with running an orthodox monetary policy based on high interest rates, accompanied by periodic attempts to attenuate its inevitable social effects. Partly thanks to a series of corruption scandals, the Socialist vote collapsed, allowing the right to enjoy a landslide victory on their return in 1993. Excluded from Parliament, the National Front found itself at times having to manoeuvre adroitly on unfavourable terrain; its criticism of French deployment in the war against Iraq (1990–91) appeared to surrender the patriotic ground to Mitterrand and Chirac, while its opposition to ratification of the Maastricht Treaty on European Union (1992) left it in no more than a supporting role in a heteroclite coalition which included the Communists, the left wing of the Socialist party and the populist wing of the Gaullists. Crucially, however, the Front rarely surrendered the initiative in its drive to expand the limits of what it was acceptable to say about race and immigration, inducing leaders of both left and right to follow it after 1988 as they had before.

Michel Rocard: the politics of pragmatic consensus

The parliamentary elections of 1988 which, as we saw in Chapter 3, eliminated all but one of the National Front's deputies, nonetheless returned 27 Communists on a similar 10 per cent share of the popular vote, thanks to the greater concentration of the Communists' strength and their strategy of standing well known local figures, usually mayors, in their working-class strongholds. Ironically, since the Socialists fell short of a majority by 13 seats (Mitterrand himself not having helped their cause by publicly warning that an absolute majority for one party would be a bad thing), there existed on paper the mathematical possibility of a new left-wing coalition. Neither the Communists, preferring the role of opposition, nor Mitterrand, with his campaign promise of an 'opening to the centre', were interested. However, although the Christian-inspired component of the UDF felt sufficiently inspired by the events of the year to form their own parliamentary group, the Union of the Centre (UDC), they refused to agree to a programmatic pact with the Socialists. The new Prime Minister, Michel Rocard, accordingly fell back on politicians who had last held office under Giscard in the 1970s, including the ill-starred former minister responsible for immigrant workers, Lionel Stoléru, adding figures from outside mainstream politics such as the ecologist Brice Lalonde and the media darling and founder of the charity Médecins Sans Frontières, Bernard Kouchner. At the head of a government of which one-third was non-Socialist, Rocard set about implementing the programme outlined by Mitterrand in his presidential manifesto, the 'Letter to all the French', combining a rigorous economic policy with measures to help the new poor: 'austerity with a human face' (Ross and Jenson 1989, p.7).

Following his personal penchant for consensus politics the Prime Minister consulted widely with social forces outside Parliament and negotiated with the opposition parties in an attempt to compensate his minority situation by constructing fleeting majorities on the merits of each individual project. This produced rapid resolution of the conflict in New Caledonia and unanimous approval of a new supplementary benefit for those who had fallen through the social security net, called the Revenu Minimum d'Insertion (RMI), while a watered down wealth tax, replacing the 1982 version abolished in 1986, was carried with the help of Communist votes against combined RPR–UDF–UDC opposition (Lovecy 1991). A further tax of 1.1 per cent on all incomes, intended to fund the epic deficit in the health and social security budgets, narrowly squeezed through against a vote of no-confidence put down by the opposition.

The government stood firm against pay demands fuelled by a brief economic upturn in the autumn of 1988. Strikes by public sector workers and Paris transport staff, co-ordinated by rank and file committees rather than the unions, became drawn-out and bitterly fought affairs thanks to Rocard's insistence on lengthy negotiations on the detailed points at issue rather than conceding across-the-board increases (Elgie 1991); his popularity with the left electorate was irreparably damaged when troops were employed to provide transport in the capital and the police allowed to break up nurses' demonstrations.

On immigration policy, Rocard hoped to achieve consensus by persuading the conservatives to commit themselves to positive measures in favour of the social integration of existing minorities, in exchange for the left's commitment to firm controls on new entries. He declined, however, to legislate on the restrictive proposals put forward by the 'Commission of wise men and women' which had been charged by the Chirac government to prepare a reform of the Nationality Code, and allowed the new Minister of the Interior, Pierre Joxe, to reverse Pasqua's 1986 measures to transfer control of entry rules from the courts to the police and administration. Naturally, Rocard could expect no co-operation at all from the National Front, which began the new septennate as it had finished the last: Le Pen's disparagement of the new Radical minister, Michel Durafour, by calling him 'Durafour-*crématoire*', was a deliberate reminder to friends and enemies of his previous dismissal of Hitler's incinerators (*four-crématoires*) as minor historical details (see Chapter 5).

Le Pen was frequently saved from having to resort to such calculated sallies, however, by actors from the mainstream who turned the spotlight on minorities on at least three occasions during the summer and autumn of 1989. Gérard Dezempte, the RPR mayor of Charvieu-Chavagneux, a village near Grenoble in the industrialised valleys of the Alps, tried to frighten local Muslims by instructing contractors to demolish an old canteen being used as a prayer-room while nine people were still inside it. After Dezempte's election as mayor in 1983 the municipality had acquired ownership of the land on which the prayer-room stood and given the Muslims notice to quit; his re-election in 1989 followed a campaign in which he claimed that a mosque would turn Charvieu into a magnet for Muslims and halve property values in the commune. For their part, local Muslims recounted how they had bought land on which to build a community centre, only to be refused planning permission by an administration which had even managed to prevent an Algerian sports club from using the town stadium (*Le Monde* 18, 19, 20, 27 August 1989).

The affair threatened to escalate when Friday prayers were held in the garden in front of the town hall, in the presence of delegations from leftist unions and associations including the MRAP, SOS Racisme and the CFDT, and the local NF organiser was kept in the police station for a night after discharging his shotgun (loaded with grains of rice) at a group of youths who he claimed had insulted him. Next, Bruno Mégret turned up in Charvieu, holding a press conference at which he congratulated the mayor for having 'done what no NF mayor would have dared to do', and announced:

> Islam can only be present in France if it is marginal ... Our country will not escape the law of nature which means that there is no possible peaceful coexistence between ethnic and religious communities which are radically different. (*Le Monde* 27 August 1989)

Meanwhile, however, the local prefect, on the orders of the Interior Ministry, had reminded the mayor that the Republic guaranteed freedom of conscience and the free exercise of religion and that the commune had no right to oppose the opening of a mosque either directly or by manoeuvres. Suitably chastised, Dezempte promised to erect pre-fab buildings on the site of the destroyed prayer-room and to provide two classrooms for the 276 children temporarily deprived of their school-support classes, proposing for good measure the purchase for future needs of a large villa in the centre of the commune (*Le Monde* 29 August 1989).

A few weeks later, the opportunities open to headstrong mayors tempted to play politics with community relations were further illustrated at Montfermeil in the Paris suburbs, where the 'independent conservative' Pierre Bernard threatened to cut off canteen, heating and cleaning services, paid for by the municipality, from two nursery schools which had disobeyed his instructions not to register foreign children. Once again, pushed by a campaign uniting the CFDT, SOS Racisme and local parents' associations, the prefect called in the recalcitrant mayor and instructed him to abandon his plans, but not before the 'threat' of overcrowding by 'immigrants' in suburban schools had been well aired by the popular press and a demonstration in support of Bernard had been attended by the local RPR deputy, Eric Raoult (*Le Monde* 12, 17 October 1989).

The Headscarf Affair

If the Charvieu and Montfermeil affairs obliged anti-racists to develop the arguments needed to combat a couple of minor local politicians hovering between the conservative fringe and the National Front, the major *cause célèbre* of that same autumn, the so-called Headscarf Affair, found the Muslim minority under attack simultaneously from the right *and* from the left. On 18 September three pupils of Maghreb origin were excluded from their secondary school in Creil, some 50 km to the north of Paris, for wearing their headscarves in class, their Gaullist headmaster Ernest Chenière arguing that the secular principles on which state education was founded excluded the wearing of religious symbols or garments. When the case was taken up by anti-racist associations, the girls were first allowed back into lessons when they agreed to drop their scarves on to their shoulders in the classroom and then excluded once more when they reverted to covering their hair. In a debate which raged for nearly three months every editorialist and leader-writer found it necessary to register his or her opinion, while political parties, apart from the National Front, maintained an embarrassed silence, a sure sign that they were internally divided. Indeed, when the Education Minister, Lionel Jospin, finally told the National Assembly, in the last week of October, that he had instructed Chenière to drop his ban and allow the girls to return to school, he was applauded from the UDC benches and attacked by Socialist deputies and fellow ministers (Gaspard and Khosrokhavar 1995, pp.21–2).

The reason for this apparent paradox was the left's strong attachment to the principle of secular education which, ever since the banning of all religious instruction from state schools in the 1880s, had formed part of republican leaders' historic drive to extirpate Catholic influence from all areas of life. The Communist *L'Humanité* had already on 7 October reversed its original sympathy for the girls by putting the matter in this light. When the Catholic primate Cardinal Lustiger suggested in *Le Monde* (21 October 1989) that some girls' decision to wear the scarf perhaps represented no more than a form of juvenile assertion of identity, like the wearing of dreadlocks, and called for an end to the 'war on Beur adolescents', he provoked the wrath of that part of the left whose self-assigned mission was to defend the lay character of state education from religious encroachment. The Socialist Party secretary Pierre Mauroy (a former schoolteacher as well as former Prime Minister) declared that the French should not have to submit to fundamentalism (*Le Monde* 24 October 1989), while the teachers' unions unanimously condemned Jospin's decision, as did his cabinet colleagues Jean Poperen and Jean-Pierre Chevènement, the latter a leader of a rather nationalistic and autarchic current in the Socialist Party who warned that the 'right to difference' would turn France into a new Lebanon (Vichniac 1991, p.50). But the left's most astonishing over-reaction was expressed in a joint open letter to Jospin from a group of five intellectuals, including Régis Debray, Alain Finkielkraut and Elisabeth Badinter, published by the *Nouvel Observateur* (26 October–1 November 1989). Labelling the headscarf a symbol of patriarchal oppression, they described Jospin's decision as 'the Munich of the republican school-system', implying that they regarded the stigmatised girls as hostile forces whom the Minister was attempting to appease. Recalling that French democracy was synonymous with the republican form of government, they went on:

> [The Republic] is not a mosaic of ghettos where the law of the strongest is dressed up as freedom for all. Devoted to free enquiry, linked to the expansion of knowledge and relying only on the natural light of human reason, the republic's foundation is public education. That is why the destruction of the school system means the destruction of the republic itself. (cited in Gaspard and Khosrokhavar 1995, p.23)

In the following weeks this article was widely quoted and commented on in the media. For an important and influential section of the left, three small squares of cloth had now become synonymous not only with the destruction of the school system but with the end of a century or more of French civilisation!

Jospin and his supporters were able to retort that if Islam was to be deplored because it oppressed women, then the exclusion of Muslim girls from state schools would only reinforce that oppression, restricting them to the home or to private Koranic schools. The emancipation of Muslim women, furthermore, was likely to be all the more secure if conquered by the women themselves, rather than by state imposition – especially if the latter was at the cost of playing into the hands of the National Front. Later research would in any case confirm that, among girls and young women who chose to wear the scarf, those who felt pushed into it because of family and peer pressure were a small minority, while wearing the scarf rarely implied acceptance of more unambiguous forms of oppression such as polygamy and arranged marriages which were in any case little practised in France (Gaspard and Khosrokhavar 1995, pp.34–68).

But the most incongruous aspect of the whole affair was the credibility given to the idea that France was on the threshold of an irreversible choice between conflicting models of society, with the girls of Creil cast as the vanguard of a flood of their co-religionists waiting only for a signal before flocking to school in 'traditional' dress. As the National Front's Bruno Mégret put it, 'We will have to ask ourselves the question, should France have to adapt its principles to suit the immigrants, or is it the immigrants who should adapt to the customs and rules of our country?' (*Quotidien de Paris* 18 October 1989). Yet only 30 per cent of a sample of Muslim parents polled at the height of the affair favoured allowing the headscarf to be worn in school, a proportion which had fallen to 22 per cent five years later, with 44 per cent against and 30 per cent indifferent (*Le Monde* 30 November 1989 and 13 October 1994). The number of girls who sought to wear the scarf to school was tiny, rising from a few dozen to 2000 during 1993–94, according to the Education Ministry. Even the rival figure of 15,000, floated by Pasqua's Ministry of the Interior in 1994, when set against the 350,000 girls from Muslim families who were attending state schools daily without controversy (Hargreaves 1995, pp.129–30), served to underline the unreality of the alleged threat to republican norms. In political terms, the Creil case evoked no mobilisation at all in the Maghreb communities which form the vast majority of Muslims in France. The families at the heart of the case are thought to have been influenced by the so-called National Federation of Muslims of France (Gaspard and Khosrokhavar 1995, p.16), a tiny organisation founded in 1985 and representative mainly of French converts to Islam. During the entire affair, the one national demonstration in their defence, attended by 500–600 people on 22 October, was jointly organised by the Voice of Islam, a tiny pro-Iranian group and the, mainly Turkish, Islamic Association of France (Hargreaves 1995, p.128). In mainstream French politics, however, the effects of the affair were immediate and direct. The right of young girls to choose to wear the scarf was defended by SOS Racisme, a youthful anti-racist campaign largely inspired and financed by the Socialist Party and given publicity by the sponsorship of a clutch of Socialist-friendly cultural and media personalities. But it was soon disavowed by some of its former sponsors, including the veteran feminist Gisèle Halimi, and then betrayed by Mitterrand who, having cynically identified with SOS in order to garner the youth vote and help secure his own re-election, had no further use for such a lively and radical movement. His announcement on television in December that the number of immigrants in France had now passed the infamous 'threshold of tolerance', was said to have left many SOS members 'traumatised' (*Le Monde* 9 January 1990). Not to be outdone, Jean-Marie Le Pen declared that all immigrants, legal or otherwise, who had entered France since 1974, should be deported and that workers who wanted to be reunited with their families would have to go home: 'nobody ever promised them that they could stay indefinitely' (*Le Figaro* 6 December 1989). Speaking in Lyons at the height of the affair, Le Pen hailed the city as the capital of resistance to 'Islamic occupation', just as it had been against German occupation during the war (*Le Monde* 28 November 1989). In September opinion polls had shown immigration to be the issue ranked eighth in importance by potential voters; in the aftermath of the Headscarf Affair it was second only to employment (Mayer 1991, pp.116–17). In November, running on the slogan, 'No to the headscarf in schools, no to mosques', Jean-Pierre Stirbois' widow, Marie-France, won a sensational parliamentary by-election victory in Dreux, polling 61 per cent of the second-round vote. The Dreux result, following a good performance in the June European elections, ended the premature optimism which had some commentators interpreting the Front's performance in the March local government contests (2.5 per cent nationally, 10.1 per cent in its targeted urban areas) as a setback. When Parliament held a debate on integration in the spring of 1990 the Front's poll support rose to 18 per cent, its highest ever rate (Mayer 1991).

Although these events rendered all the more urgent Rocard's attempts to build a cross-party consensus on immigration policy, the conservative parties' response was lukewarm. Their 'round table discussions' with the Prime Minister at Matignon in April and May achieved little, due to their reluctance to be seen by voters as involved in co-legislation with the Socialists. Instead, the RPR devoted the spring to running a petition campaign demanding reform of the nationality law, which culminated in the presentation of a bill in the Senate on 21 June (Fysh 1991). The right could hardly oppose, however, the creation in February 1990 of a High Council for Integration, made up of top civil servants, academics and politicians, with a brief to study the situation of marginalised minorities and to propose remedies for the worst cases of exclusion, nor the channelling of extra resources into the processing of political asylum applications, with the aim of reducing the time it took to deal with them from an average of three years to six months, a reform which in time had the effect of reducing the number of refugees seeking asylum in France (Hargreaves 1995, p.21). Given a period of political calm, Rocard must have hoped that the effects of these practical measures would in time reassure minorities that they were welcome in France and deprive the NF of grist for its mill. Unfortunately, another year of political drama was to disappoint him on both counts.

On 9 May 1990 the whole political establishment again united in condemnation of Le Pen after his latest long television interview on *L'heure de vérité*. There was nothing new in the NF leader's complaints about the influence of Jews in the media, but when, the next morning, 34 graves in a Jewish cemetery in Carpentras were found with swastikas daubed over the tombstones, with one of the corpses, that of an 80-year-old man, having been exhumed and impaled, a wave of anti-NF feeling swept the country. In the previous months the Front had displayed its anti-semitism with increasing effrontery. In September 1989 Claude Autant-Lara, an NF Euro-deputy, told *Globe* magazine that Simone Veil played on her status as an Auschwitz survivor to curry favour with the public, regretting that the Nazi genocide had spared 'old mother Veil' (*Globe* September 1989). In a television debate in December Le Pen had openly baited the Jewish minister Lionel Stoléru, remarking that he was an official of a France–Israel friendship society and asking if it was true that he had dual nationality. Later, when the subject turned to the illegal employment of immigrant workers, Stoléru boasted that he had himself taken part in raids of the Sentier area of Paris, a district with a large Jewish population. 'Really? So you could carry out a *rafle*?', interjected Le Pen, deliberately employing the term used to describe the 1942 round-up of Jews by the Vichy government, prior to their dispatch to the death camps (*Libération* 6 December 1989).

In the week that followed the Carpentras outrage over 50 demonstrations against racism and anti-semitism were held across France, including a 200,000-strong march through Paris on 14 May, headed by the leaders of all the mainstream parties except Giscard. In Parliament a Communist deputy, Jean-Claude Gayssot, successfully moved a Bill making public contestation of crimes against humanity an offence (Hansson 1991, pp.42–3). The government ordered that a documentary film about the Holocaust, *Nuit et Brouillard*, be immediately screened on national television, a number of mayors plucked up the courage to ban the National Front from meeting on municipal premises and sanctions were taken in schools, in universities and in the police force against extreme right-wing sympathisers (Mayer 1991, p.117). A text by six leading academics calling for sanctions against lecturers associated with Holocaust revisionism (*L'Evénement du Jeudi* 28 June 1990), met with success when a professor in Lyons was fined by the courts and disciplined by his university for a negationist article.

In short, in response to the Carpentras outrage anti-racists did what they had failed to do during the Headscarf Affair: they united in defence of a stigmatised minority community and managed to put the Front on the defensive. Although the NF ran a long campaign proclaiming its innocence[2] and denouncing the anti-NF mood as a Jewish plot, the party's poll rating fell from 18 per cent to 11 per cent in a month. The mood did not last, however: by July the Front's standing had returned to pre-Carpentras levels (Mayer 1991, p.118) and in November the party, with 48.5 per cent of the second-round vote, narrowly failed to win control of Nice in a city by-election provoked by the surprise departure of the previous mayor to South America.

The Gulf War

If the Headscarf Affair largely worked in the National Front's favour, the Gulf War at first represented something of a challenge. Barely ten weeks after the desecration at Carpentras, Saddam Hussein's troops invaded Kuwait and Le Pen astonished his opponents by spurning the opportunity to whip up anti-Arab fervour, declaring that French soldiers should not have to 'die for Kuwait' and that the conflict was primarily an Arab affair. Clearly out of phase with the party's supporters, who in August offered a higher rate of support for George Bush (82 per cent) and US military action (75 per cent) than supporters of all the other parties (*Le Monde* 26, 27 August 1990) the leadership's stance could be seen on one level as a gamble based on the assumption that public opinion would turn against the war once French casualties mounted (Marcus 1995, p.124).

Le Pen had to deal with internal dissent from members whose first reaction was to support French troops in whatever action they had been deployed, bringing Pierre Sergent into line although losing another politbureau member, Jules Monnerot, who resigned over the issue. But within the party, non-intervention pleased the most bigoted anti-semites, since the US-led venture to dislodge Saddam was widely seen as serving Israeli interests as well as US global ambitions; and the revision of the pro-US line which had seen the party support the US bombing of Libya in 1986 was part of a wider strategic aim to counter the impression that it was simply a xenophobic single-issue movement of 'simple-minded, visceral anti-Arabs', while presenting Le Pen as a 'man of peace' (Bruno Mégret, *Libération* 29 August 1990). In November the Front's leader tried to fashion an image as a statesman by heading a delegation of far-right

2. It was not until August 1966 that a group of skinheads with links to the far-right PNFE confessed to the desecration.

members of the European Parliament which was greeted in Baghdad by Saddam Hussein and his Foreign Minister Tariq Aziz, Le Pen later claiming credit for rescuing 63 French hostages, although their release had been decided some weeks earlier (Marcus 1995, p.123).

At the same time the party's members and supporters, who found themselves on the same side as the Communists and a branch of the Greens, were challenged to adopt a more sophisticated perspective on events than the populist racism which had drawn them to the Front. During the war of nerves accompanying the build-up of US troops, the party's cadres convinced a large part of the periphery that in a post-Communist world the greatest threat to nation-states was posed by 'mondialism', represented in this instance by US imperialism and the state of Israel (*Le Monde* 30 August 1990). By October 1990 as many as 67 per cent of NF voters believed that military intervention in the Gulf was unnecessary (Simmons 1996, p.102). On 23 January 1991, Le Pen was able to tell a rally of 4000 supporters that the war was

> ... an international police operation executed with the complicity of our political authorities to benefit the interests of foreign powers dressed up as the defence of international law

an argument which Le Gallou elaborated two days later in a *Le Monde* article in which he took a lofty tone to warn of the dangers of driving the Arab world into a defensive block, not forgetting to mention that the son and grandson of former president de Gaulle took more or less the same view, as did his former Foreign Secretary, Couve de Murville (*Le Monde* 25 January 1991).

The war, which finished on 28 February, revealed once more both the sense of vulnerability of some members of the population of north African origin, regardless of age or social situation, and their mixed feelings about the need for an organisation which could represent them (see Chapter 6). It had also given the National Front an opportunity to enhance the range and quality of its links with its periphery and boosted Mitterrand's popularity, but done nothing to raise the standing of the ruling Socialist party, one of whose leaders, Chevènement, had resigned as Defence Minister on the eve of hostilities. The mainstream parties failed to profit from the Front's momentary discomfiture after Carpentras and during the war, partly because of revelations about the shocking amount of financial corruption in which they were involved (see Chapter 9) and partly because of internal discord. The Socialist Party congress held in Rennes in March 1990 was a disastrous, acrimonious affair dominated by faction-fighting as various rivals – Jospin, Fabius, Rocard, Mauroy – began jockeying for position in what was to be a long battle for control of the party as Mitterrand neared retirement. The year before, the RPR and UDF had been destabilised by the activities of a group of 'renovators' who wanted to dissolve the public's impression of their parties as perpetually warring electoral machines, by ditching the two historic leaders, Giscard and Chirac (Bresson and Thénard 1989), one of them, Michel Noir, being elected mayor of Lyons against the hierarchs' wishes. Their revolt fizzled out when a dissident list put up at the June 1989 European elections won only 8.4 per cent of the vote, Giscard's score of 28.9 per cent for the official RPR–UDF list leaving him firmly in the saddle. In the RPR, however, Chirac was forced to accept the constitution of rival factions at the party's conference in February 1990, an historic first for the Gaullist movement. Although he and general secretary Alain Juppé won the day, two party heavyweights, Charles Pasqua and Philippe Séguin, won the backing of a third of conference delegates for their demand for a return to the populist roots of Gaullism, and would remain thorns in the leadership's side (Fysh 1993).

Stealing the National Front's clothes

It had always been assumed that Rocard, who had never been a member of Mitterrand's circle, would not last the full five-year legislature. With the Gulf conflict safely over, the President duly sacked him on 15 May 1991, entrusting the task of restoring party fortunes before the regional elections due the following spring to his friend and protégée, Edith Cresson. An experienced and combative politician who had publicly scrapped with the farmers' and small business lobbies when serving successively as Agriculture and Industry Minister in the early 1980s, Cresson made her reputation in Châtellerault in the 1983 local government elections by becoming the only Socialist to defeat a sitting conservative mayor. A Mitterrand loyalist first and foremost, she was not a player in the internal party politics which had disfigured the Rennes congress in the previous year, nor was she a product of the elite civil service training schools, from whose extensive and distinctly masculine old-boy network she could expect no favours. If, by sending her to Matignon, Mitterrand secretly hoped that she would not only rally the party and the voters but emerge as a presidential contender in 1995, then it was a gamble in which the odds were impossibly long. In office for only ten months, she became the most unpopular of all the Socialist prime ministers, neither voters nor colleagues warming to the abrasive and populist style which had her telling journalists she 'didn't give a damn' about the value of the Stock Exchange, questioning the virility of British men and calling for economic war against the Japanese, whose impressive industry she likened to that of ants.

Lamentably, Cresson tried to compensate for her isolation by announcing that her government would get tough on immigration. Planes would be chartered, she boasted, to deport illegal immigrants. With her comments greeted by Mégret as vindication of what the NF had been saying for years (*Le Monde* 10 July 1991), the anti-racist association the MRAP found it necessary, in the same week, to express its 'stupefaction' at a Communist Party leaflet which reiterated familiar stereotypes about the immigrant population being prone to drug dealing, crime and delinquency while taking advantage of the social security system at the expense of French families (Shields 1994, pp.241–2). Suddenly it seemed as if everyone was trying to drum up extra votes by outbidding the NF. On 19 June, Jacques Chirac had told a meeting of supporters in Orléans that there was an 'overdose' of foreigners in France and that 'having Spanish, Polish and Portuguese workers in our country poses fewer problems than having Muslims and blacks', who, according to him, lived with three or four wives and 20 or so children in council flats, earning three times more in social security payments than the combined wage of an average couple 'naturally' without even working. 'If you add to that the noise and the smell', Chirac concluded, French workers were understandably driven mad (Plenel and Rollat 1992, pp.331–3). In September, in the much less spontaneous setting of an article in the *Figaro-Magazine*, Giscard deliberately echoed an NF slogan, referring to the immigration 'invasion', and endorsed one of the main planks of its programme, reform of the Nationality Code to prevent the children of immigrants becoming French by virtue of their birth on French territory (Plenel and Rollat 1992, p.333).

Such unanimity allowed Le Pen to laugh off condemnations of his racism and anti-semitism and proclaim himself to be at the centre of the political spectrum, 'because with certain expressions, Messrs Chirac and Giscard d'Estaing have considerably outflanked me' (Plenel and Rollat 1992, p.341). True to form, however, the Front took the debate a stage further. In November Mégret made a chilling statement in which he referred to the French people as 'a species' and condemned the 'disappearance of human races by generalised cross-breeding' (*Le Monde* 5 November 1991). Two weeks later he unveiled a new 50-point plan according to which all immigration would be banned, French nationals would have priority access to jobs and council housing; immigrants would be ineligible for the RMI or family allowance; companies would be taxed for employing immigrants; a new product label would be introduced marked 'made in France by the French'; anti-racist legislation would be scrapped; ethnic ghettos would be 'dismantled'; the construction of mosques would be brought to a halt and the opening of Islamic centres and schools restricted; the children of immigrants would have to pay for their education and would be subjected to classroom quotas; a revision of schoolbooks would be conducted to 'banish the incessant cosmopolitan references'; nationality would be based on parentage and a future National Front government would revise naturalisations granted before its own election to office, thereby imitating the actions of the Vichy government in the 1940s. Although the plan was roundly condemned by the Socialists, the government, as if to emphasise that its role was to follow not to lead, effectively implemented point 46 of the NF plan by passing a law that December which authorised the setting up of detention centres for asylum seekers. A delighted Mégret taunted the PS, asking whether government policy would henceforth be inspired by the Vichy regime or whether condemnation of the Front's measures had now been proved unjust (*Le Monde* 22, 23 December 1991). With mainstream politicians from all parties trying to outdo each other in running ahead of the National Front's bandwagon, the suspicion that it was winning the battle of ideas was borne out by a SOFRES poll published in *Le Monde* in October: 32 per cent of respondents declared their agreement with the Front's ideas, against only 16 per cent in December 1988, 17 per cent in May 1989 and 18 per cent in September 1990. The party's influence had never been stronger (Perrineau 1997, p.72).

Indeed the four years since the 1988 presidential had seen the Front make significant progress in embedding itself in the grass roots of French politics. When the six-yearly town council elections took place in March 1989, the party managed to present its own lists in 143 out of the then 219 towns with a population of more than 30,000, as well as in more than half of the towns of 20,000 plus (214 out of 390). Altogether the NF was present in elections in 306 of the 900 towns of more than 9000 inhabitants; in 192 cases they ran under their own banner, while in the remaining 114 cases they coalesced with other right-wing forces. Once again the 'mainstream' played its part in legitimising the Front as a respectable player in the political game, for in 28 cases the NF was able to form a joint list with the UDF or the RPR (Birenbaum 1992, pp.166–7). Nationally, the party won only 2.5 per cent of the votes cast in the first round, for it was not yet strong enough to stand in every tiny commune. But in the 143 larger towns where it was standing it scored 10.1 per cent. Altogether it returned over 1000 municipal councillors, not a bad haul for a party which was starting virtually from nothing, with then probably no more than 15,000 members, and which lost no time in setting up organisational structures to deal with the practical and ideological training of these local ambassadors many of whom were inevitably relatively recent recruits (Birenbaum 1992, pp.165, 169). A few months later, in June, the Front comfortably repeated its success of five years previously in the breakthrough European elections, winning 11.73 per cent of the vote and sending ten deputies to the European Parliament. It was thus with some degree of optimism that the party approached the regional and county council elections in the spring of 1992. Ahead of the campaign, the Front set itself the target of gaining control of Provence–Alpes–Côte d'Azur in the south-east, aiming to show, according to Mégret, that the party was capable of running a large region, 'and tomorrow, France' (*Libération* 31 August, 1 September 1991). Although it failed in its specific target, nationally the Front's performance was its best ever in an election of this kind, up 4 per cent on its 1986 score at 13.6 per cent, topping 15 per cent in five of France's 22 regions, and returning representatives, 239 in all, to every regional council. Not surprisingly, faced with this seemingly enduring break in the established pattern of four-party politics, many political scientists were by now poring over the data which would reveal who were the voters propelling this upstart party into national prominence.

Who votes National Front?

Although the National Front's electoral breakthrough was greeted with alarm by those who were well aware of Jean-Marie Le Pen's long career as an extremist agitator (Plenel and Rollat 1984; Lorien *et al*. 1985) many other commentators downplayed the movement's chances of making any durable political impact. Some identified the NF as a 'single issue' party, which would diminish in importance once the 'immigration question' declined in salience. Others saw it taking the Communist Party's place as a focus of anti-system opposition, offering the possibility of a 'release' for frustrations, 'more expressive than instrumental' (Jaffré 1988). After almost a decade in which the party consistently polled upwards of 10 per cent in a variety of national elections, there were still those like the *Guardian*'s Paul Webster who predicted that the organisation might follow precedents, 'in which the extreme right-wing parties inflate themselves like bullfrogs before blowing up in their own contradictions' (*Guardian* 24 March 1992), while more sophisticated observers believed that the party had reached an impasse, unable to break through the 15 per cent barrier (Habert *et al.* 1992, pp.159–60).

In what follows we will consider in turn the grounds on which NF voting can be understood variously as a superficial reaction against immigration, as rather unpolitical protest by the economically marginalised, or as a reactivation of an old extremist electorate. We then show how the party's ability to attract support from all social groups, in all geographical areas, coming from a variety of political horizons allowed it to survive and prosper until and even beyond a debilitating split in its ranks occasioned by the expulsion of the party's then number two, Bruno Mégret, in 1999. We conclude by showing that the core of the party's voters are motivated by more than just a visceral racism, are ideologically committed to it and vote for it in election after election, serving as a pole of attraction to ever-widening circles of more peripheral supporters whose disparate discontents are adroitly exploited by party propaganda. The party's fortunes are far more likely to depend on its leaders' manoeuvring and the reactions of its opponents than on supposed structural barriers to its growth.

'Contact racism'

The fact that the Front began by polling its highest votes in departments with large concentrations of foreigners seemed to support the assumption of a causal relationship between the two. For the demographer Hervé Le Bras, who claimed to be able to predict the NF vote in different regions on the basis of an equation (Le Bras 1986, p.216),

$$\text{NF vote } (\%) = 6\% + [1.7 \times \text{foreigners } (\%)] + \text{trace element}$$

the coincidence between Le Pen's electorate and the distribution of immigrants was 'remarkable and terrifying'; '... wherever they had immigrants before their eyes they voted Le Pen; where they didn't, they voted for the "gang of four"' (Le Bras 1986, p.64).

Certainly survey evidence at the time showed that NF voters cited immigration as the most important factor motivating their vote. Over 70 per cent of those who voted NF in the March 1986 general election did so (Mayer 1987, p.891) but this in no way proves that *contact* with immigrants is the source of such ranking. Voters may be hostile to immigrants because of what they believe or know about them indirectly, or because such hostility is part of an ideology they adhere to for other reasons.

It soon became clear that the correlation between the NF vote and the number of immigrants was highest in urban agglomerations; in 1984 the party won an average 14.1 per cent of the vote in the 36 French cities with populations of more than 100,000, as against 11 per cent in the whole country, so that problems of urban decay or social exclusion could have been just as important as the presence of immigrants in explaining the vote. Furthermore, a study of the 1986 vote in Marseilles showed that support for the Front was concentrated not in the areas with the highest proportion of immigrants but on their margins, often in areas with no strong local political tradition (Bon and Cheylan 1988, p.264). In Toulouse, similarly, the Front's zones of strength, largely populated by middle-class voters, apparently formed a ring around the area of highest immigrant concentration, where the NF vote was weak. These observations led some commentators to the conclusion that voting NF was the result of a 'halo effect' produced by the rumours, fears and fantasies bred in some voters by *indirect* contact with an immigrant concentration (Perrineau 1985, p.29).

Yet even this modified version of 'contact racism' was undermined by the evolution of the party's vote in Paris between 1984 and 1986. If Le Bras' equation were valid, Paris, with the densest concentration of immigrants in France, would also record the highest share of the vote scored by the NF, instead of the ninth highest in 1984 and only the 20th in 1986. Paradoxically, in the 1984 European elections there was a definite correlation between the NF vote and the presence of immigrants from the Iberian peninsula, concentrated in the city's western districts, but practically no correlation between the NF vote and the presence of north African immigrants in the north-eastern areas of the city. Two years later, the position was reversed; there was strong support for the Front in the north-eastern districts, but the party's vote in the areas inhabited by Spanish and Portuguese had declined. Neither the 'halo effect' nor direct contact racism explained this evolution. After all, as the study's author wondered, why would it take the voters of the north-east quarters of Paris until 1986 to become aware of the immigrant population living nearby? The riddle is solved when it is realised that the 1984 vote did not signify hostility towards Spanish and Portuguese but the mobilisation behind Le Pen of the well-heeled population of western Paris when faced with a choice between the Socialist government and a conservative list headed by the moderate Simone Veil. The 1986 vote reflected west-end voters' return to the conservative fold and the Front's attraction of voters in poorer areas where the city's working-class Maghrebi population happened to be concentrated. The vote in those districts correlated more closely with overcrowded housing (+0.81) or the proportion of workers in the population (+0.69) than with the Maghrebi presence (+0.52); the study's author persuasively concluded that the party's success was due to some combination of political or socio-economic factors which went beyond the single issue of 'the presence of foreign communities on national soil' (Mayer 1987, p.898). Anti-immigrant sentiment had indeed existed for decades before large numbers of people felt moved to vote NF in the mid-1980s. The 66 per cent of survey respondents who believed that there were too many north Africans in France in 1984 were only a few more than the 62 per cent who had thought the same in 1968. It was less a question of immigration explaining the Front's electoral breakthrough than of Le Pen, with the collusion of the established political parties, propelling the immigration issue to centre stage. As Schain reminds us, political issues 'do not emerge but are constructed as part of a political process' (Schain 1987, pp.238–49). The search for votes by mainstream politicians unable to alleviate the stresses and strains provoked by the ending of the long post-war boom led them, as we saw earlier in this chapter, to scapegoat immigrants in a way which reinforced and helped legitimise Le Pen's message. In this, as Husbands (1991b, p.392) and Birenbaum (1992, p.16) have suggested, they may have been aided by those commentators who relayed the idea that immigrants, just by existing, were themselves to blame for the Front's early successes.

A protest vote?

Those who have suggested that a vote for the National Front might be termed a protest vote have used the term in a number of senses. Was the party a vehicle for the particular grievances of groups which had in the past supported anti-parliamentary extremism? Could its rise be explained by the declining ability of the Communist Party to channel anti-system attitudes, or was it due to the rising despair of those social groups suffering most from social and economic difficulties in the 1980s?

The first question to settle was whether the NF vote was a re-edition of the support received by short-lived protest movements such as Pierre Poujade's shopkeepers' revolt against taxation during the 1950s and Jean-Louis Tixier-Vignancour's unsuccessful attempt to rally Pétainists and colonialists against de Gaulle in the 1960s. In fact the 20 departments voting most strongly for Le Pen in 1984 correlated not at all with Poujade's best scores in 1956 and only partially with Tixier's best performances in 1965, largely thanks to the 'massive presence' of repatriated former Algerian settlers in the south-eastern departments where both the NF and Tixier did well (Lorien *et al.* 1985, pp.218–19). While Poujadism was an overwhelmingly provincial movement which mobilised a distinct social category over an issue which concerned it directly, the Front's support was urban and, as we shall see below, became very diverse, mobilising voters across class boundaries. Although the partial overlap with Tixier's results did indicate that Le Pen's movement was attractive to those who had supported Pétain or fought in vain against Algerian independence, NF success extended well beyond the traditional enclaves of extremist voting. A line running from Caen in Normandy to Montpellier in the centre of the Midi divided the NF areas of strength in the north and east of the country from the royalist and Catholic heartlands in the west and south-west which had been the bastions of the extreme right ever since the Great Revolution of 1789. This novelty was underlined by the pattern of religious practice; the proportion of NF voters who were regularly or occasionally practising Catholics was much lower than the proportions among either pre-war anti-parliamentary movements like the Action Française or the conservative mainstream voters of the 1980s (Plenel and Rollat 1984, p.122).

While these findings were being digested, an argument was sometimes heard which explained the rise of the Front by the decline of the Communist Party, the latter's collapse allegedly leaving only the NF as a conduit for anti-system protest (Jaffré 1986, p.229). Certainly, the Front's electoral breakthrough occurred after a period of some years during which there was mounting evidence of voter dissatisfaction with the 'normal' political game. In 1977, 42 per cent of respondents in an opinion poll believed that politicians were not concerned with what ordinary people think, a figure which grew to 51 per cent in 1983. At the same time, positive attachment to mainstream parties diminished, as did support for an important role for parties in the political process (Schain 1987). Significantly, NF supporters display more cynicism than those of any other party in their attitude to the establishment. A 1984 opinion poll reported that 72 per cent of them thought that 'once elected, politicians forget their promises', a view shared by only 42 per cent of a sample of the population as a whole (Plenel and Rollat 1984, p.127); over half of Le Pen's electorate in 1986 believed the main parties to be incapable of solving the issues of the day (Jaffré 1986, pp.225–6), and 76 per cent of those who voted NF in the 1992 regional elections claimed to want to use their vote to express dissatisfaction with government policy (Bréchon 1993, p.55). Such disillusionment extends to attitudes about institutions other than parties or the government. In 1987, 56 per cent of NF sympathisers had 'no confidence' in the civil service, compared to 39–41 per cent of those of other parties, and 33 per cent had no confidence in the school system, compared to 14–18 per cent of sympathisers of other parties (Ranger 1989, pp.140–3). All this seems to indicate that part of the reason for the growth and stabilisation of the NF's vote is indeed that it has acted as a conduit for generalised anti-system attitudes. The Communist Party's ability to do the same may have been hampered by its participation in the first Mitterrand government, which allowed it to be lumped together by NF propagandists into the 'gang of four'. Yet vote-switching by disillusioned Communists played a negligible role in the Front's electoral breakthrough; in all the elections from 1984 to 1988 the party attracted no more than between 2 per cent and 5 per cent of those who had voted PCF in a previous contest (Husbands 1991b, p.408).

One should also be wary of explaining the NF breakthrough by reducing it to an apolitical cry of despair by rootless sections of the population whom the economic crisis had caused to lose their traditional cultural references (Jaffré 1986, pp.224–6). Certainly, the cynicism about politics of many NF voters goes together with generally poor social integration and largely pessimistic attitudes both about the future and their own place in society, which foreseeable economic conditions are hardly like to allay. But such people are those who are least likely to vote, so a party limited to such a constituency would be permanently vulnerable to collapse. This is far from being the NF's case. Its best scores in the mid-1980s were not in the areas which were suffering most from the recession – the north and west, Lorraine and the Parisian basin – but the comparatively affluent eastern borders and the Mediterranean coast. Within those regions, support was strongest neither in the most bourgeois nor in the most working-class areas but in districts

> ... no longer really perceived as working class, not yet identified as middle class. Their population is formed in part by white-collar workers, shopkeepers and the self-employed, sometimes of working-class backgrounds, often descendants of European immigrants, whose upward social mobility has been halted by the crisis. (Bon and Cheylan 1988, pp.270–1)

This intuition that the NF vote expressed the voice of 'the dissatisfied middle classes' rather more than it did the helplessness of 'victims' (Bon and Cheylan 1988, p.442), was supported by analysis of voting in the 1988 elections, which showed that National Front supporters were far more likely to be upwardly mobile than destitute and more likely than supporters of other parties to own their own home, run their own business or have a private income. The self-employed and shopkeepers who voted Le Pen in 1988 more often came from a working- or lower-middle-class background than an upper-middle-class or bourgeois one. Likewise, the large numbers of workers attracted to the Front's cause in 1988 were overwhelmingly skilled workers and foremen (Mayer and Perrineau, 1990).

Evolution of the National Front vote

While predictions that the NF would remain confined to the role of safety valve for directionless protest or soon fade away like its extremist predecessors proved faulty, there was plenty of evidence by 1988 that the Front was gathering support from such a variety of sources that it was likely to be around for some time to come. In one respect the pattern which emerged at the European election in 1984 was set for the succeeding decade and a half: the Front's electorate was *sui generis*, combining some features traditionally found in the supporters of the conservative mainstream with others usually characteristic of the left. Until the 1995 presidential election, the Front had in common both with the mainstream right and previous extreme-right movements higher than average support among the middle-class self-employed typified by shopkeepers, garage owners, small factory owners and the like (see Table 3.3). Unlike the right, its electorate has been markedly more masculine than feminine, a trait historically typical of authoritarian movements and, until recently, of the left. Except in 1989 (when a multiplicity of lists were available to choose from) the Front has generally polled higher among the two youngest age groups than its score in the population as a whole, while its declining popularity in the 65+ age group marks quite a sharp distinction between it and the mainstream right, which usually appeals to an older electorate.

The party seems to have experienced three main phases of development in its appeal to different social classes. In 1984, a European election with no direct impact on domestic policy, it was to an extent a vehicle of protest against the Socialist government by affluent voters whose choices were limited by the conservatives' decision to run a single list under Simone Veil. That year, Paris, Lyons and Marseilles all recorded their highest NF votes in their most bourgeois districts (Le Gall 1984, p.46). While those voters returned to the conservative fold for the parliamentary election of 1986 when the fate of the government was in the balance, 19 per cent of professionals and senior managers again voted strongly for Le Pen in the first ballot of the 1988 presidential election, knowing that the outcome would only be decided on the second. From that date, however, the party also began to poll strongly among the less well off, consistently scoring a higher share of the vote among manual workers than its share in the population as a whole. Its slightly weaker performances among white-collar workers and middle managers reflect its tendency to do less well among those who have more than basic educational attainment. The

Table 3.3   Sociology of the National Front electorate

To be read as follows: in 1984, the NF won 14% of the votes of men

	1984 (1)*	1986 (2)	1988 (3)	1988 (2)	1989 (1)	1993 (2)	1994 (1)	1995 (3)
Men	14	11	18	12	14	14	12	19
Women	8	9	11	7	10	13	9	12
18–24	10	14	16	15	9	18	10	18
25–34	11	10	17	9	8	10	15	18
35–49	12	11	17	8	12	13	10	15
50–64	12	9	11	10	15	13	12	17
65+	10	6	12	10	12	13	7	9
Regularly practising Catholics	14	7	7	5	15	12	8	10
Irregularly practising Catholics	6	8	16	10	12	12	6	12
Catholics not practising	13	12	17	11	12	13	13	18
No religion	5	7	9	9	10	15	11	14
Farmers, farmworkers	10	17	13	3	3	13	4	16
Self-employed shopkeepers, manufacturers	17	16	27	6	18	15	12	14
Professionals, senior managers	14	6	19	10	11	6	6	7
Middle managers, office workers	15	11	13	8	9	13	9	16
Manual workers	8	11	19	19	15	18	21	30
Inactive retired	9	8	12	9	13	12	9	11
Self-employed	13	13	21	7	10	12	6	11
Employed in the public sector	8	8	11	9	7	12	4	15
Employed in the private sector	15	14	17	13	14	16	17	21
Unemployed	–	–	12	–	–	–	28	25
Not seeking work	–	–	12	9	13	12	9	11
Total	11	10	14.5	10	12	13	10.5	15.5

*   1 = European election   2 = Parliamentary election   3 = Presidential election

Source: SOFRES exit polls; Perrineau and Ysmal 1995, p.250. (SOFRES group *chefs d'entreprise* with artisans and shopkeepers)

erosion of its appeal among farmers, professionals and top managers during 1993–95 was doubtless due to the candidature of the maverick upper-class conservative Philippe de Villiers whose base was in the rural west. Despite minor variations, therefore, it is clear that one of the secrets of the Front's success from 1988 to 1995 was its ability to win votes among all occupational groups.

The 1994 and 1995 elections seemed to mark in startling fashion the beginning of a third phase of development. In winning 21 per cent and then nearly 30 per cent of the workers' votes, the Front proved on each occasion twice as popular among workers than among the population as a whole. Its 1995 score, making it in one sense the 'foremost workers party of France', reflected a higher than average increase in its vote (compared to 1988) in a range of industrial regions, formerly favourable territory for the left, stretching from west and north of Paris to Alsace. In all, 46 per cent of the NF vote was made up of blue- and white-collar workers, making it by far the most plebian electorate of any candidate, even the Communist Robert Hue receiving only a third of his votes from the same sources. A quarter of the unemployed also voted Le Pen in 1994 and 1995, twice the proportion who had done so in 1988 and again more than supported any other party. To at least one observer some old industrial working-class communes seemed 'to have cracked socially and politically' under the impact of 'long term unemployment and the difficulties of life in districts faced with a real process of disintegration of the social fabric'. Evidence of a correlation between the Front's gains and a fall in Socialist voting in the areas in question led him to announce the arrival of 'Left-Lepenism' (Perrineau 1995a, p.246–9). Such a dramatic shift in the nature of the Front's support certainly required serious attention, but there was as yet no hard evidence that the masses were about to turn to fascism as a solution to their material problems; immigration and law and order continued to rank just behind unemployment but ahead of any other economic factor in voters' accounts of their reasons for choosing the NF. In contrast, supporters of the Socialist and Communist leaders, Jospin and Hue, and of the fringe left candidates, Laguiller and Voynet, when added together still amounted to a larger number of individuals who cast votes on the basis of the fight against unemployment and poverty and the defence of welfare legislation and their standard of living. During the 1990s, it was certainly true that the Front made most of its electoral advances among working class and unemployed voters, going on to win 30 per cent of the manual worker vote in the 2002 presidential election, along with 38 per cent of unemployed voters. But there is no evidence to suggest that these voters considered themselves on the left. The majority of workers voting Le Pen consistently identified themselves as either right wing or 'neither right nor left' (Mayer 1999, pp.96–7). These voters were distinguished primarily by a sense that they were at the bottom of the social scale and that their prospects were bleak. In 2002 Chirac and Jospin picked up their highest levels of support among people who considered their situation in life was improving. In contrast over a quarter of Le Pen voters considered themselves to be 'disadvantaged' while 31 per cent felt that their situation was getting worse (*Libération* 23 April 2002). Furthermore, there was as yet no evidence that the shift in voting support had been matched by a corresponding shift in party membership, while the party's battle to build a mass base amongst trade unionists had yet to be won.

If the ability to win votes from all social classes was one of the key aspects of the National Front's successes, another was the spread of its geographical support. In the 1984 European elections, it established bastions in the south and south-east from which it was never subsequently dislodged, beating the left into third place in a number of towns and winning more than 20 per cent of the vote in Marseilles. But it also scored more than 10 per cent of the vote in 44 of France's 96 departments. Eight years later, in the 1992 regional contest, the party won at least 5 per cent of the vote in all departments, passing 10 per cent in 67 and 15 per cent in 27 of them, mainly located along the Mediterranean coast, in the Paris suburbs, the north-east and the Rhône–Alpes region. The strength of party organisation at the grassroots was demonstrated in the difficult parliamentary elections of 1993, when a slight retreat still left the Front with more than 15 per cent of the vote in 19 departments (compared to eight in 1988), and more than 20 per cent in each of the four southern departments which contain some of France's largest cities, including Nice, Marseilles and Toulon. In 1995, Le Pen extended his vote in the industrial areas of the north and in rural France: only in Chirac's department, the Corrèze, did it fall below 7 per cent. Finally, in 2002, Le Pen the presidential candidate consolidated his vote in his core areas of support but also made new inroads into rural areas such as Champagne–Ardennes and the Beaujolais and for the first time topped the poll in the industrial Nord–Pas-de-Calais region (*Le Monde* 23 April 2002). Le Pen the parliamentary candidate (his youngest daughter Marine) followed this up by leading four NF candidates in this region into the second round, where only one of them had previously passed the 12.5 per cent first-round barrier (*Le Monde* 18 June 2002).

In addition to its sociological and geographical range, the Front regularly attracted voters previously attached to a variety of political traditions. One-third of 1981 Mitterrand voters chose the NF in the 1986 parliamentary election (Jaffré 1986, p.226) and 12 per cent of his 1988 voters chose Le Pen in 1995 (Perrineau 1995a, p.257). Transfers from those who had previously voted right or centre carried on throughout the 1980s, a third of those who voted for conservative lists in 1986 switching to the NF in 1988. This regular expansion of the NF electorate has necessarily given it something of a composite air. One result of this heterogeneity was that it increased the potentially destabilising influence of Front supporters in the second round of presidential elections, once their first-choice candidate, Le Pen, was eliminated. In 1988, 19 per cent of them plumped for Mitterrand and 65 per cent of them for Chirac on the second round. Seven years later, 28 per cent chose Jospin and 21 per cent abstained or spoiled their ballot. The 51 per cent who chose Chirac were enough to see him elected, but with a much weakened popular mandate (Perrineau 1995a, p.257).

National Front voters: core and periphery

More significantly, however, the composite political provenance of the party's voters implies that the NF leaders' key strategic task (which we explore more fully in Chapter 5) is to draw fresh supporters into their ambit and win them permanently to their own camp. Evidence of their success is that NF voters are uniquely more committed to the ideas of the party than to the personality of their leader (contrary to some expectations) or their party label; 79 per cent of NF voters in 1988, and 60 per cent in 1995, gave as the main reason for their vote the ideas and proposals of their candidate, against only 59 per cent and 45 per cent respectively of the electorate as a whole (Mayer and Perrineau 1990, p.171; Perrineau 1995a, p.254). The themes which party supporters identify as motivating their vote have varied little in a decade, 'national preference', repatriation of immigrants and law and order being placed as high on their agendas as they were prominent in NF propaganda in 1985 and 1995 (Lorien *et al.* 1985, p.221; Perrineau 1995a, pp.252–3). NF voters are also the most loyal of any electorate: 90 per cent of those who voted for the party in 1988 claimed to have done so in 1986 (Husbands 1991b, p.409), while 81 per cent of Le Pen's 1995 support had voted NF in 1993 (Shields 1995, p.32).

Researchers have identified a solid core, making up about a third of the Front's electorate, consisting of people who have voted for it in election after election and who are distinguished from the less consistent periphery by being older, more urban, more male and more affluent, as well as by identifying more readily with the organisation, with its programme and with the extreme-right label. In attitudes and values they are more politicised, more ethnocentric and more authoritarian than the periphery (Mayer and Perrineau 1990, pp.176–8). The party's grassroots organisations have been able to construct a relatively secure electoral base around this committed and reliable hard-core of supporters. Profiting from the fragmentation during the 1980s of the various social structures which previously held together life in France's urban centres, from the Communist Party to the various secular associations on the periphery of the French left, NF activists were able to weave themselves into the fabric of communities, offering opportunities for conviviality to those who had none and creating a periphery made up of a series of concentric circles with different modes and degrees of attachment to the core (Mayer and Perrineau 1993, pp.69–71). This is all the more important in that NF voters as a whole are more socially isolated and more distrustful of state institutions (except the police and the army) than the rest of the population, have a social life largely restricted to their own family and are less likely than other voters to take part in collective protests or solidarity action. In survey after survey they have proved to be more pessimistic about the future than other voters (76 per cent compared to 53 per cent; Perrineau 1988, p.26). Of potential NF voters, 40 per cent feel insecure in their own homes, compared to 29 per cent of the population as a whole. Among voters who score highly in surveys on the pessimism scale, and who also have a low protest or associative potential, or a lack of trust in institutions, support for the NF rises to over 20 per cent (Mayer 1993).

Four different levels of attachment of the periphery to the core were explored by a study based on a series of interviews with NF voters in the Lyons suburb of Vénissieux (Nadaud 1996). On the outer edge of the National Front family is the protest voter, socially integrated but politically fragile, who wants to express discontent but does not identify with the NF or its ideas. Less peripheral are 'malaise' voters, driven by a sense of despair, socially very isolated individuals who feel trapped, unable to progress and whose choice is motivated not by ideological attachment to the Front but by feelings of social humiliation and failure. These two groups effectively vote NF by default, because they see no other way of expressing their frustrations. They have little knowledge of the Front's programme, are first-time NF voters and are generally uncomfortable, even ashamed, about their choice. A more integrated group, won to the Front in 1988, are right-wing although not extremist voters who identify with the NF's nationalism, its 'outsider' status and its stand on law and order, but who remain critical of the Front and do not consider it to be a party of government. These voters are politicised, socially integrated, professionally satisfied and enjoy a good standard of living. Nadaud, like Mayer and Perrineau, finds that the hard-core NF voters consider themselves on the extreme right of the political spectrum and have a very strong sense, based either on class or race, of belonging. They are overtly racist, identify wholeheartedly with Le Pen and express their support for the Front without hesitation or shame.

Further progress by the party clearly depends on how successfully the more peripheral voters can be converted into core voters or members. In recent years opinion polls have recorded a steady polarisation of attitudes to the Front. The number of 'don't knows' has shrunk so that, while support for Front ideas has grown, so also has the number of people opposed to it. Between 1983 and 1997 the proportion of survey respondents who considered Le Pen's organisation a 'danger for democracy' rose from 38 per cent to 75 per cent, and there have been similar increases in the number of those willing to describe the Front as racist, sectarian and incapable of governing (*Le Monde* 25 October 1991, 20 March 1997). What this does not tell us, however, is what such people would do to defend democracy, or whether they even care about it. NF voters certainly have little time for it. In Dreux in 1989, 49 per cent of those whose votes had secured the NF candidate's emphatic by-election victory were of the view that 'democracy means disorder' (Bréchon 1991, p.73), while over three-quarters of the NF electorate in the 1997 parliamentary elections believed that democracy was working badly in France, as indeed did 48 per cent of all voters. In these circumstances, being labelled 'a danger to democracy' is hardly an automatic turn-off for those tempted to vote for the Front. Indeed, being held at arm's length by the establishment is exactly what the Front's leaders want, as we will explain in more detail in Chapter 5.

An idea of the party's scope for future expansion in votes and members can be gained if it is remembered that by 1995 a quarter of the French population had probably voted NF at least once (Soudais 1996, p.10). A series of opinion polls during the 1990s reported between 18 per cent and 32 per cent of respondents willing to say they agreed with Le Pen's ideas (*Le Monde* 20 March 1997); on the single question of immigration, in the 1990s, endorsement of the party's programme has fluctuated between 25 per cent and 38 per cent in tune with political events (*Le Monde* 2 January 1991, 20 March 1997). Taking all that into account it seemed realistic to judge in 1997, as we did in the first edition of this book, that the Front could count on a potential electorate of around 30 per cent of the population. In the same year a French commentator set the bar as high as 36 per cent (Perrineau 1997, p.192). These judgements appeared to be called into question by the dip in the party's fortunes in the 1999 European elections at which the recently split Front presented two rival lists. On the other hand the extent to which a modern political party which has established a clear public image can go on adding to its votes even while suffering organisational difficulties was shown by Le Pen's remarkable comeback in the 2002 presidential election when his 16.86 per cent was enough to eliminate the then Prime Minister and put himself into the second round. The addition of Bruno Mégret's vote gave the fascists a combined total of 19.2 per cent, shattering their previous record of 15 per cent in 1995. Whether the party can improve on this and go on to fulfil its potential will depend partly on the actions of their opponents, which we will assess in Chapters 6 and 7, and on how well they manage to recover from the split in their own ranks, which we discuss in Chapter 9. Before that, it is time to look more closely at the origins and nature of this new party which had so rudely shattered the framework of French politics in the 1980s. Who were its leaders? What were their aims and beliefs and from which political tradition, if any, did they come? To these questions we now turn.

4
Le Pen and the Extremist Tradition

The process of coming to terms with the National Front has been hampered by French historians' long-standing reluctance to acknowledge that French society could produce fascist political organisations. For a long time after World War II the 'consensus' view (Irvine 1991, p.294) was that not only French fascism but also the crimes of the occupation period were imported phenomena (Girardet 1955; Plumyène and Lasierra 1963; Burrin 1984, 1986; Berstein 1984). For René Rémond, the most influential of consensus historians, genuinely fascist organisations rooted in France were marginal, while other, more significant movements merely took on surface characteristics of fascism in the spirit of the age (Rémond 1982, pp.217–23). The collective tendency to shore up the republican myth by refusing to face up to French collaboration with the Nazis has been challenged by foreign historians such as Robert Paxton, who detailed the Vichy regime's involvement in the crimes of the occupation (Paxton 1972), and Zeev Sternhell, who argued that France, far from immune to fascism, incubated its own protofascist tradition in the nationalist leagues of the late nineteenth century (Sternhell 1978). More recently, Robert Soucy has shown that during the inter-war period fascist organisations won widespread support in France (Soucy 1995).

However, although the reality of inter-war fascism is now indisputable, a new variant of the old consensus identifies the NF not with fascism, but with a vague and nebulous form of right-wing extremism referred to as 'national populism' (Taguieff 1984, 1986; Winock 1990; Milza 1987, 1992; Perrineau 1993, 1995a). The NF is thus held to be the latest manifestation of a peculiarly French authoritarian tradition which has emerged periodically under different names, gaining mass support in times of crisis only to fade away rapidly when stability returned. Le Pen's precursors, therefore, are seen to be 'populist' leaders such as Boulanger or Poujade rather than, say, Mussolini or Hitler. We believe that use of the term 'national populist' tends to fudge the differences between distinct political phenomena by emphasising shared surface characteristics, such as propaganda techniques and style, while neglecting both doctrine and social and economic contexts. The label may be useful in illustrating the cultural influences on the NF, without proving affiliation to a political tradition, if indeed national populism can be termed a tradition. In the next chapter we give our reasons for believing that, *as a summary of its doctrine*, the term 'national populism' is unhelpful in defining the National Front. In the second half of this chapter we show that *as a political organisation*, far from being called into being by a passing crisis, the NF is the product of a long and conscious process of regeneration in which fascist activists, defeated and discredited in 1945, attempted to rehabilitate themselves and adapt their political project to a changing environment. It is undeniable, however, that the extremist tradition in France is an important component of the political culture in which the NF has been constructed. Le Pen and many of his associates have been life-long activists in extremist causes and they can collectively lay claim to a diverse heritage, the themes of which they deliberately exploit. We therefore begin with a survey of the intertwining doctrinal and political evolution of the extreme right from the 1880s to the occupation.

Three crises: MacMahon, Boulanger and Dreyfus

The parliamentary Republic which was declared in 1871 and consolidated gradually in the 1880s and 1890s was the third such experiment after two short-lived false starts in the 1790s and 1840s. For much of the time since the Great Revolution of 1789 the country had been governed alternately by two different monarchies and two 'empires', headed by rival claimants of the Bourbon, Orleanist and Bonaparte dynasties. When they were out of power and not in exile, their respective supporters habitually formed a distinctly disloyal opposition aiming to overthrow the regime in place and replace it with one of their own preferred design. Paradoxically, the constitutional framework of the new republic, established piecemeal from 1870 to 1875, was largely the work of monarchists, divided between Legitimists nostalgic for the divine right of kings and the more constitutional Orleanists; each hoped that the constitution's provisional nature would afford time to resolve their differences. Sweeping Republican success in the elections of 1876 dashed these hopes, inducing the monarchist-sympathising President MacMahon to exercise his power to dissolve the chamber; when fresh elections in 1877 simply confirmed the Republicans' victory MacMahon was forced to resign and the Republic had surmounted its first crisis – a trial of strength between a would-be 'strong man' and the representatives of the people. For the next 65 years President, Prime Minister and government were subjected to the whims of a National Assembly which threw up and threw over 98 governments.

Their weakness and instability, matched by the corrupt wheeling and dealing of the deputies, provided ammunition to many of those who would attempt to overthrow the regime in subsequent years.

More concretely, in the last years of the century, religion was a major battleground, thanks to the Republicans' attempts to supplant the role of Jesuits and parish priests in education by a network of free, compulsory primary schools staffed by teachers trained according to thoroughly republican and secular principles. In 1884 they liberalised divorce and after the turn of the century tore up Napoleon's Concordat with the papacy, claiming back church 'property' for the state and discontinuing the payment of parish priests. Catholic outrage during the 1880s was all the more dangerous in that the Pope forbade them to take part in politics so that their only hope of turning back the tide was to overthrow the regime itself. The Republican establishment also came under fire for its failure to liberate Alsace and part of Lorraine, ceded to Prussia after military defeat in 1871. Leading the attack was the jingoistic poet Paul Déroulède's League of Patriots, founded in 1882, which, as well as burnishing the hope of an eventual revenge over the Prussians, proposed the creation of a 'citizens' police' to help root out spies, agitated against foreign workers and devised schemes of 'patriotic' education, in which military tradition, gymnastics and target practice would occupy an important place. Eventually the German question sparked a crisis which seemed to imperil the very survival of the Republic, thanks to the appointment as Minister of War of a certain General Boulanger, whose reputation as a patriot had earned him the nickname of 'General Revenge'. In 1887 he was summarily dismissed amid fears that his undiplomatic bluster might actually provoke a real war. Boulanger's pique and the ambitions of the disgruntled Bonapartists and monarchists who plied him with money, led him to launch a spectacular campaign against the 'system', calling for the election of a constituent assembly to inaugurate a new regime capable of standing up to France's enemies, in which the power of Parliament would be severely limited by a strong President chosen by universal suffrage and with the power to resort to referenda on issues of 'national' importance. The general contested a string of by-elections, his success snowballing during 1888 as he resigned his mandate after each victory in order to stand again. His greatest and final triumph came in the capital on 27 January 1889 when, after a poll in which he won nearly a quarter of a million votes, an excited crowd urged him to march on the Elysée. But the government reacted vigorously, arresting leaders of the League of Patriots and changing the law to prevent a candidate standing for election simultaneously in more than one constituency. By April Boulanger had fled abroad; two years later, bankrupt and brokenhearted following the death of his wealthy mistress, he committed suicide on her grave in Belgium.

Although its programme was clear enough, Boulangism could hardly be said to have had a doctrine, unless attacking the parliamentarians for their 'incapacity, low intrigues and tedious debates' or demanding a republic 'composed of something other than a collection of ambitions and greeds' (Thomson 1968, pp.87–8) could be counted as such. Neither did it command an organisation able to withstand the loss of its leader or energetic police persecution. Rather than marking the foundation of an authoritarian tradition, Boulangism is indeed best seen as the temporary convergence of a variety of discontents; financed by aristocrats and adopted as a saviour by the frustrated 'patriots', the general was equally indebted to the agitation of the left-wing *L'Intransigeant*, which stirred up the workers and artisans of the teeming Parisian suburbs, rendered fertile ground for protest politics by economic stagnation and a swelling flight from the land (Seager 1969; Hutton 1976; Rutkoff 1981; Nord 1986).

The Dreyfus Affair

At the turn of the century, however, the atmosphere of civil war created in the narrow political and intellectual elite by the Dreyfus Affair did allow the extreme right again to make progress towards establishing a more homogeneous doctrine and threw up an organisation, the Action Française, which would be a key intellectual and political point of reference right up to World War II. Since the mid-century, anti-semitism had been a part of the political discourse both of the left, via anarchists such as Proudhon who equated Jews with big capital, and of the Catholic right, via the likes of the Assumptionist Order's *La Croix*, which informed its readers in 1887 that the Jews were plotting to introduce income tax in order to impoverish the peasants and then buy up all the land. The impetus of Boulangism, indeed, had owed something to the popular belief that Jewish financiers had conspired to bring about the crash in 1882 of the Catholic-owned bank, the Union Générale. A key figure in the development of populist anti-semitism was Edouard Drumont, a journalist and pamphleteer whose bestseller, *La France Juive*, published in 1886, was the prototype for some ten to twenty such works published every year for the next three years, while his French Anti-semitic League, founded in 1889, likewise spawned a number of imitations. Drumont attempted to appeal both to 'conservative Christians' and 'revolutionary workers', lamenting the dissolution of 'old France' by the corrosive power of money and proposing the confiscation of Jewish property and its use in assuaging the sufferings of the people. These fantasies were regularly relayed to a mass audience by Drumont's *La Libre Parole*, which achieved a daily circulation of 200,000 within months of its foundation in 1892 (Girardet 1983, pp.141–57).

The Jew-baiters had a chance to assess the effect of their propaganda when Alfred Dreyfus, a Jewish army captain from Alsace, was arrested in 1894, convicted of selling secrets to the Germans and within months despatched 'in perpetuity' to French Guyana. In mounting his defence, Dreyfus' family and friends accused the army and politicians of collaborating in a cover-up of evidence which would establish Dreyfus' innocence. The flamboyance of their attack on the 'honour of the army' in Zola's celebrated article, *'J'accuse'*, helped provoke a rapid escalation of anti-semitic violence, with 69 recorded outbreaks during January and February 1898, in which Jews were insulted, chased, beaten, had mud thrown at them and their shops and homes damaged. In a few cases crowds of more than 500 took part in riots which went on for up to a week. Prefects' reports singled out Catholic clubs, Catholic school pupils and religious orders as instigators of the violence, while the anti-semitic leagues worked overtime to egg them on (Wilson 1982, pp.106–24). The suicide of an army officer awaiting trial on the charge of forging evidence of Dreyfus' guilt seemed to the left to make unanswerable the case for quashing the original verdict. For the anti-semites, however, Colonel Henry was not a villain but a victim. When the *La Libre Parole* opened a public subscription for his widow donations flooded in, accompanied by laconic comments in which visceral anti-semitism mixed with reverence for the army and longing for a saviour figure; old soldiers, petty bourgeois and the clergy figured prominently in the subscription lists which, added together, made up 676 pages:

From two old soldiers from 1870 and five who want revenge and hate the yids	F2.60
From an anti-semitic shopkeeper from Boulogne who hopes to see all the yids done in a saucepan	F5.00
From a rural parish priest who ardently desires the extermination of the Jews and the freemasons	F5.00
(cited in Girardet 1983, pp.178–81)	

The furore created by the Affair was forging a new extremist amalgam which embraced Catholicism, nationalism, anti-semitism and antirepublicanism but shed Boulangism's interest in direct democracy and its association with the dispossessed. Yet the Affair ended in victory for the left. Having recast his organisation in anti-semitic and anti-republican mode (Rutkoff 1981, pp.121, 162–4), Déroulède failed in a farcical attempt to march on the Elysée and stage a *coup*. Arrested, then released, he made an inflammatory speech praising the army as 'our last honour, our last resort, our supreme safeguard', calling on its soldiers to become 'the gendarmes of France against the parliamentarians'. This time he was tried and sentenced to ten years' exile (Girardet 1983, pp.176–8). Soon afterwards, Socialists and anti-clericals formed an electoral pact under a slogan which would be used on many subsequent occasions against the enemies of democracy: 'Republican Defence'. The triumphant Radicals elected in 1899 went on the offensive against the anti-Dreyfusard leagues, organised a presidential pardon for Dreyfus and romped to victory again in 1902, after which they proceeded to the crowning act of their anti-clerical programme: separation of church and state.

Theorists of reaction: the Action Française

Although the anti-Dreyfus coalition of authoritarians, militarists, monarchists, Jew-baiters, Germanophobes and militant Catholics had come together more or less by accident in the heat of battle, the Affair threw up a man, Charles Maurras, who attempted to weld these diverse doctrinal components into a coherent whole with an organisation, the Action Française (AF), which provided a home for disappointed activists ready to renew the struggle. Maurras, the deaf and pessimistic essayist and literary critic who became a life-long political agitator, believed that, if France was to recover her greatness via strong and stable government, she must do away with democracy, which led only to internal feuding, and restore a monarchy which would be 'hereditary, traditional, anti-parliamentary and decentralised'. His royalist doctrine proposed to integrate all the predilections of the counter-revolutionary right: 'Like the Catholic party', he wrote,

> the royalists are Catholics (by reason, by sentiment or by tradition) and they stand for the primacy of Catholicism. Like the antisemitic party, they are antisemites. Like the party of M. Paul Déroulède, they desire a responsible and strong administration ... Essentially, royalism corresponds to the various postulates of nationalism, it is itself the *integral nationalism*. (cited in Girardet 1983, p.203)

For Maurras, a nation conceived as an organic whole could do without the close supervision from the centre characteristic of the Republicans' traditional Jacobinism; on the contrary its solidity would be guaranteed by the freedom of provinces, grassroots 'communities' and professional corporations to run their own affairs. He criticised both the principles of liberal economy and the advocates of class struggle, saying that 'classes may be apparently hostile but deep down they are allies. All classes have an identical interest in the prosperity of the composite which they form, known as the Nation' (cited in Girardet 1983, pp.198–9).

In 'Kiel and Tangiers', part of the AF's hefty contribution to the nationalist agitation preceding World War I, Maurras denounced the Republic's foreign policy as inevitably condemned to 'gauche and debilitating manoeuvres which are more than dangerous for the integrity of our territory and the independence of our people' (cited in Girardet 1983, p.204), especially when Germany represented not only a potential military threat but also an unmatchable industrial juggernaut. 'Peaceful understanding with this nation would change nothing, on the contrary. Armed peace requires force. We have no choice, militarism must be our policy' (cited in Girardet 1983, p.207).

Those whom Maurras wished to defend were conceived as an ancient race solidly implanted in an ancestral homeland:

> This country is not an empty building site. We are not gypsies born by chance at the side of the road. Our territory was settled twenty centuries ago by the races whose blood flows in our veins. (cited in Girardet 1983, p.209)

Yet already before 1914 the Action Française was purveying a pessimistic picture of a France in the throes of decomposition and decline, thanks to the 'invasion' of foreign workers and the imagined monopolisation of the intellectual professions by Jews and other 'wanderers'. 'You wonder whether or not we are still in our own country in France ... It is perfectly clear that we will soon cease to exist if things go on at the present rate' (cited in Girardet 1983, p.209).

For almost half a century 'integral nationalist' analyses and polemics poured from Maurras' pen in the form of books, pamphlets or editorials in the *Action Française*, which became a daily in 1908, achieving a circulation of 100,000 at its post-war peak. The movement rapidly increased its following thanks both to the absorption of leaders of the Antisemitic League and to the adoption of a triple organisational structure: the Institut de l'Action Française was given the task of developing the movement's doctrine and organising public lectures; the Cercle Proudhon, set up in 1911 with the help of Georges Sorel, was intended as a transmission belt to the working-class followers of Sorel's anarcho-syndicalism; finally, the Camelots du Roi (the King's Hawkers) were a troop of newspaper vendors doubling as a protection squad for AF meetings and an assault force specialised in breaking up the university lectures and political rallies of the movement's opponents.

Yet the AF never quite succeeded in establishing hegemony on the Catholic and nationalist right. Part of Catholic opinion followed Marc Sangnier's Sillon in embracing the Republic and devoting itself to paternalist social policy. Others, while sympathetic to Maurras, gave their primary loyalty to the papacy, with which he became embroiled in a long-running polemic culminating in Rome's formal condemnation of the AF in 1926 and the placing of a number of Maurras' works and the newspaper itself on the index of forbidden reading matter. Furthermore, the Revolution had now been a part of French history for over a century and even authoritarian nationalists like the novelist, journalist and deputy Maurice Barrès could not bring themselves to believe it had never happened. Barrès, who in his youth had been an ardent Boulangist and in 1914 took over the presidency of the League of Patriots on the death of Déroulède, objected that Maurras' royalism was unrealistic since it could call on neither a credible pretender nor a supporting aristocracy able to supply the trappings of tradition which ought to help legitimise the new regime. He forced Maurras to concede that, if the monarchy were not restored by the parliamentarians themselves as a result of a crisis similar to those of 1848 or 1870, then it would have to be imposed by a military coup (Giradet 1983, pp.216–22). This began to look less and less likely when the cataclysmic impact of World War I had shaken down the thrones of two German Emperors and the Tsar of all the Russias. Even though AF activity reached its zenith in the immediate post-war years it did not develop a strategy for taking power, either legally or illegally, failing to mount serious election campaigns and being outflanked by other forces during the riots of February 1934 which forced the resignation of a frightened government. Throughout the inter-war period, indeed, changed social conditions and the contagious example of Mussolini's success in Italy seemed to render an authoritarian counter-revolution led from below by a new type of mass organisation of displaced and downwardly mobile social groups more plausible than a successful elitist conspiracy.

The paramilitary veterans' leagues

The victory of 1918 ought to have strengthened the loyalty to the Republic forged during four years of suffering. But the devastating physical and psychological effects of the war, the subsequent failure to exact the promised reparations from the defeated Germans and the inflation which eroded the value of the franc, threatening to bankrupt middle classes and government alike, all contributed to the feeling that the victory was a 'mutilated' one. Thousands of brutalised young men, their faith in the republican ideals of rationality and science shattered by the barbarism of the trenches, were targeted for recruitment by a number of leagues often originally set up to defend the interests of ex-servicemen but evolving into anti-parliamentary, sometimes paramilitary political organisations calling for order and authoritarian government. The impact of a first wave, including Georges Valois' Faisceau, modelled on Mussolini's Fascisti, and the champagne magnate Pierre Taittinger's Jeunesses Patriotes was neutralised by an economic revival following currency reform in 1926 (Anderson 1974, pp.199–201). A second wave rose in the early 1930s, peaking between 1936 and 1938 when they were plied with subsidies by employers frightened by the threat of the reformist Popular Front.

Copying the programme, paramilitary uniform and Roman salute of Mussolini, by whom they were largely subsidised, Marcel Bucard's Francistes were hampered by failure to gain wealthy backers in France and probably never won more than two or three thousand members (Soucy 1995, pp.39–40). In contrast, the Solidarité Française (SF) owed its short-lived success to the largesse of the French perfume millionaire François Coty, whose ambition was to overthrow the Third Republic and replace it with an authoritarian regime of his own design, and whose newspaper, *L'Ami du Peuple*, provided much of the organisation's leadership. It attracted tens of thousands of members in the second half of 1933, many of them drop-outs or converts from Action Française and the Jeunesses Patriotes (Soucy 1995, p.61), and helped provoke a major crisis on 6 February 1934 by joining the other leagues in protesting at the cover-up of the political elite's links with a murdered fraudster, Alexandre Stavisky. During an all-night battle with the police outside the National Assembly, nearly 1500 people were wounded and 15 killed, inducing a left-of-centre government headed by Daladier to give way in a panic to a more authoritarian one. This event, amid the anxiety provoked by Hitler's recent victory in Germany, opened up a period of left–right polarisation in French politics, illustrated on the one hand by the growth of grassroots anti-fascism and a regrouping of the left-wing parties into the Popular Front, and on the other by the spawning of organisations, such as the 10,000-strong Green Shirts, who agitated amongst the peasants, and the clandestine Cagoule which stockpiled weapons with a view to an eventual *coup*. While the Solidarité Française rapidly fell apart following the death of its wealthy founder in July 1934, the gap which it left was soon filled by another ex-servicemen's association, founded in 1927 and at first restricted to those who had been decorated for bravery in battle, whence its name, the Croix de Feu (Cross of Fire, or CF). Under the leadership of a retired colonel and minor aristocrat, François de la Rocque, membership was opened in turn to all ex-servicemen, then their wives and finally a youth movement, the 'National Volunteers', which recruited well among the military cadets being trained at the École Polytechnique and St Cyr. Total membership increased to a quarter of a million after 6 February 1934, when the disciplined attitude of La Rocque's troops was highlighted in the conservative press, and mushroomed to half a million at the start of 1936. Meanwhile CF women set up the Mouvement Social Français (MSF) to spread the organisation's influence via musical evenings, fundraising events, sports and camping holidays, as well as upper-class charity balls, of which the proceeds went to finance soup kitchens doling out free meals to the unemployed (Soucy 1995, pp.108–10).

By 1936, the combined disturbance of public order wrought by the various leagues' activities was such that a Radical government plucked up the courage to ban them, a decision with marginal consequences for the Croix de Feu, which simply changed its name to the French Social Party (Parti Social Français or PSF), and adopted the statutes and programme of a party. Nonetheless, events swung further against the extreme right in June when a massive general strike welcomed the Popular Front government into power and gave it the clout, during its year of office, to force industrial employers to concede union recognition, the 40-hour week, an overtime ban, a pay rise and two weeks' paid holidays, and inaugurate a system of intervention buying in agriculture which both helped small peasants get a decent price for their products and protected the consumer against the inflation provoked by hoarding. Popular support was so enthusiastic that it is plausible to speak of a revolutionary potential held back, ironically, by a Communist Party anxious not to antagonise Stalin's allies, the 'bourgeois democracies' (Danos and Gibelin 1986; Guérin 1963).

The employers responded to the threat from the left by increasing their subsidies to the leagues. In 1936 they ensured the survival of yet another new organisation, the Parti Populaire Français (PPF), founded by the expelled Communist dissident Jacques Doriot. Primed by donations from the Worms Bank and a small allowance from Mussolini, the PPF enjoyed regular handouts from eight other banks and the steelmakers' association, the Comité des Forges. Marseilles, Lyons and Bordeaux, where the party recorded its highest membership figures after Doriot's bastion in the Parisian working-class suburb of St Denis, were cities in which it was particularly well supported by local businessmen. The link was so naked that Jean Le Can, a Bordeaux construction millionaire, and Pierre Pucheu, bagman for the Comité des Forges, were both members of the PPF central committee – until, that is, October 1938, when the last gains of the Popular Front were wiped out and Pucheu and his backers withdrew their support. La Rocque had more success in diversifying the sources of his subsidies in order to ensure that the Croix de Feu did not become over-dependent on one or another of them. He accepted money from François Coty and, after the latter's death, from a number of electricity, steel and railway companies, the Banque de France and the Banque de Paris et des Pays-Bas. His connections also allowed him to tap support from the Duke Pozzo di Borgo and other members of the aristocratic set in the 16th district of Paris, as well as from the French royal family in exile in Belgium (Soucy 1995, pp.124–8, 135).

The PSF programme reflected the interests of La Rocque's capitalist backers more than it did those of the royalist pretender, demanding the banning of free trade unions, the right to strike and the Communist Party, whose members were likened to the 'red hordes of Stalin' and the '*danger par excellence*' facing France (Soucy 1995, pp.175–7). The party's blueprint for social organisation was hopelessly contradictory, on the one hand extolling the inherently anti-corporatist ideal of upward social mobility while on the other proposing a network of scab unions (its own Fédération des Syndicats Professionnels), whose relationship with the employers would be essentially corporatist, relying on the 'fraternal interaction of all social groups' (Soucy 1995, p.187). Likewise it suggested solving the economic crisis by cutting wages and government spending, while at the same time proposing to increase the coverage of pensions and accident insurance. The major propaganda drive was directed at the lower middle class; on one occasion during 1936 La Rocque sacrificed the support of the electricity magnate Ernest Mercier when he over-enthusiastically attacked the selfishness of the big capitalist trusts and the stock exchange (Soucy 1995, pp.126, 131, 189). In the countryside PSF activists tried to stir up the peasants against the Popular Front by claiming that their taxes went to pay for the workers' 40-hour week while they themselves got nothing (Soucy 1995, pp.132–3). The programme of Doriot's PPF displayed the same cosmetic features designed to attract elusive working-class support, while proposing a corporatist economic framework in which small businesses would be defended against cartels and nationalised monopolies. Intellectuals such as Drieu la Rochelle and Bertrand de Jouvenel used the party's paper, *L'Emancipation Nationale*, to elaborate this vision of a new society which would be a 'third way' between capitalism and communism.

The PPF and CF/PSF had much else in common. In both parties, surface commitment to democracy sat uneasily with the obligation to swear an oath of allegiance to the leader. Both adopted in varying degree the trappings of flags, fascist-style salutes and uniforms, the CF members being organised into regiments and companies, mimicking the structure of an army and often collaborating with the Catholic hierarchy in pageantry around symbols like Joan of Arc and services to commemorate fallen soldiers. Both parties maintained special bodies of shock troops for breaking up pacifist meetings and contesting control of the streets with the Communists. Both had a similar clientèle in which petty-bourgeois groups – the self-employed, shopkeepers, clerical workers and professionals – were dominant, once the substantial but localised working-class base which Doriot brought with him to the PPF had returned to the Communist Party (Soucy 1995, pp.237–9). Neither La Rocque nor Doriot described their organisations as fascist, wary of association with France's historic enemy, Germany. Both welcomed assimilated Jews into their ranks. La Rocque (like the Solidarité Française's Jean Renaud) indignantly refuted the Nazi theory of racial purity and stressed that French identity was the product of successive waves of immigration (Soucy 1995, pp.75, 153), although his supporters readily expressed their anti-semitism via the slogan 'Rather Hitler than Léon Blum!', and the denunciation of Jewish 'Bolsheviks'. The PPF evolved in a more markedly anti-semitic direction after the death in 1938 of a Jewish politbureau member, a friend of Doriot, and after the withdrawal of financial support by Jewish bankers (Soucy 1995, p.279).

Despite all these similarities it was until recently customary for historians to regard the PPF as France's 'only' serious fascist organisation (Anderson 1974, p.216; Berstein 1984), while the Croix de Feu has been held to be 'certainly not fascist' (Jackson 1988, p.253) and even a variant of conservatism which, by turning to party politics after 1936, acted as a potential barrier to fascism (Rémond 1982). Placed in historical perspective, however, it is clear that the French extreme right of the 1930s was different in nature from that of the 1880s and the 1900s. The political stances and the fortunes of the CF and the PPF were both structured by the distinctive economic and political context of the 1930s – the depression and the struggle between capital and labour. While Boulanger and his friends had wanted to overthrow the Third Republic in order to win back Alsace and Lorraine, while Maurras and his friends of the Action Française had wanted to overthrow it to prevent the release of Dreyfus, the paramilitary leagues and their backers wanted to overthrow the Republic in order to head off the threatened redistribution of wealth and power implied by Communism in general and, all too concretely, by the Popular Front in practice. The similarity between the political and sociological characteristics of the PPF, the Croix de Feu and the forces which overthrew democracy in Italy, Germany and Spain in analagous circumstances is so stark that if the label 'fascist' is applied to the cases in which they eventually triumphed, it must equally apply to the case of France where the balance was weighted against them.

That, at any rate was the calculation made by La Rocque; although he kept his troops on constant alert during 1935, frequently hinting that the decisive hour was near, he ultimately drew back, preferring to call on his ex-servicemen to accept the cuts in their pensions proposed by the conservative government, rather than risk defeat in a civil war (Soucy 1995, pp.124–5, 171–2). In the 1930s, as in previous moments of crisis, the French extreme right failed to act out the counter-revolution it had dreamed of for so long. The leagues were divided among themselves, their leaders unwilling to allow precedence to their rivals; the Popular Front was eventually dislocated by disputes over issues such as the Spanish Civil War and the need for rearmament to combat the Nazi threat, while the employers needed only the help of a conventional conservative government to wipe out most of the workers' gains of 1936 (Danos and Gibelin 1986).

Vichy

In the summer of 1940, fleeing before Hitler's tanks, an overwhelming majority of the 600 deputies and senators who managed to assemble at the small spa town of Vichy, voted to hand over all executive and legislative powers to Marshal Philippe Pétain, the octogenarian World War I hero. Initially responding warmly to Pétain, whom they saw as an incarnation of the prudent values of rural France, the bulk of the population was soon absorbed in a struggle to survive the penury resulting from a British blockade and the exactions of the occupying Nazis. Meanwhile, politicians, generals and admirals tried to win favour by ingratiating themselves with the German occupiers. The fascist ex-Socialist Marcel Déat criticised Pétain for not being radical enough and urged him to adopt a single mass party – his own Rassemblement National Populaire

(RNP), created in 1941 – to control and mobilise the population in imitation of the Nazi model. Others like Maurras and La Rocque (who rejected the idea of a single party, not wanting to dissolve his own forces into it), wanted to support Pétain without becoming closely identified with the Germans. After the war, many would justify their support for the Vichy regime by pretending that Pétain's authority over an unoccupied 'free' zone was a 'shield', protecting France from the worst 'excesses' of Nazi rule.

In truth, this victory over the Republic, achieved without recourse to mass parties and paramilitary street-fighters, allowed a small group of reactionary officials and politicians to set about implementing the programme of the paramilitary leagues, the Action Française, the church and the big bourgeoisie, at the same time brutally settling accounts with their opponents. The new regime mimicked the political style of fascism by dispensing with Parliament, purging local government and the prefectoral corps and creating a handpicked 'National Council' to advise the supreme leader, who was made the object of a personality cult and glorified in a specially written anthem. Young people were dragooned into physical training programmes and citizens urged to spy and report on their neighbours. Unions, strikes and political parties were banned. Big industrialists, including the PPF's former financier, Pierre Pucheu, were handed control of the economy, covered by a sham corporatist structure to which a handful of compliant former trade unionists and Socialists lent a fig-leaf of legitimacy. Church leaders, who affected to see in Pétain the 'instrument of providence' (McMillan 1992, p.136), were gratified by a purge of schoolteachers, the abolition of free secondary education and an attempt to impose religious instruction in state schools. Former Republican military and political leaders including Blum and Daladier were interned, subjected to a show trial, and later deported to Germany. A special force of volunteers, under the command of the ex-*cagoulard* Joseph Darnand, was given the job of tracking down Communists, Jews and freemasons. This well-armed and lawless 30,000-strong *Milice* became more feared among the Resistance than the Gestapo, responsible for the murder, among scores of others, of two former Popular Front ministers and the septuagenarian president of the League for the Rights of Man, Victor Basch.

As if all this were not bad enough, what eventually made the memory of Vichy stink in the nostrils of history was its persecution of the Jews, which was so noxious that it earned the condemnation even of the Italian occupation authorities in the south-east of the country, where many French Jews fled for sanctuary. As early as October 1940, quite unbidden by the Germans, the regime banned Jews from responsible positions in the army, judiciary, civil service, teaching, public enterprises, and a long list of other occupations. A few months later, Jewish-owned businesses were confiscated or closed down, and a Jewish 'quota' was established in schools, universities and the professions. By the summer of 1942, collaboration with the Nazi genocide was in full swing. In the months following the notorious *rafle* carried out by the French police in Paris on 16 and 17 July, 42,500 Jews, including 6000 children, were deported to Auschwitz. In all, Vichy helped send 76,000 – a quarter of the Jewish population – to their deaths in the extermination camps. French participation in this crime against humanity came about not because the Vichy regime was a German import, and not because power had been seized by a fanatical minority, for the most enthusiastic French Nazis like Doriot and Déat were never dominant, and certainly not in the summer of 1942. The crime was implicit in the powerful anti-semitic, anti-egalitarian and counter-revolutionary domestic tradition which made Vichy 'another act in the long French drama of internal conflict opened in 1789' (Paxton 1972, p.xii) and still being acted out by Jean-Marie Le Pen today.

The regime lost its last shreds of autonomy, becoming an increasingly compliant agent of Nazi repression, after Allied progress in north Africa prompted the extension of the occupation to cover the whole country. Doriot's Legion of French Volunteers against Bolshevism (LVF), formed after the German invasion of Russia in 1941, was given a government seal of approval, its members joining the 7500-strong Charlemagne division of the Waffen SS, fighting on the eastern front to defend Hitler's bunker. German pressure secured the entry of their most faithful servants, Darnand, Philippe Henriot and Déat, into the government at the start of 1944. Later, when they moved to Sigmaringen in Germany, Doriot himself was invited to join them. It is here that he is thought to have met his death, machine-gunned from an Allied plane. La Rocque, the former staff officer, had long since seen which way the wind was blowing and begun to organise an intelligence network which passed information to the British. When he was unwise enough to urge Pétain himself to change sides, he was arrested and deported; he died in 1946, his health broken by prison conditions. Maurras was tried and condemned at the Liberation, dying in 1952. During their brief moment of power, activists of the French extreme right had shown all too clearly what they were capable of. With the war over, and a generation of protagonists leaving the scene, their tradition appeared irreparably condemned by its complicity with Nazi atrocities. To survive, it would need to reinvent itself.

The survival of French fascism, 1945–72

The French extreme right traversed three distinct political contexts between the Liberation and the foundation of the National Front in 1972. The first, from 1945 to the outbreak of the Algerian War in 1954, was a period of marginalisation. The second, from 1954 to 1962, was an interlude of hectic activism conditioned by the Cold War, decolonisation and the revolt of the provincial petty-bourgeoisie. Following Algerian independence in 1962, a period of prolonged political stability reduced opportunities for activism but stimulated the search for a strategy which could bring together disappointed conservative nationalists and determined fascist ideologues – a search which culminated in the foundation of the NF in 1972 (Algazy 1984, 1989).

The defeat of the Nazis and the liberation of France marked the nadir of the extreme right's fortunes as de Gaulle's provisional government (1944–46) laid the basis of the welfare state, carried out a programme of nationalisation and re-established democratic institutions. It carried out a limited purge of Vichy officials and propagandists and initiated the prosecution of war criminals, netting a few of the culprits and sending the rest running for cover or exile. Until the mid-1950s, attempts to rebuild fascist organisations, such as Maurice Bardèche's Mouvement Social Européen (MSE), made up of ex-collaborators and representatives of European fascist groups, including Oswald Mosley, quickly ran into the sand. In scarcely more than a decade, however, conditions had changed in a way which offered extremists new opportunities. The Fourth Republic, inaugurated in 1946 by a referendum in which opponents and abstainers far outweighed those voting in favour, was regarded by many as illegitimate and transitory. Disapproving both of the reappearance of the pre-war parties which he detested and of a constitutional framework which he believed gave them too much power, de Gaulle withdrew from government and founded a political movement with a strongly nationalist flavour, dedicated to constitutional reform and his own return to power. At the same time, the onset of the Cold War and the emergence of a threatening eastern bloc camped behind the Iron Curtain signalled the Communists' adoption of a position of outright hostility to the regime. Sandwiched between these two powerful anti-system forces, a motley collection of Socialists, Radicals and Christian Democrats, themselves frequently at loggerheads, staggered from ministerial crisis to ministerial crisis, forming over 20 governments in twelve years until, hopelessly split by the Algerian War and unable to command the loyalty of their soldiers and civil servants, they gave up and called on de Gaulle to return to power in 1958.

In these changed conditions, the openly fascist Jeune Nation was able to lead violent demonstrations against French withdrawal from Algeria and to attack the Communists systematically until it was banned, went underground and set up as its legal face a student wing, the Fédération des Etudiants Nationalistes (FEN), whose elitist, racist and anti-semitic *Manifeste de la classe 60* was said to have greatly influenced nationalist circles in the early 1960s (Algazy 1984, p.195). Jeune Nation and the FEN played minor parts in the April 1961 putsch organised by rebel army generals against the government's plans for home rule in Algeria. But with the defeat of the putsch and the arrest of many of its leaders, Jeune Nation degenerated into little more than an appendage of the OAS, the Secret Army Organisation, which conducted a desperate scorched-earth campaign at the end of the war, destroying parts of the Algerian economic infrastructure, randomly murdering the civilian Arab population and attempting to assassinate pro-independence figures in France, including de Gaulle himself. The end of French Algeria created three future sources of recruitment for the counter-revolutionaries: a generation of defeated activists who experienced prison or exile before returning to pick up the threads of their nationalist commitment, part of the mainstream right disappointed in their expectation that de Gaulle would resist decolonisation, and more than a million former European settlers in Algeria, the *pieds noirs*, who uprooted themselves and embarked on an uncertain future in mainland France.

Alongside the struggle in the colonies, economic and social developments in mainland France provided other opportunities for extremist political mobilisation. Agricultural modernisation and the flight from the land, together with a revolution in transport and distribution networks, spelled doom for tens of thousands of small proprietors – shopkeepers and artisans – who were tied to disappearing rural communities or put out of business by rival supermarkets. In 1953 an obscure provincial store-owner, Pierre Poujade, formed the Union for the Defence of Shopkeepers and Artisans (UDCA), rapidly recruiting a mass membership which set about impeding the work of tax inspectors, usually by ransacking their offices, in order to bring the plight of the 'little man' to the attention of government officials. In 1953 UDCA won 3 million votes and over 50 seats in the general election but was soon riven by dissension, its founder resisting the efforts of his group's young parliamentary leader, Jean-Marie Le Pen, to turn it into an extremist party devoted to the cause of French Algeria. De Gaulle's return in 1958 soon wiped out the political challenge of a movement which had no other programme but the evasion of taxes and the denunciation of a rotten parliamentary system perceived as being in the pocket of big business.

Theorising the National Front, 1962–72

The two referenda which recognised Algerian independence and endorsed de Gaulle's scheme to make the President eligible by universal suffrage brought to an end the phase of activism linked to the rearguard struggle against decolonisation, ensured the stabilisation of the new Fifth Republic and presented the extreme right with a double challenge: the formation of a strategy for achieving power in the new political context and the elaboration of a 'modern' doctrine. While doctrine would remain a problem for some years to come, a number of thinkers used the pages of Bardèche's *Défense de l'Occident* and Dominique Venner's review, *Europe-Action*, to address the problem of winning power, by re-examining the conditions under which Mussolini and Hitler had achieved it. Their conclusion, that a long march through the democratic institutions was necessary, was eventually adopted by the founders of the National Front. In *Le Fascisme est-il actuel?*, François Gaucher argued that if the fascist flame was to burn again, 'It cannot burn in the same way, because the atmosphere has been profoundly modified' (Gaucher 1961, p.19). Assessing the structural changes which western Europe had undergone since the 1930s, Gaucher stressed that urbanisation and the flight from the land were destroying the natural habitat of the traditional values carried by the peasantry and the small-town shopkeepers and artisans. At the same time, the menace of social revolution led by the working class was receding with the emergence of a new middle class made up of managers and civil servants. As a consequence, fascists could no longer pose either as a bastion against Communism or as defenders of the social and economic standing of the petty-bourgeoisie. Gaucher concluded that it was necessary to combat the desire of certain nostalgics for a return to the era of classic fascism, while seeking to retain their support.

Another text of this period, Dominique Venner's *Pour une critique positive*, became a reference for the founders of the NF, one of whom saw it as their equivalent of Lenin's *What is to be Done?* (Duprat 1972b, p.122). Venner, a veteran of Jeune Nation, founded the review *Europe-Action* in 1963, and in May of that year reproduced the main points of *Pour une critique positive* in its pages. He argued, like Gaucher, that a frontal assault on the state was now more or less impossible and revolutionaries had little chance of winning sections of the bureaucracy to their side unless they could show that they themselves were capable of running a modern state. Cloudy allusions to the inspirational qualities of a great man were no longer enough:

> As power is in the hands of the enemy a superior stratagem is required. As numbers are lacking, quality must be targeted. As the 'great man' (besides being non-existent) has been too disparaged, we must count on the team. Quality of combatants, methodical and reasoned combat, collegiate leadership, imposing: education, doctrine. (*Europe-Action* May 1963, p.33)

Reviewing in turn the limitations of parliamentarianism, of Poujadism and of terrorist activism, Venner suggested that hard-core fascists needed to retain some kind of link with the most extreme fringes of the mainstream right, as they had during the Algerian struggle, so that they could recruit from them and attempt to turn the revolts which they led into revolution. At the same time he cautioned revolutionaries against precipitate activism, insisting on the careful preparation required to shake the ideological hold of the regime:

> Revolution is not the violent act which sometimes accompanies a take-over of power. Neither is it a simple change of institutions or political clan. Revolution is less the taking of power than its use for the building of a new society ... THERE ARE NO SPONTANEOUS REVOLUTIONS. (*Europe-Action* May 1963, pp.31–2)

From all this Venner concluded that it was time to abandon the focus on building organisations and develop instead a new, more flexible type of politics. Nationalists should seek wherever possible to take control of organisations, however small, including unions, local newspapers, even youth hostels, in order to create bases for 'the militants of a white nation' (*Europe-Action* May 1963, pp.50–1). His text also contained a plea for doctrinal renewal, complaining that fascists, royalists and Catholic fundamentalists were all subdivided into further fragments united only by negative themes such as anti-Gaullism and anti-Communism. A comprehensive revolutionary nationalist doctrine was needed, around which the extreme right could unite (*Europe-Action* May 1963, p.37).

Venner's followers were given an opportunity to test some of his ideas in practice when Jean-Louis Tixier-Vignancour, a veteran of the Vichy propaganda ministry, stood as a candidate in the 1965 presidential election. His campaign was run by Jean-Marie Le Pen, who used it as a focus for the temporary federation of a number of diverse forces including *pieds noirs*, former Poujadists, veterans of the Algérie française movement, Catholic fundamentalists, ex-collaborators and members of the mainstream right (*Europe-Action* November 1965). Le Pen also courted the FEN, Venner's Europe-Action team, and the fascist group Occident, which for a while took on the organisation of the Comités Tixier-Vignancour in the colleges. But the inherent difficulty of keeping unrepentant fascists and anti-Gaullist conservatives in the same camp proved too much, Venner and Le Pen forming a block which resisted Tixier's attempts to find common ground with the mainstream. The results of the campaign were meagre and the alliance fell apart in January 1966, Tixier blaming his low score (5.32 per cent) on Le Pen, whose record company was inopportunely charged with defending war crimes shortly before the poll. Tixier then set up the Alliance Républicaine pour les Libertés et le Progrès (ARLP) which failed to make any headway, while the more moderate elements joined the parliamentary Centre Démocrate and the extreme right-wing (*Europe-Action*, the FEN) followed Venner in forming the Mouvement Nationaliste du Progrès (MNP). The MNP contested the 1967 elections but won only 30,000 votes, fell into decline and collapsed a year later. De Gaulle's re-election in 1965 had limited still further political opportunities for the extreme right and economic growth undermined any strategy based on social discontents as increasing disposable incomes brought a new array of consumer goods within the grasp of the mass of the population. For the baby-boom generation, which had known neither the depression nor the occupation, the extremists were an irrelevance, reduced to a number of tiny sects based mainly in the universities, from which they sallied forth from time to time into pitched battles with the Trotskyists and Maoists. When Venner withdrew from active politics in the summer of 1967 the gulf between conservatives and extremists, which the Tixier campaign had temporarily bridged, seemed as wide as ever.

And yet, as it happened, another – and finally successful – attempt to end the extremists' isolation was in the offing. Occident, a grouplet infamous for its violent assaults on the left and banned in October 1968 on public order grounds, was re-founded a year later under the name of Ordre Nouveau (ON), uniting the ubiquitous Bardèche with activists of various generations including *Minute* journalist and ex-Vichy Milice member François Brigneau; Gabriel Jeantet, formerly with the Vichyite propaganda sheet *France Réelle* and Jean-François Galvaire, ex-general secretary of the Jeunesses Poujadistes and a veteran of the Tixier campaign. The new organisation's most influential thinker, however, turned out to be François Duprat, once of Jeune Nation, the FEN and Occident, and one of the most prolific of the post-war fascist activists, whose enthusiasm for the Strasserite left of the Nazi Party, the Italian fascist Jules Evola, and Léon Degrelle, leader of the Belgian Rexistes, found an outlet in a string of publications which he edited.[1] At the second ON congress in June 1972, Duprat presented a collectively written document, '*Pour un Ordre Nouveau*', which pursued the attempt, begun by Venner, to chart a course for the future of revolutionary nationalism and finished by proposing the establishment of a 'National Front' to act as a transmission belt between revolutionaries and the mainstream. Like Venner, the text's authors argued that the modern French state could not be easily overthrown since it had succeeded in wedding to itself, both materially and ideologically, large sections of the population who depended on it for their jobs or for welfare benefits. Nonetheless they believed that if Ordre Nouveau could introduce a revolutionary perspective into the corporatist revolts of farmers, professionals, shopkeepers and small-businessmen, recruits could be found. But they in turn warned that success was unlikely to be rapid: Hitler had spent 13 years in pursuit of his goal, Lenin, Mao and Ho Chi Minh nearer 30, all of them patiently learning from their mistakes and adapting to new conditions. Crucially, although their long-term aim was to overthrow democracy, both the Bolsheviks and Hitler's National Socialists had combined the use of legal and illegal means, '[i]t is not the form of activity, but the goal which characterises a revolutionary organisation. The means are solely dependent on circumstances' (*Pour un Ordre Nouveau*, p.160). Duprat's document argued that violence and unnecessary revenge attacks on the left would have to be avoided if the movement were to escape isolation and extend its appeal beyond the student fringe and into the traditional right. Characterising elections as an 'excellent instrument of struggle for a revolutionary party' (*Pour un Ordre Nouveau*, p.166), it suggested that the time was right to set up a 'National Front' open to all the extremist sects which would contest elections on a programme some way short of fascist revolution as a means of putting the fascists into contact with potential recruits, educating them, and 'transforming them in our image' (*Pour un Ordre Nouveau*, p.120). Following decisive interventions at the congress by Duprat and François Brigneau, the proposal to establish a federation of different tendencies around a basic programme, open to the traditional right and even the centre, was approved. Proposals to call the new organisation a Front National pour un Ordre Nouveau were rejected because of fears that

---

1. *Revue d'histoire du Fascisme, Année Zéro, Salut Public, Revue Internationale des Problèmes du Nationalisme, Cahiers Européens.*

the name was too extreme for the 'camouflage' required (*Cahiers Européens* 1, May 1974).

Fascist origins of the National Front, 1972–81

The Ordre Nouveau leaders installed as the Front's first president Jean-Marie Le Pen, whose long history of collaboration with avowed fascists and status as an ex-deputy and former organiser of the Tixier campaign made him the ideal potential federator of fascists and conservatives, committed to 'widening the scope of nationalist struggle by opening out as broadly as possible' (*Ordre Nouveau Hebdo* 12 October 1972). The ON members were reassured by their own leaders about the road they had embarked upon in Le Pen's company.

> The electoral road is not a game. It is not an easy road, but it's the only one which offers the hope of ending up with something serious, which can give our ideas a chance to influence reality. (*Ordre Nouveau Hebdo* 18 October 1972)

The new organisation got off to an inauspicious start, weakened by a split which saw many of the original membership depart to form a rival organisation, Faire Front, later renamed the Parti des Forces Nouvelles (PFN), which opted to support Valéry Giscard d'Estaing's presidential campaign in 1974, providing strong-arm security for his meetings. Although in the long run the PFN's attempt to recruit from the traditional right was unsuccessful, the NF was for several years overshadowed by its rival and existed in almost complete obscurity, itself recording a negligible score in the 1974 election campaign. The gradual establishment of a press, a cadre and a structure with a degree of local implantation was due in no small measure to the roles of two figures with long fascist pedigrees. The first was Victor Barthélemy, who had fought for a Nazi Europe in Doriot's LVF and worked for Mussolini in Italy in 1944, later joining Tixier, Bardèche and Mosley in founding the Mouvement Social Européen before collaborating with Le Pen in the Algérie Française and Tixier campaigns. More importantly, Barthélemy was also a former general secretary of Doriot's Parti Populaire Français who had played a leading role in efforts to form a single fascist party during the occupation (Barthélemy 1978). At Le Pen's invitation, Barthélemy set up a federative structure for the NF on the PPF model (see Chapter 5). Ordre Nouveau applauded his appointment, identifying Barthélemy as a kindred spirit (Lorien *et al.* 1985, p.105).

The other key ally of Le Pen in the mid-1970s was François Duprat who, after Ordre Nouveau was banned in 1973, operated in the NF through his own Groupes Nationalistes-Révolutionnaires (GNR), establishing a circle of influence in Rouen via regular propaganda and electoral activity. It was Duprat who organised the NF election campaign for the town councils in March 1977, using the GNR's bulletin to keep the NF's strategy firmly fixed on the parliamentary road, arguing that electoral success for Le Pen would benefit not only the NF, 'but all the national movements, who would gain a new political credibility in the eyes of Public Opinion' (*Cahiers Européens Hebdo-Notre Europe* April 1974). He also counselled the movement's members to avoid using 'incomprehensible jargon', praising Le Pen's modern and accessible language and his exploitation of up-to-date electoral issues (*Cahiers Européens* May 1974). He insisted that the NF had to avoid being labelled fascist in order not to be 'excluded from the System, not to say all significant public activity' (*Dossier Nationaliste* 1, 1974), and that explicit references to National Socialism should therefore be dropped from the movement's propaganda (*Revue Internationale des Problèmes du Nationalisme* January/February 1978).

For his part, Le Pen welcomed Duprat's group with open arms. 'The Revolutionary-Nationalists' place is at the heart of the National Front', he declared at the second NF congress, praising the GNR's attempts to unite other fascists under the Front's umbrella (*Cahiers Européens Hebdo* June 1974). When Duprat was killed by a car bomb on 19 March 1978 an editorial in the NF newspaper, *Le National*, recounted his life-long commitment to right-wing extremism, praising both his Holocaust revisionism and his 'Revolutionary Nationalist Manifesto', which argued for the need to modernise fascism. Le Pen himself led the eulogies to the Front's 'martyred brother' thus: 'Know that in any case you did not die in vain, because we will take up the torch. Your work will be continued!' (*Le National* April 1978). True to his word, every year, on the anniversary of Duprat's death, Le Pen has led a group of NF representatives to his graveside.

Duprat's group was not the only revolutionary tendency operating in the NF. When Venner's MNP broke up in 1967 its membership followed two separate paths. One section, about which we will have much to say later, eschewed 'sterile' activism and devoted itself to doctrinal development, calling itself the Group of Research and Study for European Civilisation (Groupement de Recherches et d'Etudes pour la Civilisation Européenne, or GRECE). A second group, led by Pierre Pauty and Pierre Bousquet (a member of the Jeunesses Francistes in the 1930s, later an officer in the Charlemagne division of the SS), formed Militant, which joined the NF at its foundation in 1972, its journal of the same name doubling as the NF's internal bulletin between 1974 and 1975. In the late 1970s, however, Militant and the GNR were rivalled by a group of new arrivals, the Solidarists, who had originally refused to participate in the formation of the National Front, fearing that the smokescreen of respectability would lead to compromise (*Jeune Garde* April 1975). They finally joined *en masse* in the autumn of 1977 and were promoted rapidly through the ranks following Duprat's death and the departure in 1980 of Bousquet, Pauty and Alain Renault, who had been Duprat's deputy. Solidarism was a form of Christian, corporatist, authoritarian nationalism which combined attacks on both Marxism and big capital with appeals for national, cross-class solidarity. Its main organisational emanation, the Mouvement Jeune Révolution (MJR), had fragmented into rival groups within a few years of its foundation in 1966, its remnants unable to escape from the ghetto of small-scale violence and internecine rivalry. The outstanding Solidarist was Jean-Pierre Stirbois, a former correspondent of the fascist Aginter press agency (Laurent 1978, p.132) who followed Duprat's lead in embracing the parliamentary road and working assiduously to build up his own electoral base in Dreux, a dormitory town west of Paris. Stirbois filled the gap left by Duprat at Le Pen's right hand; as general secretary of the National Front between 1980 and 1988 (until he was killed in a car accident) his meticulous attention to detail helped build up the organisation, membership and electoral strength of the party. Although the arrival of the Solidarists contributed to driving out Militant, their loss was more than compensated by a link-up with the Catholic fundamentalists, bearers of a counter-revolutionary tradition dating back (through Maurras) to the eighteenth century, vehemently opposed to the ideas of the Enlightenment and with a distinctly anti-semitic reading of Christianity. They brought to the NF not only the prestige of the unsuccessful combat waged by ex-Cardinal Lefèbvre against the modernisation of church liturgy and doctrine, but also the weekly newspaper, *Présent*, claiming a readership of 30,000. Although one of *Présent*'s founders and the fundamentalists' self-appointed chief spokesman Bernard Antony, alias Romain Marie, did not officially join the Front until 1984 (when he entered its politbureau), he endorsed Le Pen's abortive presidential candidature in 1981.

The problem of doctrinal renewal

While Dominique Venner and François Duprat played key roles in theorising and, in Duprat's case, applying the 'frontist' strategy which brilliantly succeeded in helping the extreme right break out of political isolation in the 1980s, neither succeeded in their aim of producing a modernised fascist doctrine which could generate a credible political programme suitable for the post-war context, a 'weapon of struggle genuinely adapted to the times we live in', as Duprat put it (*Année Zéro* May 1976). Convinced of the primacy of race over nation, Venner's group expressed its ideas in a form all but indistinguishable from Nazi propaganda, proposing, among other things, to purify the ruling class by segregating 'without any futile sentimentality', the 'true elite' from 'the biological dregs' (*Europe-Action* July–August 1964). Duprat and his friends, on the other hand, were aware that biological racism was a philosophical 'straitjacket' which would only serve to prolong the revolutionaries' confinement to the margin of politics, as it had helped ensure Europe-Action's demise (*Année Zéro* May 1976). They even argued that anti-semitism had been elevated by the Nazis into a political principle on the basis of the most fanciful of 'theories' (*Dossier Nationaliste* 1, 1974). Duprat found a way of distancing himself and his comrades from the Nazi genocide by organising the translation and publication in France of the basic text of Holocaust denial, the British Nazi Richard Verral's *Did Six Million Really Die?* Ultimately, Duprat was no more successful than Venner, however, in producing a coherent ideology which could justify the ideas which they both believed in: superiority of European over all other cultures, the survival of the fittest, abolition of democracy, a hierarchically organised society dominated by a self-selected elite.

It was therefore left to others, who remained outside the National Front during the 1970s, to undertake the doctrinal renewal which the Front and the movement as a whole needed if it was to succeed. These were the members of GRECE, founded by a prolific and provocative former leader of the FEN, Alain de Benoist, who, drawing on an audacious reading of the Italian Communist Antonio Gramsci, blamed the extreme right's political failures on its inability to achieve intellectual hegemony. When Venner's MNP broke up in 1968, rather than attempt to build yet another new party, the GRECEists chose to devote their energies to recasting fascist and racist ideology, seeking to conquer power ultimately by spreading the influence of what they identified as key ideas and values, irrespective of their connection with conventional politics. The success of such a strategy did not depend on mass recruitment. As the GRECE journal, *Eléments*, put it:

> ... we want to attract those few thousand people who make a country tick. A few thousand is not many in absolute terms, but a few thousand of such importance, sharing the same thoughts and methods, represent the potential for revolution. (cited in Duranton-Crabol 1988, pp.141–2)

Eschewing the mass, the GRECE strategists went in search of the elite, persuading distinguished academics to sponsor their university-style colloquia and act as the editorial panels of their reviews, *Nouvelle Ecole*, *Eléments de la Civilisation Européenne* and *Etudes et Recherches*. The group launched their own publishing house, Editions Copernic, in 1976 and exploited every opportunity to spread their views in the mainstream press, de Benoist contributing a weekly column in the news magazine *Valeurs Actuelles* throughout the 1970s and appearing, along with other GRECEists, in the monthly *Spectacle du Monde*. From 1978 half a dozen of them were writing regularly in the mass circulation weekly *Figaro-Magazine*, thanks to the sympathy of its editor, Louis Pauwels.

The GRECE's willingness to address themes like feminism, urban planning and educational philosophy, along with cultural forms such as cinema and cartoon books which had hitherto been unfamiliar territory for the extreme right, fooled many mainstream commentators into believing that these ideologues were purveyors of a genuinely 'new' right, tainted neither by fascism nor by the opportunism of conventional conservative politics. The GRECE, however, in no way represented either a break from fascism or a retreat into esoteric intellectualism. The rest of the extreme right followed their development with interest, the Solidarist journal, the *Cahiers du CDPU*, reporting in May 1973 on a camp organised by the GRECE which offered 'an advanced education in National Socialism' to participants including a number of ex-Ordre Nouveau members and former FEN activists. In the pages of *Militant*, Pierre Bousquet pointed to the revolutionary nature of the 'New Right', dismissing its 'symbolic' references to pre-Christian values as 'window-dressing', and stressing the importance of the phenomenon for all far right activists (*Militant* 8 September 1980). From October 1980 *Militant* devoted a regular column to Indo-Europeanism, one of the GRECE's favourite themes.

With 4500 members and 6000 subscribers to *Eléments*, against only 2000 two years previously, the GRECE reached the zenith of its influence as an independent organisation around 1981, when it was destabilised by the coincidence of a number of factors. An exposé of the influential role played by young GRECEists in the backroom staffs of a number of well known politicians led to a public riposte by Gaullist and Giscardian leaders who denounced the group's attacks on Christianity and the liberal roots of western political philosophy. The *Fig-Mag*'s Louis Pauwels withdrew his support, announcing his conversion both to Catholicism and to the free market liberalism associated with the so-called Reagan revolution then in full swing in the US, while taking a side-swipe at the GRECEists' alleged attempts to impose their own views. Finally many of the original GRECEists found themselves increasingly at odds with Alain de Benoist, whose hostility to the market liberalism in vogue among the mainstream Gaullists and Giscardians in the early 1980s was such that he even announced his intention to vote for the staunchly anti-American French Communist Party at the 1984 European elections. These positions did little to endear him to the owners of the mass circulation press in which, as the 1980s progressed, the GRECE presence was steadily eroded, while the group fell into a certain ideological and organisational disarray (Duranton-Crabol 1988, pp.216–22).

To individual GRECEists disenchanted by de Benoist's refusal to campaign actively against the left and ready to accompany their culturalist strategy with participation in conventional politics, the National Front became a pole of attraction which grew in strength following its electoral successes in 1983 and 1984. By the end of the 1980s former GRECEists were occupying a range of top- and middle-ranking positions in the NF. Among them was Pierre Vial, a founder and former general secretary of the GRECE, who sat on the Front's central committee, contributed to its theoretical review *Identité* and was a member of two NF think-tanks, where his work in party training brought him into contact with NF politbureau member and editor of *Identité* Jean-Claude Bardet, once of *Europe-Action* and later a member of the editorial board of *Nouvelle Ecole* and a founder of the GRECE's *Editions Copernic*. His former colleague on *Nouvelle Ecole*, Jean-Jacques Mourreau, became communications director for Le Pen's presidential campaign in 1988. Philippe Milliau, administrative director of *Nouvelle Ecole* between 1970 and 1974, became an NF councillor and in 1987 became deputy general secretary of the party's Marseilles federation. Others who transferred easily from the GRECE orbit to that of the NF include Pascal Delmas, NF central committee member, and Jean Varenne, Jules Monnerot and Jean Haudry, all patrons of *Identité*.

While the GRECE had been destabilised by the question of whether to take sides between the resurgent left and the mainstream right, another group of ideologues at first strengthened their association with the mainstream, while developing an eclectic doctrine which they labelled 'national liberalism', before they too threw in their lot with the NF after the 1988 presidential election. These were the leaders of the Club de l'Horloge, the 'Clock Club', which was formed shortly after the 1974 election with the explicit aim of providing ideas for the traditional right. Its members – their number deliberately limited to 250 – were young technocrats and intellectuals from the upper echelons of the French civil service, the professions and big business. The Club's three founder members, Yvan Blot, Michel Leroy and Jean-Yves Le Gallou, had all been members of the GRECE, and at first the Club remained more or less in the GRECE's orbit. At the end of the 1970s, however, Yvan Blot justified closer involvement in day-to-day politics by arguing that one ought always to identify and target one's chief enemy, which, in the context of the time meant the left and particularly the Socialist Party, in power after 1981. Accordingly, Leroy and Le Gallou joined Giscard's UDF and Blot the Gaullist RPR, and the trio set about organising a series of symposiums devoted to themes such as immigration, welfare, law and order and defence, to which they invited their new colleagues in an attempt to shift them to the right and to break what they saw as the welfarist and egalitarian consensus of post-war French politics. Under Blot's direction the Club's review, *Contrepoint*, regularly mixed attacks on the Socialists, penned by RPR and UDF notables, with theoretical justifications of the electorally successful Reaganite and Thatcherite programmes which combined attacks on welfare with tax cuts for the rich and tough law and order policies to contain the resultant discontents.

For a while these efforts succeeded in creating a current which avoided the counter-revolutionary, collaborationist overtones that had so hampered the extreme right in the past and won the Club an audience in the mainstream, particularly the RPR, in which Blot himself occupied the key position of head of the general secretary's office from 1978 to 1984, later working for RPR Senate leader Charles Pasqua, before taking a parliamentary seat in 1986. In French conditions, however, and faced with a redoubtable opponent in the shape of outgoing president François Mitterrand, the Reaganite formula was not a vote winner. Chirac's drubbing by Mitterrand in the 1988 presidential election was the signal for a change of personnel and a rethink at the top of the RPR, the new party general secretary Alain Juppé announcing a blanket ban on future collaboration with the NF. In these circumstances Blot realised that his period of effective influence in the mainstream right was at an end; in June 1989 he announced his conversion to the Front, immediately becoming a Euro-deputy, and later entering the politbureau and taking over party organisation in the Bas-Rhin. In doing so, he was reunited with a number of old friends with whom, in truth, he had never been out of contact. Jean-Yves Le Gallou took the post of general secretary of the NF parliamentary group between 1986 and 1988 and was soon to join the politbureau and run the party's Centre for Study and Argument; following the Front's great success in the 1992 regional elections he led its large party group on the Paris regional council. Fellow Club member Bruno Mégret, like Blot a former RPR parliamentary candidate who had for a while dabbled with a personal strategy via a network of 'Republican

Action Committees' of his own creation, had joined the Front in 1986 and become its chairman in October 1988, second only to Le Pen in the party hierarchy.

Bringing the family together

The democratic republican tradition in France has been regularly challenged by counter-revolutionaries. Yet neither the heteroclite coalition supporting Boulanger, nor Maurras' elitist royalism, nor the leagues of the inter-war years were able to gather enough support to overthrow the Republic. During the occupation French fascists strutted briefly in the shadow of Nazi rule before the Liberation and the post-war purge snuffed them out as a political force. Although the decolonisation crisis gave a new credibility to counter-revolutionary politics in the 1950s, raising the hopes of a new generation of activists, their defeat in 1962 ushered in a slow process of regeneration characterised initially by apparently insurmountable organisational and ideological divisions. Before the 1970s, none of the principal fascist organisations of the post-war period had developed a strategy suited to a period of political stability and economic prosperity; all were undone by a failure to distance themselves from sectarian violence and by an inability to develop a programme which could appeal to people outside their ranks. Brief alliances between the extremist hard-core and the conservative fringe for the duration of specific and limited campaigns were routinely followed by fragmentation.

It is against this background that we can measure the achievement of the National Front. In the 1970s Duprat and Le Pen, with the help of Barthélemy and Stirbois, built on the strategic analyses of Bardèche, Gaucher, Venner and Duprat himself in consolidating the electoral strategy and a new structure which integrated in steady succession recruits from the GNR, Militant, the Solidarists, the Catholic fundamentalists, the GRECE and the Clock Club. A significant stage in the process of bringing the family back together was reached in the early 1980s when the Front was rejoined by two former collaborators, both founder members of the NF who had followed the Faire Front dissidence in 1973: François Brigneau, whose post-war career had established him as the extreme right's leading anti-semitic journalist, and Roland Gaucher, a former member of Marcel Déat's pro-Nazi RNP, later a leader of Ordre Nouveau and the PFN. A roll-call of the membership of the NF political bureau in the 1980s confirms the Front's extraordinary success in federating all the post-war currents of right-wing extremism. It included André Dufraisse (who died in 1994), a founder of the National Front and former member of Doriot's PPF, of the Charlemagne division of the Waffen SS, and the OAS; Roger Holeindre and Pierre Sergent, both convicted OAS terrorists; Jacques Bompard, ex-Occident; and various Solidarists, including Jean-Pierre and Marie-France Stirbois, Christian Baeckeroot, Alain Jamet and Michel Collinot. Another historic activist, Pierre Pauty, once of Europe-Action, the MNP and Militant, having left the organisation in 1980, later returned to the NF and sat on its central committee. Continuity with the past was also provided by the newspapers and magazines which formed an extended circle of support and sympathy for the Front, without being formally part of it. Among them were the magazine *Minute*, whose owners included François Duprat's former deputy in the GNR, Alain Renault, once a leading member of both Ordre Nouveau and Militant (*Politis* 18 January 1990), and the *Choc du Mois*, run by other remnants of the old Ordre Nouveau leadership. Another publication, cited by the Front as part of its satellite press (Front National 1992, pp.481–2), the quarterly magazine *Enquête sur l'Histoire*, was edited by the former leader of Jeune Nation and Europe-Action, the author of *Pour une critique positive*, Dominique Venner. Clearly the NF became far more than a temporary emanation of 'national populism', responding to and drawing its strength from a temporary conjunction of circumstances. It achieved what no other organisation of the French extreme right was able to achieve. It created a federation of the inheritors of various branches of the extremist family who, through their celebration of a shared past, allowed it to pose plausibly as the inheritor of *all* the counter-revolutionary movements in French history which fought more or less unsuccessfully against the democratic republic.

It was not enough, however, to bring about an organisational regroupment and adopt a parliamentary strategy. To escape from obscurity into the mainstream, the party also needed a coherent doctrine offering an analysis of what was wrong with contemporary society, plausible suggestions for changes and an organisation which seemed capable of carrying them out. These are the subjects of our next chapter.

5
Anatomy of a Fascist Party: Ideology, Strategy, Organisation

Overtly or not, all political parties operate with a doctrine, a number of propaganda themes and a model of party organisation geared to a strategy for achieving power. In conventional politics, most parties' organisations and strategies reflect their common adherence to a pluralist doctrine in which party competition is unhindered, citizens are free and equal to vote and stand for election and the parties themselves pledge to respect the verdict of the ballot box. Most also pledge to maintain and foster freedom of enterprise and the private ownership of wealth, still further limiting their doctrinal differences to the point where they seem to be distinguished only by the emphasis they place on selected propaganda themes. In France it has recently become more and more doubtful whether even the Communist Party can be counted an exception. Some accounts of the French National Front implicitly situate it within the same consensual model, treating National Front doctrine as more or less synonymous with its propaganda themes – a 'confection' (Marcus 1995, p.102) designed to appeal to public opinion in pursuit of an electoral strategy differing little from those of conventional parties, while the NF's extremely detailed attention to organisation and party discipline amounts to no more than the application of 'modern management methods' (Marcus 1995, p.45) to the same end.

In the case of the National Front, however, there are strong grounds for doubting that the relationship between doctrine, propaganda themes, strategy and organisation fits the liberal pluralist norm. Later in this chapter we show that the party's organisational structure corresponds to a strategy which goes beyond the mere peaceful accumulation of votes and indeed expects NF ideas to triumph in a context of dramatic social upheaval. Before that, we identify the key components of National Front doctrine, understood as its assumptions about the nature and potential of human beings, its explanation of what is wrong with French society when compared to an abstract ideal, what changes ought to be made, and what means ought to be used to bring about the required changes.

Not all aspects of Frontist doctrine are exposed in equal detail to the gaze of the general public, the party preferring to use propaganda themes selected for their compatibility with 'normal' electoral competition and to train its members to employ a manufactured 'soft' discourse which hides the party's real intentions behind a carefully constructed mask. Taken together, the combination of doctrine, strategy and organisation add up to an enterprise which, far from being 'just another party' seeking to garner votes out of the temporary discontents of a popular electorate, aims at the destruction of democracy itself.

National Front doctrine

The evolution of National Front doctrine can best be understood in terms of the partial reconciliation between the activist and ideological wings of the extreme right which had become separated in the 1960s with the founding of the Group of Research and Study for European Civilisation (GRECE). By the end of the 1970s this group, led by Alain de Benoist, had created a veritable philosophical system, the founding premise of which was its refusal of what it called the 'universalist' belief that all humans derived from an original single model, in favour of the 'nominalist' conviction that the observable differences between all the different social and ethnic groups on the planet were irreducible and could not be traced back to a single common denominator. On the one hand they rejected any philosophies – including economic liberalism and political democracy – which posited a common human nature irrespective of the individual's rootedness in a particular society with its given formal and informal rules; on the other, they rejected any philosophies – including Socialism and Christianity – which posited or pursued the equality of men. The GRECE ideal was that of humans nurtured and 'rooted' in communities which integrated the individual 'as an organism integrates the organs which compose it within a higher order' (de Benoist, reprinted in Lepage 1980, p.572), a community which all instinctively were ready to defend, and whose destiny they were fated to share.

While the NF leaders periodically criticised the GRECE's non-engagement in day-to-day politics, by the end of the 1970s many on the extreme right were ready to applaud what they saw as the group's success in disconcerting the left by its 'brilliant tactical innovation' in creating a new philosophical framework which could be applied to almost any facet of social life with a consistency which had hitherto only been claimed by Marxism (Bardèche 1979, pp.17–18). But since the NF was the inheritor of a number of distinct currents of extremist thought a would-be comprehensive philosophy like that of the GRECE was likely to offend some of its members on some points and was unlikely to please all of them all at once. While its condemnation of Socialism and political democracy were part of the extreme right canon, its hostility to economic liberalism was not easily understood by those activists for whom praise of private enterprise was both the inverse of Socialism and a useful transmission belt to the interests of the petty-bourgeoisie. Its attack on Christianity was likely to be unacceptable to the guardians of the Maurrassian tradition represented in the NF by the Catholic fundamentalists. For these reasons, it appeared to some that the Front was inescapably prevented from achieving doctrinal coherence by the 'coexistence of multiple ideological currents ... which have rallied to the NF without however having coalesced into the same mould' (Taguieff 1986, p. 44), and that the only thing which kept the factions united was the presence of Le Pen, as if his moral or intellectual authority could achieve in the 1980s and 1990s what they were unable to achieve in the 1960s. Such accounts probably underestimated not only the ability of the leaders of the various currents to get along together in pragmatic fashion but also the importance of the common doctrinal framework provided for them all by the GRECE. The problem of free market liberalism was dealt with by the leading thinkers of the Clock Club (Club de l'Horloge), who also theorised a highly conditional acceptance of the French Revolution designed to mollify the followers of the Maurrassian counter-revolutionary tradition. From this emerged a characteristic NF doctrine eclectic enough to bind the factions together yet coherent enough to be interpreted and used by the membership in their day-to-day propaganda.

Racial supremacy

The GRECE had its roots in the FEN and Europe-Action and inherited from these groups a belief in racial superiority. Early GRECE publications insisted on the primacy of inherited genetic characteristics and the necessity of biological revolution, championing eugenics as a means of improving public health (Duranton-Crabol 1988, pp.325–6) and proposing the elimination of 'pathogenic' elements such as Jews and blacks, referred to as 'lobotomised Europeans' by one of the organisation's publications, *Race et Intelligence* (Chebel d'Appolinia 1987, pp.325–6, 410). During the 1970s, however, biological racism did not seem to pay electoral dividends in France; writing in *Défense de l'Occident*, Pascal Yague drew attention to the frequently heard phrase, 'I'm not racist but ...', proof, according to him, of both the strength of the 'System', in that it was able to impose its vocabulary on individuals, but also its weakness, since it could not change the thoughts which lay behind such expressions (Yague 1973, pp.50–63). Even in Marseilles, where the local Ordre Nouveau branch had campaigned for years against the large local immigrant population, Duprat noted that potential sympathisers had been scared off, 'traumatised by the issue of racism' (*Cahiers Européens*, no. 1, May 1974). By 1976, fearful of an anti-racist backlash, the NF had already toned down its discourse, claiming to be against immigration, not immigrants, and proposing 'humanitarian' measures such as repatriation schemes and financial penalties for those who hired immigrant labour (*Cahiers Européens* 24 August 1976).

It was therefore natural that the NF leaders greeted with enthusiasm GRECE guru Alain de Benoist's abandonment of the principle of heredity for the notion of 'culture' as an explanation of ethnic differences. Animals were governed by heredity, he argued, their behaviour being programmed by genetically imprinted instincts. By contrast, men had been able to liberate themselves partially from their inherited genetic codes by filtering and abandoning certain aspects of instinctive behaviour, a process which amounted to the creation of a culture. In consequence de Benoist proposed to drop the word 'race' from the extreme right's 'scientific' vocabulary and substitute that of 'ethnic group' (*ethnie*), with the differences between such groups no longer seen as biologically inherited but depending on participation in a common culture, itself formed over thousands of years by the influence of space and climate (Bardèche 1979). For the veteran fascist Maurice Bardèche:

This substitution of the idea of culture for the idea of heredity is the pivot on which rests the whole renewal of right-wing thought which the GRECE proposes. (Bardèche 1979, p.19)

Bardèche did not feel obliged to give up his biological fantasies, continuing to believe in 'inequalities scientifically proved by intelligence quotients' (Bardèche 1979, p.18), and the rhetoric of cultural difference continued to share the pages of GRECE publications with favourable references to sociobiology and eugenics (see 'Biologie: Vers un eugénisme populaire?', *Eléments* December 1992). But the switch allowed the GRECE and its fellow-travellers to reserve such views for a relatively restricted audience while publicly presenting their ideas in a manner designed to deflect opprobrium, even claiming the mantle of anti-racism since they pretended to respect equally the specific capacities and achievements of all ethnic groups (Duranton-Crabol 1988, p.108; Bardèche 1979, p.19). In the hands of the NF, this flexible new 'culturalism' provided a sliding scale of racism, ranging from simple suspicion of the outsider to the labelling of 'foreign' as 'dangerous', to the desirability of racial segregation and selection and finally to racial supremacy.

When Le Pen says, as he does frequently, that he prefers his daughters to his sisters, his sisters to his cousins and his cousins to people from another family, his rejection of what is outside or foreign is at this basic level apparently both instinctive and harmless. The next stage of the argument is to insist that rejection of the foreign is not only instinctive but salutary. In an article titled 'Exclusion: a law of nature', the Front's theoretical review, *Identité*, shows a picture of lymph cells attacking cancerous cells, with the caption, 'Biology, like medicine, shows that the living world is perpetually struggling against what is foreign to it: cancerous cells, viruses, parasites, etc.' (*Identité* September/October 1990). For Le Pen, the exclusionary 'law of nature' is a vital defence mechanism not only against foreigners but also against sick members of the host society. Human progress, he tells us,

> ... is based on struggles, selections; we are able to defeat – with difficulty – hunger because we have selected the best kinds of wheat, corn, rye, because we have planted them in the best land, etc. (Le Pen, cited in Taguieff 1989a, p.188)

In the same vein he invokes a Darwinian struggle for survival between nations:

> Nature assigns all living things living zones suitable for their aptitudes and affinities. The same is true of men and peoples. All are subject to the same hard struggle for life and space. The best, that is to say the most able, survive and prosper as long as they remain so. (Le Pen, cited in Taguieff 1989a, p.186)

Furthermore, in this struggle for survival, degeneracy and defeat are threatened not only by military conquest but also by

> ... a planetary levelling down, a generalised cross-breeding aimed at the definitive reduction of the differences which exist between men and in particular ... racial differences. (Le Pen, cited in Marcilly 1984, pp.185–6)

By the late summer of 1996 the NF leader decided that it was time to say publicly what it had hitherto only been possible to deduce from a close examination of his writings. At the end of August he referred to the notion of racial equality as 'absurd', later citing the Olympic Games as a prime example of the 'obvious inequality' between the black and white 'races'. In response to the inevitable press outcry he followed up by asserting that 'all races are equal but some are more equal than others' (*Le Point* 21 September 1996).

The ideal society

The National and European Heritage

The GRECEists' model of the ideal form of social organisation is based on research by a distinguished French historian and linguist, Georges Dumézil, who theorised that only peoples who spoke Indo-European languages developed a tripartite separation of social functions into those which possessed a sacred character, those concerned with warfare, and those concerned with economic activity. According to Dumézil, in ancient times the Indo-European peoples established a hierarchy between these different functions, with the sacred at the top and the economic at the bottom, and developed codes which forbade the personnel concerned with religious, military or economic affairs to step outside their own domains. Not only the GRECE but also their emulators in the Clock Club adopted this model, Le Gallou adding the mystic touch that the tripartite division of social functions corresponded to the human organs of brain, muscles and mouth (Le Gallou 1985, p.144), and Yvan Blot suggesting that the sacred functions were to be regarded as not only religious but those concerned with the demarcation and celebration of identity and sovereignty (Blot 1985, p.201). These tasks were – or should be – the responsibility of the state, and consequently state officials ought to be at the pinnacle of the hierarchy of functions. The National Front's adoption of GRECE ideas on the European heritage was revealed in its 1985 programme:

> Throughout their long history, European cultures and nations have always distinguished three great social functions: the function of sovereignty, the function of defence, the function of production. (Le Pen 1985a, p.49)

The discovery that Indo-European societies were alone in systematically separating the three functions left the way open for GRECE and the Front to argue (against the protests of Dumézil) that European nations share a distinctive superiority to all the others. In 1984, for example, Le

Pen declared: 'We believe in the superiority of western civilisation ... the necessity of its authority in the world, tempered with Christian charity and European humanism' (Le Pen 1984, p.73). A 1988 NF internal bulletin added rather lamely, 'We have faith in the civilising mission of European peoples and, above all, of the French people' (Front National 1988, p.9), leaving French nationalism in a somewhat supporting rather than a central role in the party's doctrine, a position perfectly acceptable to the Front's Maurrassians, who stress the political expedience of the idea of the nation rather than its fundamental importance.

> The rational ideal would be that a single people of the same race, speaking the same language, should live on the same territory. That has rarely occurred in practice in history, and it is not my ideal.
>
> For me, the fundamental element in the life of men is at bottom the notion of a *community of destiny* [emphasis in the original]. What determines powerfully the organised life of men is a certain feeling, a certain wish to live together ...
>
> ... I observe that today, amid the general collapse of values, men have a tendency to gather round the idea of the nation, which is a protective idea. (Marie 1985, pp.43–4)

The idea of the *community of destiny*, which stresses shared culture and history ahead of place of birth or nationality is equally compatible both with nationalism and, when the Front leaders wish to stress it, with a certain pan-Europeanism. Accordingly it is difficult to accept unreservedly the view that the National Front is above all concerned with 'the survival of the French nation and French identity' (Marcus 1995, p.101). In day-to-day politics the Front undoubtedly chooses to concentrate its propaganda on what threatens its idea of France. But propaganda – which may be elaborated to appeal to the electorate or to attack an opponent – should not be confused with doctrine. The key principles which give both GRECE and National Front doctrine coherence are those of an anti-egalitarian form of social organisation which the Front believes France should adopt, not the uncomplicated dogma of 'my country, right or wrong'. After all, both Pétain and de Gaulle claimed to stand for the survival of the French nation and French identity but they had rather different ideas of France. We cannot define National Front doctrine unless we can say which of these traditions – or another – it resembles. It is no more satisfactory to characterise the Front's doctrine as 'national populist', akin to Reaganism or Thatcherism, which is the preferred formula of a large body of opinion in France (Taguieff 1986, p.46, and see Chapter 10). If it is not unambiguously 'national', the Front's doctrine can be even less convincingly described as 'populist' – although its style and elements of its propaganda may well be. Populism as doctrine would imply a denigration of elites and a preference for giving power to the people. The Front may well denigrate contemporary French elites, as part of its populist tactics, but its doctrine is far from hostile to elites as such and is no great friend of democracy.

Tradition, hierarchy and elite leadership

All the ideological currents within the NF are perfectly at home with the GRECE notion of 'rootedness' in a community of destiny, an organic society the members of which are linked by a common attachment to its territory by ties of blood and tradition and by the cult of heroic deeds (Vaughan 1982, p.61). As the NF newspaper put it in 1978, '[a]ll Frenchmen are brothers linked to a common destiny, they must occupy the place in the social hierarchy that their merit and talent justify' (*Le National* March 1978). The same organicist conception was evident in party propaganda in 1984,

> The supreme truth, biological reality, demands that the individual should not be arbitrarily detached from his line, which is what the left wants, because he is inseparable from it. (*Front National* 1978, p.44)

and repeated in 1996 by the NF chairman Bruno Mégret, for whom '[w]ithout links of blood and destiny there are neither peoples nor nations' (Mégret 1996, p.157).

For Pierre Vial, as a leading member of GRECE writing in the 1970s, the class most likely to defend a community's interests and identity, and therefore most fitted to occupy the sovereign functions, was the aristocracy, because it had the strongest sense of rootedness, while the bourgeois and the worker were both more concerned with owning than with being: 'aristocrats attempt to preserve what they are, bourgeois endeavour to preserve what they have' (Vial, cited in Vaughan 1982, p.64). Likewise, the spokesman for the Catholic fundamentalists, Romain Marie, believes that

> [e]very democracy worthy of the name generates an aristocracy. Aristocracy is nothing other than the emergence of the best. And then you need an authority to crown the whole edifice. (Marie 1985, p.40)

Applying this frame of reference to day-to-day politics in the 1980s, the party justified its attacks on contemporary political leaders by 'the necessity of giving life back to the authentic elites rooted in our people, who will take over from the corrupted oligarchies' (Front National 1988, p.12). Almost a decade later, Mégret was still convinced that the restoration of the sovereign function, essential for the regeneration of society, could not be carried out by existing elites, which were 'stale, turned in on themselves, timorous and apparently only concerned with their own preservation' (Mégret 1996, p.29).

How, according to the Front, should elites be selected? Certainly not by democratic means, if the GRECE attack on liberal principles is followed consistently, for in western society, according to de Benoist,

> [s]ince there is no principle of authority which is aloof and transcendental, power is no more than the *delegation* by individuals, whose votes are *added together* whenever elections come around. The 'sovereignty of the people' has nothing whatsoever to do with the *people as people*, but is the indecisive, contradictory and manipulable sovereignty of the individuals who compose the people. (de Benoist, reprinted in Lepage 1980, p.572)

Like the GRECE, the NF recommends the methods used in the heroic past when elites were forged by the trials of war, along with the greatest of ancestral European values:

> ... that of surpassing oneself, of combat, of competition, of emulation, that which permits conquest, discovery, that which leads to pushing back one's limits ... A virtue which made our European world the greatest civilisation which the earth has known. (Mégret 1996, p.50)

The concept at the heart of the National Front ideological system, linking the elements of cultural and racial supremacy, organic community and hierarchy, is identified by Le Gallou in an article in the party's theoretical review: it is 'anti-egalitarianism', which forms the cornerstone of the party's 'intellectual, political and moral counter-revolution' (Le Gallou 1991, p.20). In one respect the Front's anti-egalitarianism continues the extreme-right tradition of anti-Communism. Like its predecessors, the NF has tirelessly exploited the Communist bogey to oppose strikes, trade unions and any kind of redistribution of wealth or power based on class mobilisation. But, faced with the bogey's declining credibility during the collapse of Soviet power, the Front was quick to develop new anti-egalitarian themes. It has particularly targeted what it calls the new 'ideology' of the 'Rights of Man', allegedly developed by the French Socialists to give themselves some political stock-in-trade, via anti-racism and the fight against 'exclusion', now that they no longer promise the 'break with capitalism' (Mégret 1990, pp.23, 40). The Socialists' allegedly predominantly anti-racist message leads Mégret to identify a new bogey to be knocked down, 'cosmopolitanism', which pursues its egalitarian ends via the effect of racial mixing, and has become 'the key question of the end of the 20th century' (Mégret 1992, p.7). In creating 'a world without nations, without frontiers and without races', cosmopolitanism aims to 'make differences and identities disappear, to exalt inter-mixing, crossbreeding and the melting-pot and to uproot cultures and ethnic groups' (Mégret 1990, p.36). Egalitarianism is deplored in a third sense, in terms of the features of the world economy, when it is sometimes referred to as mondialism. The principle of free trade is compared to a system of communicating vessels: just as one vessel, containing more water than another, will be emptied of some of its liquid to bring about parity, so the opening of frontiers between two unequally developed countries will lead to a strengthening of weaker economies at the expense of richer nations, an 'egalitarian logic' which is blamed for the destruction of traditional economies, rising unemployment and falling wages (Mégret 1996, pp.138–9). This global form of egalitarianism is allegedly supported not only by the left but also by US imperialism, via international competition, and seen as a deliberate political project aiming at the creation of a 'universal empire' (Milloz 1992, p.82), fomented, according to Le Pen, by freemasonry and 'the Jewish international' (*Présent* 11 November 1989).

Economy and society: between free enterprise and social control

While the themes addressed so far – racial supremacy, organicism, anti-egalitarianism – undoubtedly constitute the core of the party leaders' doctrine, which in turn closely parallels the system of ideas developed by the GRECE in the 1970s, there was an important point on which the NF parted company from the GRECE's founder and leader Alain de Benoist. This was the question of the relationship between private enterprise and the state. In the Gaullist era it became habitual for much of the French right to launch attacks against American culture and economic power in which de Benoist's tilting at afflictions such as Hollywood, US financial backing for French ecologists, and the refusal of the US to sell uranium for the French nuclear programme, did not seem out of place (Duranton-Crabol 1988, pp.105–6). But he went much further, deploring the way in which capitalism had spread itself all over the globe, extinguishing local and ancient cultures in its path and imposing a 'bourgeois' obsession with money-making. Liberalism was even blamed for Communism itself, thanks to the influence on Marx of the classical economists' conception of an 'economic man' always motivated by his own best material interests, a concept dismissed by de Benoist because neither liberal nor Communist doctrines grounded the interest individuals were supposed to seek in convincing value systems which, according to him, could only be provided by the cultures of definite communities (de Benoist 1979, reprinted in Lepage 1980, pp.569–70). Such a blistering attack on capitalism was hardly calculated to appeal to the petty-bourgeois clientele attracted to the extreme right during the Poujadist phase of the 1950s. Indeed in 1978 the Front published a programme, *Droite et Démocratie Economique*, which was at odds with de Benoist's views. In its preface, Le Pen extolled both free enterprise on the basis of the traditional conservative slogan 'no political freedom without economic freedom', and the role of profit as guarantor of investment and jobs, not hesitating to demand the privatisation of state-owned companies and the distribution of their shares among the citizens. Using Maurras' dictum, 'Politics first', to argue that it was pointless to discuss the type of society one preferred unless the nation's survival was assured, he went on:

> ... we know that this cannot result from turning in on ourselves but, on the contrary, from a vigorous offensive which only the economic system based on free enterprise, competition and emulation is capable of providing. (Le Pen 1985a, p.10)

At the end of the 1970s there was thus an obvious incompatibility between those who followed de Benoist and the Front's clear liberal departure from the corporatist ideas which had inspired previous generations of extremists. That this incompatibility did not prove fatal to a rapprochement between the Le Penists and those influenced by the GRECE was largely due to a more subtle interpretation of the doctrine of the three functions by Jean-Yves Le Gallou and the Clock Club. De Benoist vigorously defended the state's right to guide the economy, complaining that the liberals wanted to reduce it to the role of

> ... maintaining order and security ... protecting the money men at the same time as leaving them complete freedom of action – in short it is no longer to be the *master*, but the very *slave* of those who, understanding better 'economic laws', ... are precisely better placed to

organise the world in their own best interests. (de Benoist 1979, reprinted in Lepage 1980, p.571)

According to Le Gallou, however, although Keynesianism was based on the idea, 'in itself justified', of general regulation of the economy by the political sphere, it was operated by pragmatists who had no overall grasp of the relations between the sovereign and productive functions and necessarily degenerated into the reverse of the distortion analysed by de Benoist, namely 'statism',

> ... a society which is at the same time mercantile and bureaucratic, dominated by economic concerns and commercial values, in which the economy is put under direct control, and the state substitutes itself for private actors. (Le Gallou 1984, p.154)

It also meant a loss of prestige for the sovereign function, with the state lowering itself to negotiate with its own employees and the special status previously reserved for the armed forces and civil servants extended to the directors of nationalised firms and various other hangers-on. The confusion of roles thus led to a double drawback – the citizen's loss of freedom was matched by the state's loss of authority (Le Gallou 1984, p.155). Le Gallou's formulation, first published in 1977, left the Clock Club on the same wavelength as the National Front, ready to participate in, and indeed advance, the emerging 'liberal' critique of past political practice by arguing that the state's sovereign functions should be restored and the authority of its agents strengthened at the same time as the *extent* of its authority should be rolled back to allow economic actors greater freedom. As it happened, this rapprochement between the 'new' right and the liberal revival was at first carried out – in the pages of the Clock Club's journal, *Contrepoint* – in association with activists from other parties, notably the RPR (Fysh 1990, pp.338–53), while de Benoist himself gravitated into iconoclastic isolation (see above Chapter 4), and it was not until the mid-1980s that the key Club leaders decided that they would join the Front. Nonetheless, their justification of the liberal revival via the theory of the three functions removed any barriers to former GRECEists wanting to join the Front but inhibited from doing so by de Benoist's intransigence. Le Gallou's formula confining the state to its 'regal' functions (sovereignty and defence) and leaving economic actors free to operate within their own domain quickly appeared in the 1985 party programme, which stressed that the state's fundamental role was to ensure the safety of the community and of individuals in the face of internal and external dangers (delinquency, disturbances to public order; threats from foreign states ...)

while, '[a]s for the whole business of producing material wealth, this is a question for individual initiative, within the general framework of laws governing society' (Le Pen 1985a, pp.49–50).

This was not the end of the story, however. The relatively free play of market forces *does* continually disrupt the ability of states to control what goes on in their territories, and the National Front, like all other parties, has to retouch the broad principles of its economic doctrine from time to time. By the end of the 1980s, the free market 'Reagan revolution' had run out of steam while in France the would-be ultra-liberal Chirac administration of 1986–88 had retreated in disarray. At the beginning of the 1990s public opinion was alerted to the consequences of the ever-diminishing barriers to free competition by the debate over moves to closer European Union and intense US pressure to deregulate the agriculture and audiovisual markets in the context of a 'world order' transformed by the collapse of the Soviet empire. Reacting to some of these developments and anticipating others the NF ideologues, led by Bruno Mégret, himself an ex-Clock Clubber, went back on their free enterprise enthusiasm and re-emphasised the *anti-liberal* aspects of their doctrine, though without losing sight of its anti-egalitarian core:

The logic of multinational companies provokes restructuring and mergers which give birth to footloose industrial conglomerates exploiting the limits of different states' jurisdictions.

... This mondialist structure ... leads to the uniformisation of national communities ... Its crushing weight is felt in society generally, where it enjoys wide powers in many areas. For example the Maxwell press empire ...

Such developments are contestable and harmful. Certainly, economic liberalism is capable of creating wealth and bringing prosperity, but it is only legitimate if it safeguards the life of national communities and respects their identities instead of destroying them. (Mégret 1990, p.47)

In 1996 the party's Scientific Council repeated this critique of the 'mondialist' international economic system and, while continuing to extol free enterprise within national boundaries, called for 'a new protectionism' to shield France from the effect of its operation externally (Le Pen 1996, p.131).

Pagans against Christians

One of the features of its doctrine which gave the GRECE an innovatory air was its wholesale condemnation of Christianity's share of responsibility for the ills of modern society, stemming from its two principal alleged vices, monotheism and egalitarianism. Each were held to have accelerated the fall of the Roman Empire, Christianity taking the role of the 'Bolshevism of antiquity' by undermining the structures of the family and the polity. Subsequently Christianity was said to have contributed little of value to European culture, the most important achievements in science and art occurring 'not within Christianity, but rather in most cases against it' as Europe emerged from the Middle Ages (Vial, cited in Vaughan 1982, p.63). In the modern era, monotheism is said to have been at the root both of imperialist drives, which were legitimised by the conquerors' conviction of possessing the truth, and of totalitarianism, because individuality is subordinated to the authority of an all-powerful God. Although their self-avowed 'paganism' gave de Benoist and his friends a certain novelty, the theme of a return to the sources of European culture had parallels with the 'blood and land' mysticism developed by the Nazis to foster identification with the timeless German '*Volk*'; indeed there is some evidence that the term 'Indo-European' was a deliberate code for the unmentionable 'Aryan' in early GRECE texts (Seidel 1981, p.49). And these pagans practised what they preached: the pages of the GRECE reviews in the 1970s advertised for sale silver replicas of the hammer of Thor and called on the faithful to attend the regular celebrations of the winter and summer solstices, complete with the baring of bodies to the sun's rays and the singing of homage to the dead and those yet to be born. Marriages were said to be celebrated by the exchange of daggers, meritorious work by GRECE local groups rewarded by the right to guard a ceremonial bronze sword. In the summer of 1979, 30 or so GRECE leaders met some of their European co-thinkers at Delphi in Greece to swear an oath 'under the sign of Apollo' to do their utmost to work for the revival of European culture (Duranton-Crabol 1988, pp. 50–4).

All of this was quite literally anathema to the Catholic fundamentalist current in the NF whose political allegiance goes to the counter-revolutionary tradition of Maurras' Action Française and whose leader, Romain Marie (*aka* Bernard Antony), deplores the 'hatred of Rome' of some of his fellow party members and has denounced the 'philosophical error' of nominalism which is in flat contradiction with the Christian conviction that all God's children 'partake of the same human nature' (Marie 1985, pp.120–2). But until the 1999 split NF-watchers sought in vain for signs of serious conflict between such seemingly opposed currents. This was undoubtedly because of their shared sense of belonging to the same extreme-right family. The split was in any case not caused by ideological conflict, as we explain in Chapter 7. Marie himself was an ardent supporter of Algérie française and a member of the MJR in the 1960s; in the 1970s he was founder and chief organiser of the association Chrétienté-Solidarité, with a mission to organise anti-Communist agitation on behalf of Christian minorities in the former eastern bloc and the Middle East. With Jean Madiran, another pillar of the fundamentalists, he founded in 1982 the newspaper *Présent* which daily deploys its Christian charity in vituperative attacks on the Jews. Moreover, despite being in favour of a 'Christian social order', Marie is surprisingly pragmatic about how this could be set up in France, conceding that, '[y]ou can't make a Christian order just with laws. If society is not Christian, there can't be any Christian laws' (Marie 1985, p.39).

Although naturally in favour of Catholic education, he accepts that to demand its official restoration in all French schools would be 'an imbecile utopia' (Marie 1985, p.77). As for Rome's ban on fertility control,

> [a]s a Christian, I adhere totally to the teaching of the church. As a politician I condemn abortion absolutely. But contraception is another matter. I believe, like St. Thomas Aquinas, that one shouldn't pass laws which one hasn't got the means to enforce ... Contraception is a question of morality. The state doesn't have to get involved in what doesn't concern it. Let's leave to the church what belongs to the church and leave to the state what belongs to the state. (Marie 1985, p.99)

The same reasoning is applied to divorce, which is a 'regrettable evil' but which the state should not attempt to outlaw (Marie 1985, pp.99–100). Such pragmatism goes far to explaining why the columns of the Catholic press are open to 'pagan' contributors from time to time and why neither the pagans nor the fundamentalists have made doctrinal differences grounds for attempting to split the party.

Monarchy or Republic?

In a country in which attitudes to the Great Revolution of 1789–99 have such emblematic importance for the political traditions of both left and right, this was another question which potentially posed a problem for the cohesion of the National Front's system of ideas. We have already seen (in Chapter 4) how Maurras' obstinate clinging to his monarchist doctrine divided him on one side from Republicans like Barrès and on the other from the fascists. The Maurrassians in the NF, however, have been much more pragmatic, appearing by the 1980s to attach no more than symbolic importance to the monarchist strand of their doctrine. At the same time the Clock Club leaders set about portraying the Revolution as a part of authentic French tradition, thus avoiding for the NF as a whole the isolation to which Maurras was ultimately condemned, while at the same time making their interpretation of the Revolution so limited and conditional as not to upset the Maurrassians.

Romain Marie refers as a matter of course to Maurras as the founder of his own political tradition (Marie 1985, pp.32, 38–9, 44, 92, 97). Like Maurras, he 'execrates' the French Revolution, while his conceptions of the representation of interests (Marie 1985, pp.41–2, 58), of decentralised 'communities of destiny' (Marie 1985, p.45), mirror those of the Action Française leader. Above all, his conception of authority evokes the divine right of kings:

> If authority depends on the vagaries of opinion, it is in effect founded on nothing. For me as a Christian, there is no stable morality but that which is linked to God's commandments, there is no stable authority but that which is linked to something higher than itself. (Marie 1985, pp.37–8)

But Marie and his friends are not alone in the NF in their admiration of Maurras, who commands general respect as a symbol of elitist opposition to the Republic. Le Pen himself cites him from time to time; even Bardèche, a fairly straightforward admirer of inter-war fascism and far from a Maurrassian, has paid him a noble tribute (Bardèche 1979, pp.20–1). Moreover, closer examination reveals that Marie's monarchism, while it provided a striking metaphor for a hierarchically organised society, was in effect no more than that:

> I don't believe at all today in a restoration of the monarchy. Let's not dream ... I am in politics in order to defend step by step a certain number of values within the framework of the laws currently in force. To go on infinitely about the best regime in French history is pointless. (Marie 1985, p.38)

If Marie's acceptance of the republican form of regime is an entirely pragmatic one, that provided by the Clock Club is much more sophisticated. Following Furet's revisionist reading of the events of 1789–99, the Club argue that one of the central ideas of mainstream French political culture, namely that the social struggles of the revolutionary period revolved around the universalist and abstract notion of equality and the Rights of Man, is nothing more than a myth imposed by succeeding generations of leftist historians. In reality, according to them, the Revolution was about the revival of the ancient liberties enjoyed by the Franks before they were confiscated by an invading monarchy. It expressed not a new dawn, but continuity with the past, the reassertion of a sense of a specific and rooted community, not an abstract ideal (Blot 1985, pp.189–215). The Club accepts 1789 therefore as part of its embracing of the nation's heritage and for the same reason, unlike de Benoist, they acknowledge the significance of Catholicism as an important part of French cultural tradition. From all this it followed that by 1989, when the French establishment celebrated the bicentenary of the Great Revolution, differences between the traditionalists, who followed Romain Marie, and the 'new' right, represented by the Clock Club leaders occupying the key places in the NF intellectual establishment, had been reduced to a minimum. Neither side had any reason to object to the line laid down by Le Pen:

> Everyone in the political class is preparing to celebrate the bicentenary of the 1789 Revolution ... Why not? France is made up of 4000 years of European culture, twenty centuries of Christianity, forty kings and two centuries of a Republic. The National Front accepts all of France's past. (cited in Taguieff 1986, p.28)

The question of the Revolution raises a related doctrinal problem. It is sometimes suggested that the Front necessarily faces a difficulty in reconciling voluntarism and anti-voluntarism in the extreme-right heritage, that is the difference between traditionalists – who wish to preserve what exists – and constructivists – those who desire to create a new society (Taguieff 1989a, p.192). In this schema, the Maurrassian tradition is anti-constructivist because it is founded on the rejection of revolutionary pretentions to construct a new society of rational design in place of the natural order of the *ancien régime*. But if Maurras was 'anti-constructivist', so also are the thinkers of the 'new' right, with their adulation of the Indo-European heritage. While there is a clear philosophical gulf between these different species of traditionalism and the more grandiloquent versions of a 'new order' invoked by some of the fascists of the 1930s, it has not caused any headaches for the main NF ideologues. They lump together Jacobinism, Marxism, social democracy *and* fascism into the same 'constructivist family', alternately denouncing 'fascist' features of socialism and stressing the left-wing origins of a Mussolini or a Doriot in order to distance themselves from the record of fascism in power (Marie 1985, p.63; Blot 1992, pp.67–8). This is both consistent with the anti-egalitarian thrust of the Front's doctrine as a whole and at the same time disingenuous for, as Taguieff himself concedes, *any* political project which seeks to affect contemporary reality can be accused of constructivism in some sense. The Front's own proposals to fine employers of immigrant labour or introduce preferential votes for heads of large families are examples of attempts to construct a new reality, whether this be seen as part of a sweeping rational plan or the working of human free will in endlessly responding to new situations (Taguieff 1989b, p.194). Le Pen himself has provided a formula which neatly avoids the so-called 'dilemma':

> There's a big debate between those who believe in a natural Order, which they see as flowing simply from the nature of things, and those who believe in an Order constructed by men. Men of the right believe in an Order constructed by men who are informed by the experience of Tradition and the past ... (Le Pen 1984, p.79)

This formula leaves entirely open the possibility of selecting the lessons of the past from within the fascist experience, should it seem appropriate.

Propaganda and press

Like most parties, perhaps more than most, the NF does not try to explain the whole of its doctrine to all the voters all the time. We may call the aspects which it selects and offers for public debate at any one time its propaganda themes. Many of the proposals contained in its programmes are perennial favourites of the authoritarian right, such as the restoration of the death penalty, the banning of abortion, the promise to put more police on the beat and give them more guns, the teaching of respect for morality and tradition in schools. But the party has become adept at shifting the emphasis among these core themes or adding new ones (the environment, social policy, mondialism) in line with changing political conditions. Furthermore, its crude populism has been given a more sophisticated gloss since the foundation in 1986 of Jean-Yves Le Gallou's Centre for Study and Argument, whose role was to present the Front as a credible alternative to the mainstream and tap into prevailing moods.

Having captured a corner of the political market, thanks to its crude and reductionist proposal to deport immigrants as a solution for the problems of unemployment, crime, falling educational standards and even the balance of payments crisis (Le Pen 1985b, p.223), the party gave its anti-immigrant stance a more sophisticated veneer by developing the policies of 'national preference', which would give French nationals priority in housing, education and employment while stripping immigrants of political rights (Le Gallou 1985), and the 'Savings-Return Plan', whereby immigrant workers would pay their social security contributions into a savings account to which they would have access only on returning to their country of origin (Le Pen 1985a).

But the Front is always on the look-out for an opportunity to move the goalposts. Having set the agenda on issues like aided repatriation, the nationality code, and the treatment of applicants for asylum, the Front presented, in 1991, a new '50-point plan' which outflanked all other parties with yet more radical proposals such as reversing recently granted naturalisations or demanding that immigrant-origin children pay for their schooling (see Chapter 3). Five years later, when the Juppé government sent riot police to break up the occupation of a church by immigrants campaigning for residence rights, Le Pen moved smartly further still to the right, proclaiming loudly and often his belief in racial inequality.

On themes other than immigration, the Front has been willing to adapt its propaganda in order to tap into prevailing moods. When environmentalism emerged as a major issue the Front proclaimed itself the greenest party in France; in 1992, as the popularity of the Socialist Party plummeted, the Front made a play for its electorate by unveiling a 51-point social programme (*National Hebdo* 26 March 1992). At the height of the liberal vogue of the early 1980s Le Pen was presented as the 'French Reagan', a champion of small businesses and 'popular capitalism', promoting an ultra-liberal programme which contained proposals to deregulate the labour market, extend the working week to 45 hours with no increase in pay and make social policy entirely dependent on market forces (Front National 1978). The backlash against monetarist economics which took place in the early 1990s, confirmed by Bill Clinton's 1992 election victory, prompted the Front to change tack and incorporate a fierce critique of free trade and a new emphasis on protectionism and social policy, including a defence of the minimum wage and the 39-hour week, into its programme (Front National 1993).

These developments were part of a more generalised change in the emphasis of NF propaganda which took place in the early 1990s. With the collapse of the eastern bloc and the decline of the French Communist Party depriving the Front of its stock-in-trade Communist bogey, it began to argue that the defining cleavage of the 'new world order' was no longer between left and right but between the national camp and anti-national forces (Robichez 1992). Le Pen attempted to embellish the Front's jingoistic nationalism by espousing the Gaullist vision of a community of sovereign nations: 'nationalists of all countries unite!' he declared (*Libération* 24 September 1990), inviting comparisons with post-Communist leaders such as President Landsbergis of Lithuania in the NF press, which even described him as 'the French Yeltsin'. The Front's analysis of this global conflict between nationalism and mondialism led it to oppose the Gulf War and seek cordial bilateral relations with Arab nations, and then to reject the Maastricht treaty in 1992. The Front's apocalyptic perspective on the so-called 'new world order', discussed below, infused NF propaganda with a more radical tone in the 1990s, illustrated by its adoption of the slogan, borrowed from Jacques Doriot's PPF, 'Neither right, nor left, French!' as the party's attacks on the 'gang of four' gave way to denunciations of 'the system' as a whole.

The distinction between the explicit and implicit messages of the Front is paralleled by the distinction it makes between its official publications and the 'sympathetic' press. 'Official' NF propaganda aimed at the general public is contained in the programmes and books which the party leadership publishes from time to time, in the posters and leaflets drawn up by the party's Propaganda Workshop, and in the twice-monthly Letter of Jean-Marie Le Pen, containing a message from Le Pen, details of local NF activities and a leaflet designed to be reproduced and distributed by the local branches, accompanied by a commentary explaining its significance. The Front also has its own telephone information line, Radio Le Pen, and produces a fortnightly cassette of around an hour and a half's duration, *National-Vidéo*, sold for 150 francs. This contains reports on the principal activities of the NF leadership, such as Le Pen's visit to Iraq in 1991 and the visit of a National Front delegation to Madrid for a commemoration of Franco's death. Commentaries on the main issues of the day have included a 'counter-inquiry' into the Carpentras affair in May 1990.

'Unofficial' propaganda is disseminated via weekly magazines like *Minute-la-France*, *Le Choc du Mois* and *National Hebdo* which form part of the Front's extended family, peopled by former collaborators and representatives of the hard core of the extreme right. After 1987 the Front stopped referring to *National Hebdo*, which claims a weekly circulation of 100,000, as the party's official newspaper, for tactical reasons (interview with Roland Gaucher, 21 May 1993). This allowed the Front to deny responsibility for the fascist sympathies and anti-semitic paranoia of a newspaper in which it became a majority shareholder after 1994 and which party members could be seen selling all over France every week, giving it a much wider circulation than any of the 'official' publications.

Until 1993 *National Hebdo* was edited by Roland Gaucher, former member of Marcel Déat's pro-Nazi Jeunesses Nationales Populaires. Prior to the 1999 split the paper retained strong links with the old guard of the French extreme right under his successor Martin Peltier, via regular columnists like the former collaborator, François Brigneau, and Jean Mabire, author of several works celebrating the SS. Gaucher has never seen any reason to apologise for his war-time activities:

> It's a phase that I do not renounce at all and during the course of which I learnt a lot. (interview with Gaucher, 21 May 1993)

During the occupation, using his real name, Roland Goguillot, he wrote for Déat's newspaper, *Le National-Populaire*, calling for brutal reprisals against the Allied 'barbarians' and lambasting intellectuals who flinched whenever 'the skin of some little Jew was scratched' (*Le National-Populaire* 3 June 1944). Forty years later he still believed that 'Communism has subjugated and continues to subjugate people. Nazism and to a lesser degree fascism have given to the near totality of their youth reasons to exist' (*National Hebdo* 11 May 1984).

National Hebdo performs three important functions for the NF. It pursues party campaigns with gusto. It acts as an organisational focus, providing a forum for debate, a tribune for leading NF members and bulletins on the Front's activities. It helps educate members and supporters, introducing them to the party's dual discourse, discussed below, and mapping the Front's political heritage, via sympathetic articles on the Vichy regime and far-right icons from Maurras to Venner.

The paper is the inheritor of a long tradition of populist anti-semitism originating with Edouard Drumont, whose ideas are considered more valid than ever (10–16 April 1997), and kept alive by Drumont's acolyte, Henry Coston, and the professional anti-semite, François Brigneau, whose weekly column, whether defending Nazis such as Rudolf Hess (27 August–2 September 1987) or collaborators like Paul Touvier (28 April–5 May 1994), returned with unfailing regularity to his obsession with the Jewish conspiracy myth. For over a decade Brigneau waged a nasty campaign against the Jewish journalist Anne Sinclair, '*née*', Brigneau repeated incessantly, 'Schwartz', and in the pay of 'occult forces' (24 November–30 December 1987). When he was ordered to pay damages to Sinclair following a particularly odious slur, he called it 'the vengeance of Shylock' (27 April–2 May).

Since the Front is unable to express its views as openly as Drumont was, *National Hebdo* helps NF members to understand the significance of the leadership's coded language. Throughout the summer of 1988 *National Hebdo* ran a campaign which denounced the government's policy of opening up to the centre as a Jewish-Masonic plot to prostrate France before international capitalism. Prime Minister Rocard and the centrist Raymond Barre were identified as agents of international Jewry and freemasonry in the pay of the Bilderberg group and the Trilateral Commission, supposedly funded by multinational companies in the pursuit of a 'cosmopolitan world order' (7–13 July 1988). Attention was drawn to the influence exerted on the government by Jews, such as Interior Minister Pierre Joxe, and Lionel Stoléru, a 'notability of the Jewish community in France' (14–20 July 1988): '... there is something rotten in this French Republic', the paper argued, 'where the Stolérus *not only exist*, but prosper' (14–20 July 1988, emphasis added). When, in the autumn of the same year, Le Pen finished an attack on the non-Jewish Radical minister, Michel Durafour, by calling him 'Durafour-*crématoire*,'[1] it seemed like a sick and rather bizarre joke, but in the context of *National Hebdo*'s campaign it made perfect sense to NF members. The episode followed a pattern whereby the ground for the leadership's outbursts are prepared by the Frontist press so that their full significance is understood. When, at the end of August 1996, Le Pen declared that he believed in racial inequality, he was echoing an idea developed over the entire summer in *National Hebdo*, beginning in late June when Brigneau declared that the ability of Jews to win positions of influence offered daily proof of 'human inequality' (20–26 June 1996).

Another branch of the press which until the 1999 split gave broad overall support to Le Pen and the Front was a group of publications run by Catholic fundamentalists, including *Présent*, *Itinéraires* and *La Pensée Catholique*. Although some of the Front's Catholics, such as Gaucher and Brigneau, followed the dissident archbishop, Marcel Lefebvre, when his sect split from the Catholic Church in 1988, the Front's fundamentalist current remained in the Church, where it believed it would have more chance of influencing other Catholics. *Présent*, with a claimed circulation of 30,000, distributed mainly by subscription, is proudly described by its

---

1. *Four-crématoire* is the French word used to refer to the ovens used to incinerate the corpses of Jews murdered in the Holocaust.

contributors as 'the first daily newspaper of the nationalist right since 1945' (interview with Alain Sanders, 14 September 1992). Deeply anti-semitic, frequently denouncing the 'power of the Jews', who allegedly conspire to run the world through organisations like the *B'naï B'rith* and 'Jewish big banking which has kept France under its dictatorship for 45 years' (cited in *Le Matin* 19/20 September 1987), it is edited by Jean Madiran, a leading fundamentalist and former member of *Action Française*, much admired by Maurras himself (Camus 1997, p. 234). *Présent* carries regular contributions from across the far-right spectrum, from Bruno Mégret to Henry Coston, and pursues, like *National Hebdo*, NF propaganda campaigns, in particular against abortion.

The strategy of the dual discourse

The former GRECE and the Clock Club members in the National Front leadership have used their awareness of the importance of language as a weapon of struggle to make the Front's messages more sophisticated and shift the terms of public debate in their own favour. 'Language is a subtle form of code,' according to Bruno Mégret, 'in choosing a word we place our thoughts, sometimes against our will, in a ready-made ideological frame-work' (Mégret 1990, p.166). Armed with this insight, the Front deliberately employs a dual discourse, one official and explicit, presenting itself as a legitimate part of the political establishment, the other unofficial and implicit, reflecting its anti-democratic, authoritarian agenda. The veneer of respectability must be sufficiently opaque to fool opponents and observers, but transparent enough to avoid deceiving its own members. The strategy is spelled out in a bulletin from the party's National Training Institute:

> To appeal to people we must first of all avoid making them afraid and creating a feeling of repulsion ... You can argue the same thing with as much vigour in a language which is measured and accepted by the public at large. (cited in *Actuel* June 1990)

The document offers examples of the kind of language members of the Front should use; instead of saying 'wogs out', they should talk about 'the return home' of 'third world immigrants'; they should not talk about 'class', but use the term 'socio-professional category', not refer to 'anti-racist groups' but 'the immigration lobby' and so on. The party's own propaganda reveals the extent of the former GRECEists' influence; whereas in the 1970s the party's paper railed against 'unsociable minorities' and claimed that France had become 'a dumping ground for good for nothings, degenerates, delinquents and criminals' (*Le National* February 1973), two decades later, its programme suggested that 'the return home of immigrants will have to take place in decent conditions, in liaison with their country of origin' (Front National 1993, p.48).

This strategy has played its part in imposing the Front's own agenda on the political mainstream. In 1990 Mégret triumphantly listed a number of the organisation's expressions, such as 'the establishment', 'cosmopolitanism', and the 'Lebanonisation of France', which had become common in public debate (Mégret 1990, p.166). By the early 1990s, references to 'levels of tolerance', the 'invasion' of immigrants, and the 'noise and smell' of foreigners, were no longer the vocabulary of an isolated racist minority: they had become the language of statesmen.

But as well as subverting the mainstream the ambiguity of the Front's discourse also deliberately creates a tension between the organisation and its periphery, between 'hard' and 'soft' support, seeking to address sympathisers where they are and take them where the Front wants to go, converting them to the Frontist world view and enlarging its hard core. To this end the party leaders are adept at using language heavy with codes and euphemisms, which asserts and subverts simultaneously, relentlessly pushing debate into previously 'unacceptable' areas. The undisputed master of this technique is Le Pen himself. In one register he will talk of culture,

> ... where different races, ethnic groups and cultures exist, I take note of this diversity and variety ... I cannot say that the Bantus have the same cultural capacity as Californians ... (Le Pen 1984, pp.167–8)

In another, in a bizarre style which oscillates between the grandiose and the vulgar, evoking the obsessive themes of male paranoia, his audience will have no difficulty in recognising the racial stereotype of the invading and lascivious North African,

> who'd push open your door, drink your whisky and who, before asking you to sleep somewhere else, would say to you, 'Do you know I'm interested in your wife?' (*Le Point* 18 September 1983)

In order to express its anti-semitism the NF leadership uses a series of code words to invoke the role of the so-called 'Jewish international': 'stateless and anonymous capitalism', 'obscure forces', 'the cosmopolitan lobbies' and so on. Once the role of international organisations has been understood, Le Pen confided to *National Hebdo*,

... we have at last a key which allows us to understand international politics, we understand at last the role of the UN, UNESCO, the Brussels commission, of all the agencies and circles, from the Bilderberg to the Trilateral via all kinds of clubs. (*National Hebdo* 26 October– 1 November 1995)

In a country in which open incitement to racial hatred is punishable by law, Le Pen's dismissal of the Nazi genocide as a 'detail' in the history of World War II was no slip of the tongue but a calculated raising of the tension between the NF hard-core and the periphery. The remark was bound to provoke condemnations and resignations from the party, but everyone who stayed in had jumped an important hurdle, raising the threshold of what was 'acceptable' for Le Pen to say. Some supporters were lost, but others were moulded in the Front's image. Le Pen's provocative response to the scandal bears this out. He compared the 'Le Pen Affair' to the Dreyfus case in an article whose title, '*J'Accuse*', deliberately evoked Zola's historic polemic in defence of the wrongly accused army captain (*National Hebdo* 1–7 October 1987). A year later, he kept the issue on the media front pages with the 'Durafour-*crématoire*' 'joke'. Instead of playing down Le Pen's outbursts or attempting to neutralise the widespread outrage which they provoke, the Front uses the fall-out to repeat and expand its message to its periphery by attributing the uproar to Jewish influence in the media. The Front persistently protested its innocence following the Carpentras desecrations of 1990, claiming that the whole business was engineered by a hostile media to discredit the party, yet Le Pen was prepared to use the affair both to trivialise the act at the heart of the furore and to demonstrate his contempt for Jews. Referring to the Jewish former Prime Minister Laurent Fabius' description of the exhumed corpse, which had been impaled through the anus, Le Pen remarked that, '[t]his word, in the mouth of Mr. Fabius, sounded somehow like a rhyme' (*Le Monde* 3 July 1990).

Le Pen is often derided as a vulgar buffoon, but his buffoonery is calculated. Like the professional wrestler in Roland Barthes' *Mythologies*, Le Pen imitates the Greek tragedians, walking forward pointing at his mask. The wrestler acts out a sham performance but constantly draws attention to the pretence, inviting the audience to share the joke. Using codes and innuendo, waving his arms, inviting laughter, mocking his opponents, Le Pen holds up a mask. 'I am the new Dreyfus', he proclaims when accused of anti-semitism. He proposes to banish AIDS victims to *sidatoriums*, referring to them as *sidaïques* in a deliberate evocation of the Vichy term for Jews, *judaïques*. 'I am a Churchillian democrat', he declares. Some see a blustering fool, some see a man accepting pluralism and parliamentary democracy, others, including the initiated – and here is the danger – see a man pointing at his mask as he advances.

National Front strategy – political change and the parliamentary road

The considerable energy devoted by the Front to standing for office and campaigning for votes has fooled more than a few commentators into refusing to consider it an anti-democratic force. Even if one overlooks the strategy of the Front's fascist founders, however, there remains plenty of evidence that, in the minds of the present NF leadership, the road to power is not the dutiful progression through the institutions of the French Republic to which they feign allegiance. On the contrary, by their unremitting attacks on the other parties they do all they can to undermine the parliamentary system, the final collapse of which they expect to occur in a context of profound social upheaval.

On various occasions Le Pen has left open the possibility of his organisation taking up a more revolutionary strategy should circumstances demand it. Justifying the overthrow of a Socialist government by the Pinochet coup in Chile in the early 1970s, he judged that it would be the 'right and the duty' of the army to restore order should a similar situation arise in France (*La Croix* 28 September 1973). 'We must be respectful of legality while it exists', he told the party's national congress in 1982. 'We are an army in civilian clothes, but it's not good for us to parade about with weapons' (*Le Monde* 2 November 1982). 'I will in no way allow France to be ruined,' he told the Turkish newspaper *Gunes* (12 November 1984), 'we are ready to use arms, to go to war if necessary, to prevent this possibility'. In 1986, predicting a violent reaction from his supporters if the Chirac government amended the electoral law, drastically reducing the number of NF deputies, Le Pen warned that, '[w]hen legal means are lacking, extremist methods find themselves legitimised' (*Le Monde* 16 September 1986). *National Hebdo*, the party's 'unofficial' paper, has frequently advertised guns and ammunition and its activists' guide (not be confused with the 'official' party members' guide, *Militer au Front*) carries sympathetic articles on fascist groups such as Ordre Nouveau and L'Oeuvre Française, quoting Lenin and the Spanish fascist José Antonio Primo de Rivera to the effect that the aim of every activist is to take power, if need be by legal means. A 30-page section on the police and the courts advises activists how to operate within the law and what to do when arrested, with particular attention paid to anti-racist legislation and the possession of arms. Activists are told which weapons they can legally carry and generally advised to be cautious in this regard, for France is 'not yet' ripe for insurrection even though

> ... all committed activists must keep in mind that the use of arms can one day be envisaged. This would then become the last resort of legitimate defence if all other forms of struggle proved useless. (*National Hebdo* 1990, p.90)

Privately, party leaders are more than willing to outline their apocalyptic vision of the breakdown of 'order' in France. Jean-Claude Bardet, politbureau member and editor of *Identité*, believes that

> ... our societies are very fragile, what's more they are a lot more fragile than we think. Everything functioned when the economy functioned. As soon as the economy no longer functions everything is challenged. Everything ... (interview with Jean-Claude Bardet, 12 May 1993)

In this situation Bardet envisages a growth in support for the Front,

> ... in complete upheavals, where there is profound despair, where people say, 'but really there are no solutions apart from that one,' you will see that there are extraordinary turnarounds. People ... who totally change their standpoint, people who will be willing to come and give their support, their expertise ... (interview with Jean-Claude Bardet, 12 May 1993)

But in order to profit from this potential cataclysm, the Front has to remain unsullied by participation in 'the system':

> If it wants to retain its image as a necessary solution, if it wants to remain the only thing the French people can lean on when everything really turns bad in their minds, then it must obviously avoid becoming pally with Mr Chirac, or with Mr Balladur, or with Mr Barre or with Mr Giscard d'Estaing. (interview with Jean-Claude Bardet, 12 May 1993)

Roland Gaucher offers an even more blood-curdling scenario of global dimensions:

> Despite attempts to crush it, the national phenomenon has made an absolutely spectacular breakthrough, which is continuing at the

moment in Yugoslavia, a terrible conflict but one before which mondialism is powerless ... Can we avoid being infected by this phenomenon, that's to say an intense nationalist explosion and extremely advanced economic contradictions? I personally do not think so. (interview with Roland Gaucher, 21 May 1993)

These views were endorsed publicly with unprecedented explicitness by Le Pen in September 1996, when he warned the Front's youth wing to expect to experience moments of great crisis:

> but crisis is the great midwife of History. When situations are blocked, it's generally the drive of human nature which forces a breakthrough into new times ... Now it is certain that only the National Front can tear this country from decadence ... There is a time when all that will end, and that will be the revolution. The extreme left is preparing for it ... So I believe that you too should prepare yourselves, because at a certain point the worm-eaten structures of our system are going to collapse. (*Le Monde* 17 September 1996)

Party organisation

Given that its leaders have such an apocalyptic vision of the way in which political change will come about, it is hardly surprising that the National Front organised itself in a rather different way from other parties. The account which follows describes the situation as it was until the split in 1999. In Chapter 9 we assess how badly the organisation was affected by the departure of Mégret and the bulk of the party's cadre. On the one hand, the NF adopted a conventional structure not dissimilar from those of other parties, made up of national and local committees geared to running for office and winning votes. On the other, it attempted to extend its influence into the social fabric via a network of federated satellite organisations, in which the emphasis was not on winning voters but on party members gaining influence in the social networks in which they find themselves, which they would be able to exploit in the event of social upheaval.

The conventional party structure was headed by the party president, Jean-Marie Le Pen, assisted by a general secretary, Bruno Gollnisch, responsible for the apparatus and local branches and the chairman, Bruno Mégret, responsible for propaganda, education, communication and the party think-tanks. The official decision-making body of the organisation, the political bureau, was formally elected by the central committee, but its membership usually reflected the respective strengths of the party's various ideological tendencies: the 'new' right (Yvan Blot, Jean-Yves Le Gallou, Bruno Mégret, Pierre Vial), the Catholic fundamentalists (Romain Marie) and the Solidarists (Christian Baeckeroot, Michel Collinot, Marie-France Stirbois); other members included long-time friends and collaborators of Le Pen (Dominique Chaboche, Jean-Marie Le Chevallier, Jean-Pierre Reveau), along with young party *apparatchiks*, members of the so-called *Génération Le Pen* who had risen up through the ranks of the organisation (Martial Bild, Carl Lang, Franck Timmermans). The central committee, convened annually, had 120 members, elected by the National Congress.

The authority of the president was unassailable. Former members, some of them driven out of the party after having the temerity to present ideas of their own, have described how politbureau meetings could turn into Le Pen's public bullying of a dissenter in a session of ritual humiliation in which none of those present dared to challenge the leader to his face (Piat 1991, pp.152–3; *Le Monde* 8 October 1988). In 1995 Le Pen flagrantly contravened party rules when he ensured that Gollnisch was co-opted by the political bureau rather than elected to his new post by the larger central committee. For a long time it suited those who wanted to make a career in the Front to maintain the equivalent of a Stalinist personality cult. The Catholics, despite their fundamentalist rigour, chose to overlook the fact of Le Pen's divorce, and a calculating intellectual such as Mégret pretended to recall that on first meeting Le Pen,

> ... I felt something indefinable rise up in me, something that we call confidence. Had this been sparked off by his talent for persuasion, the sharpness of his analyses or the strength of his convictions? I still do not know. In any case, I was overcome by a simple certainty: this was a man who makes history! (Mégret 1990, pp.9–10)

The NF described its own internal structure as a 'human pyramid' (*Le Guide du Responsable*, no. 1, 'Organisation', p.93); with each level of the apparatus subject to a hierarchy which reduced internal democracy to a minimum. The members were organised into branches under the control of a branch secretary appointed by the secretary of the next-highest level, the 'federation' corresponding to the French local government unit, the department. The federation secretaries were in turn appointed by the political bureau. The role of the annual departmental conferences was to review progress made and discuss technical matters; they were meant to prepare for what was supposed to be the annual congress by drafting motions and appointing delegates. But only three congresses were held between 1985 and 1994, so opportunities for debating and voting on the party's policies were somewhat rare.

Great stress was laid on education and training. Each region organised day schools for branch officials on implantation, propaganda techniques and the overall leadership of a branch. The members were trained in, among other things, discipline, self-defence, and spelling; special sessions were organised for would-be elected representatives. Ideological development was overseen by Bruno Mégret's Délégation Générale via the National Training Institute, which provided an example of successful co-operation by militants of different ideological sensibilities. The Institute was run by the Catholic militant Romain Marie, assisted by Pierre Vial, a pagan and founder member of the GRECE. Instructors included Jean-Claude Bardet, Bruno Mégret and Jean-Yves Le Gallou of the 'new' right, but also Franck Timmermans, a party *apparatchik*, and the Royalist Georges-Paul Wagner. The Délégation Générale also ran the organisation's modest publishing house, the Editions Nationales, and produced the NF's theoretical journal, *Identité*.

The activities carried out by the branches depended on their respective size and strength. Typical local events included dances, fêtes and dinner-debates, considered useful in terms of both fund-raising and establishing links with local employers and dignitaries; lectures given by a national party or sympathetic local figure, and public meetings, to which non-members were invited; book-signings by NF members or sympathetic authors; small gatherings in members' flats, used to recruit or integrate new members, at which party videos were generally shown. The six booklets distributed by the general secretary's office to the branches, covering every aspect of an NF member's responsibilities, leave the reader in no doubt as to where authority lay in the party: 'the hierarchical decision, once taken, is sovereign' (*Le Guide du Responsable*, no. 1, p.69). The meticulous, often pedantic instructions left absolutely nothing to individual initiative. The subjects covered range from advice on how to set up a local branch, how to recruit, how to organise market-place sales of the NF and satellite press, how to organise a meeting, a dinner-debate – 'choose a restaurant with French cuisine (no pizzas, Chinese, etc.)' (*Le Guide du Responsable*, no. 3, 'Convaincre', p.9) – a disco – 'avoid African music' (*Le Guide du Responsable*, no. 3, 'Convaincre', p.24) – and how to write a leaflet. Forty-five pages were devoted to the art of putting up posters, ten pages spent explaining how NF branches should organise the traditional sale of lilies of the valley on 1 May. The members' guide devotes 13 pages to instructing members what to reply when Le Pen is accused of being a racist, a fascist, an anti-semite, a torturer, and so on.

The satellite organisations

The Front's highly centralised conventional party structure was supplemented by a parallel network of affiliated and 'unofficial' groups with a greater or lesser degree of independence from the party, developed in pursuit of a strategy pioneered for the Front in the 1970s by Jacques Doriot's former lieutenants in the Parti Populaire Français, Victor Barthélemy and André Dufraisse. Like the PPF, the National Front seeks to develop a network of activists with influence in a variety of milieux, giving the party the potential to depart from its electoral strategy and take to other forms of struggle when the leadership judges that the time is right.

The biggest and most independent of the satellite networks was the Catholic fundamentalist diaspora, linked to the NF in the person of Bernard Antony, alias Romain Marie, political bureau member and founder of *Présent*, the Centre Henri and André Charlier, which organises an annual summer school and pilgrimages of over 50,000 people to Chartres, and Chrétienté-Solidarité. According to some estimates this organisation, with 2000 members and 4000 subscribers to its review, has a sphere of influence spreading to some 100,000 people (*Le Nouvel Observateur* 12, 18 April 1990). Fervently anti-communist and dedicated to forging international links with Catholics, Chrétienté-Solidarité was in regular contact with reactionary Catholic groups in the Lebanon, Indo-China, Croatia, Lithuania and Central America. In 1989 it helped organise the first official visit of Nicaraguan Contra leaders to Europe. In El Salvador Chrétienté-Solidarité was on good terms with the army and the hierarchy of the ruling ARENA party, despite the regular slaughter of Catholic priests by government death squads (Camus and Monzat 1992, pp.163–5). The fundamentalists' campaign against abortion is taken on to the streets by two organisations, SOS Tout-petits (Save the Little Ones) and the League for Life, the latter set up and controlled by the National Front (Soudais 1996, pp.210–11).

The most integrated satellite organisation was the NF's youth wing, the Front National de la Jeunesse (FNJ), which claimed a membership of 15,000. The FNJ served two purposes: to recruit students between the ages of 16 and 25, and to develop the future leadership of the NF. To this end the FNJ organised a regular summer school with workshops on various aspects of party activity. In 1990 the NF set up its own student union,

Renouveau Etudiant, which has established strongholds in traditionally right-wing universities such as Assass (Paris) and Lyon III, and which won around 5 per cent of the vote in the 1995 student elections. A similar body, Renouveau Lycéen, targeted secondary schools.

The Front's effort to rival the left by building networks among the French people at work was overseen by the Fédération Nationale Entreprise Moderne et Liberté (FNEML), taken over by Jean-Michel Dubois following Dufraisse's death in 1994. Some 15 FNEML 'circles' were targeted on banks, the health service, education, the civil service, manufacturing and the transport industry, organising the Front's sympathisers with a view to recruiting them into the party, raising funds and spreading the party's influence generally. By the early 1990s Dubois claimed a membership of 8600 for the circles, with each annual subscription costing between 150 and 200 francs (Hennion 1993, pp.47–8). The Front also attempted to win support among railway workers, taxi drivers, dockers, lorry drivers and sailors and airline pilots. An NF union section on the Paris metro (RATP), the Cercle National RATP, claimed to have recruited a thousand members within its first three years of existence, before it was banned in June 1996 because of its overtly political nature. In its stead the NF launched a new initiative, the Cercle National des Travailleurs Syndiqués (CNTS), aiming to unite NF supporters who already belonged to trade unions in a single federation.

During the 1980s the Front made concerted efforts to establish a base in the police force, infiltrating organisations such as La France avec sa Police, set up by the RPR in 1989, the Comité Sécurité Solidarité Police, founded in association with Jean-Pierre Stirbois and Le Pen, and the best-known right-wing police union, the FPIP (Fédération Professionnelle Indépendante de la Police). So successful were these efforts that by 1995 the Front was able to set up Front National Police, winning one in seven votes in the professional elections held at the end of the year. In some areas, notably in southern France, the NF vote approached 50 per cent. Before the split in the party's ranks, the FNP was the fourth largest of 18 police associations, gave the Front permanent union officials and a voice on appointment panels.

The culture of violence and vigilantism which pervades the Front was translated into organisational form by bodies such as the Cercle National Amitié et Sécurité, which aimed to defend the French and their belongings against street crime. This culture was not confined to fringe elements in the party: the ex-GRECEist MEP and cultivated dandy Yvan Blot argued in 1995 that a national guard should be constituted to keep control of France's suburbs (*National Hebdo* 9–15 November 1995) and Le Pen himself was protected by a 2000-strong security force, Direction Protection Sécurité (DPS). In a similar vein, but with a more long-term perspective, the Front set up organisations which might be considered embryonic militias. These were the Cercle National des Combattants (CNC) and the Cercle National des Gens d'Armes (CNGA). The CNC was run by Roger Holeindre, convicted OAS terrorist and a founder member and former vice-president of the Front. Among his organisation's professed aims were the promotion of the patriotic ideal and the 'material and moral defence' of war veterans who identified with the values of the National Front (Front National 1992, p.433). The CNC claimed 5000 members and had a chateau and grounds at its disposal for activities in which the 'physical, moral and patriotic training' of members' children and their friends was combined with inculcating 'respect for the history of France and its glorious past' (CNC leaflet, author's collection).

The Cercle National des Gens d'Armes was to organise amongst the police and the army. Despite claiming to be non-political it was equipped with a newsletter, *Le Glaive*, which made plain its support for Le Pen and purveyed the same drivelling anti-semitism found in the rest of the NF-sympathetic press. The Cercle's intended role is spelled out in an article in *Le Glaive* by Bernard Lefèvre, a co-founder of the Comité de Salut Public in Algiers in 1958:

> ... is it not to save lives and defend the Common Good of the nation as soon as there is a threat from beyond its borders or from within the country? (*Le Glaive*, no. 1, second trimester 1990)

The author's idea of the threat to the 'Common Good' is spelled out in the rest of his article: the rising immigrant population, the development of urban ghettos, the pressure brought to bear by the '*mondialiste* economico-financial conglomerate', the threat to the Catholic Church from a government apparently more concerned with protecting foreign religions, and the menace to French culture in general posed by 'cultures from elsewhere, and often from the depths of barbarism' (*Le Glaive*, no. 1, second trimester 1990).

The December 1995 strike movement encouraged the Front to redouble its efforts to sink deeper roots in the associative network of French society. Early in 1996 the Cercle National des Pré-retraités et Retraités (for those over or nearing retirement age) launched a campaign over pension rights and the Cercle National des Corps de Santé, originally formed in 1989, reinvigorated by opposition to Juppé's health reforms, relaunched its efforts to spread NF influence in the health service. In schools NF influence was propagated by the Mouvement pour l'Enseignement National (MEN), which claimed by 1996 to have won 2500 recruits in three years, thanks to 'violence in school, arguments over the Islamic headscarf and the rise of illiteracy' (*Libération* 3 January 1996). In 1996 party members stood for election in 35 of France's 600 municipal housing associations under the banner of Front National des Locataires (FNL), calling for priority for French families in the allocation of housing and winning between 10 per cent and 30 per cent of the vote.

Another of the Front's initiatives reflecting the influence of the Communist model was Fraternité Française, formed in 1988, which sought, like the Communist Secours Populaire, to provide aid for those in poverty. The Fraternité Française association in Marseilles was run by Agathe Sabiani, daughter of Simon Sabiani, the former PPF boss in the city. In the same vein, the FNJ formed the Association de Recherche pour l'Emploi des Jeunes in 1994, which claimed, in its first year, to have found jobs for 80 people (*Le Monde* 28 December 1995). At the other end of the social scale, the Front exploited the potential financial support available from its sympathisers in business and the upper classes, thanks to a list of 3000 correspondents in small- and medium-sized businesses compiled by Dubois (*Le Figaro* 1 February 1990). His Cercle Alexis-de-Tocqueville, founded in 1991 along with Henri Josseran, a former member of the OAS and Occident, and Jean-Michel Schoeler, a member of the RPR and one-time adviser to Interior Minister Charles Pasqua, succeeded in February 1992 in organising an event at the Grand Hôtel de Paris at which 200 figures close to the RPR chose Le Pen's company for dinner, rather than Jacques Chirac's (the RPR had organised a dinner the same evening). A number of leading business figures were present, among them François d'Aulan, former head of the champagne company Piper Heidsieck, Jacques Henriquet, international director of Renault-Véhicules Industriels, Alain Mosconi, director of Fiat Auto-France and Jean-Louis Giral, one of the leaders of the French employers' organisation, the CNPF (Hennion 1993, pp.16–17). Another link between Le Pen and potentially wealthy backers was provided by the Renaissance Circle, which shared the address of the Cercle Alexis-de-Tocqueville. Founded in 1970 by Michel de Rostolan, a former member of Occident who became a National Front deputy in 1986 and later sat on the NF central committee, the Renaissance Circle also organised dinner debates and distributed annual prizes for literature, the arts and economic affairs. Its patrons included Pierre-Christian Taittinger, of the eponymous champagne empire and former vice-president of the Senate, and Jacques Malard, president of the Monoprix supermarket chain.

Conclusion

This analysis of its doctrine, strategy and organisation should have shown that the National Front is about far more than a revival of far-right or national populist ideas. Le Pen's organisation represents the most successful attempt at rebuilding a fascist party since the war. Its strategy combines successful participation in the electoral game with the construction of a network of sympathisers and affiliated bodies which grant it the capacity to change course dramatically in response to events. The ambiguities of the Front's discourse, the deliberate slips of its leader and the notoriety of so many NF members are, in this context, as necessary for the Front as the respectability it has so assiduously courted. These are the keys to understanding the nature of the Front and the scope of the danger which it represents.

6
Youth and Anti-Racism

Youth and social exclusion

In July and August 1981, the Minguettes, the largest housing estate in the Lyons region, in the commune of Vénissieux, had a population of 35,000: 30 per cent immigrant, 20,000 under the age of 25, 4000 unemployed, 1500 of the 10,000 flats empty. For nearly two months, under the avid gaze of an army of press and television crews, there were almost daily clashes between police and groups of youths trying to release the energies for which French industry had no use by racing and burning stolen cars.

> Clashes in Maghreb districts. Hot week-end in Lyons. Three people, among them two police officers, injured in Villeurbanne and Vaulx-en-Velin ...

> Mini-riot at the Minguettes: 150 residents confront police who had come to arrest three burglars: 2 injured ...

> For a hundred days complete and total anarchy has reigned in the concrete canyons of Vénissieux, Villeurbanne and Vaulx-en-Velin. Joy-riding, thefts, muggings, vandalism ... arson ... all go unpunished!

From the beginning, thanks to the pages of the conservative daily *Le Figaro*, and the staged images of the television cameramen, for the French public the situation of immigrant-origin youth in sink estates on the outskirts of big cities was synonymous with a law-and-order problem (Llaumett 1984, p.14; Jazouli 1992, pp.19–26, 36, 78; Bouamama 1994, p.38).

The urban riot, however, has only been the least organised – albeit the most media-exploitable – of immigrant-origin youths' responses to the political and social situation in which they have found themselves. The last two decades have seen them form their own cultural and community associations and deploy a variety of forms of struggle including hunger strikes, a series of national marches, lobbying and campaigning in elections, in support of demands covering protection from deportation, the punishment of racist crimes, the nationality law, education, the right to vote, housing conditions, military service, political asylum and above all, their treatment at the hands of the police and justice system. The key slogan of their first national march: 'against racism and for equality' underlined the dual nature of their activities: on the one hand self-defence but in addition a struggle against other dimensions of inequality in French society in which they ought logically to have found allies from the mainstream left.

The emergence of immigrant-origin youth on to the political stage prompted a flood of literature of two kinds. Racists inevitably seized on the 'criminality' evident in explosions like that of the Minguettes to add to their lists of reasons why it was necessary to block new immigration and/or send 'home' those who were already in France. Social science researchers have responded by marshalling evidence of the considerable degree to which the behaviour and values of the host society have been adopted by immigrant-origin youth. (Though this does not necessarily mean that the basis for *political* conflict between the two is disappearing.)

It is fairly easy to debunk the assertion that the assimilation of immigrants into French society is 'impossible' on account of their belonging to an 'Islamic world, in the throes of a religious, political and demographic revival' (Griotteray 1984, pp.103–4, 115). For one thing, the heterogeneity of Islam in France, with separate mosques for Turks, north Africans and other Muslims is such that 'nowhere is there an organised clergy of undisputed leadership capable of imposing religious edicts (*fatwa*)' (Roy 1994, p.57). For another there is a wealth of evidence that the children of north African families have adopted 'western' attitudes to dress, food and music, have little knowledge of or interest in Islam and little sympathy for traditional attitudes to family life and relations between the sexes (Roy 1994; Gonzalez-Quijano 1987; Hargreaves 1990; Cesari 1993). A 1987 survey of a sample of children of Muslim parents in the Paris region showed that only 5 per cent belonged to a religious organisation, less than half planned to raise their children in the same way that they had been brought up, while 84 per cent of them found 'cohabitation outside marriage acceptable'. Another study found nearly 90 per cent of young Maghrebis willing to contemplate marriage outside their community, in spite of their parents' reproval of such marriages, and 10 per cent of girls and 38 per cent of boys rejecting the traditional gender roles which assign authority to the father in Arab households (Hargreaves and Stenhouse 1991; Hargreaves 1995, p.111). Among young

Muslim women such attitudes are reflected in their membership of associations formed to combat polygamy and clitoridectomy or counter-readings of the Koran which impose restrictive dress codes on women (David 1991).

When Charles Pasqua writes (1985, p.51) that 'natives are becoming fewer and fewer, while foreigners are multiplying and multiplying in geometric progression', it is easy to show that, on the contrary, the longer they live in France, the fertility rates of foreign women approach closer and closer to that of the host society (Desplanques and Isnard 1993). When National Front authors wax lyrical about the ineffable French cultural heritage so threatened that 'little French children become strangers in their own country' (Mégret 1990, pp.185, 202; Le Gallou, cited in Hargreaves 1987, p.55), it is possible to remind them that 'French' culture has always been made up of cross-border borrowings and exchanges and that more than half of Arab parents use French to communicate with their children, who for their part have begun to turn out novels in a mixture of localised slang, French and English (Hargreaves 1995, pp.92, 103, 106). One author concluded from all this that all that remains of the 'so-called Arab "communities"' are 'a few festive observances within the family (the sacrifice of a sheep to mark the end of Ramadan for example) and the sense, confirmed by the attitude of others, that one is an "Arab"' (Roy 1994, p.60).

The poor fit between ethnic and religious parameters of identity (not all Arabs are Muslim, not all Muslims are Arab) together with the sociological and cultural convergence of immigrant-origin youth with French youth are clearly factors likely to limit powerful autonomous political organisation by immigrant populations in France. Episodes like the Minguettes, however, revealed the existence of a subculture shared by immigrant-origin *youth* in which rebellion against second-class lifestyles formed an important strand. As we show in an examination of immigrant-origin youths' situation in schooling and the job and housing markets and in relation to the police and the justice system, their mobilisation derived, not from a sense of ethnic community but from a burning sense of injustice ignited by a shared experience of racism and exclusion and the internalisation of the dominant *French* value system based on equality of all citizens before the law (Lapeyronnie 1987, 1991).

Later in the chapter we look at the difficulties which obstructed the emergence of a national movement of immigrant-origin youth and their failure to make a decisive contribution to the creation of a national anti-NF campaign. In part these arose from a sociological evolution corrosive of group unity, specifically the emergence of a middle-class elite of north

African origin which fostered a sense of community identity only to the extent that it was useful for its own social advancement (Wihtol de Wenden 1994; Geisser 1992; Cesari 1993; Roy 1994). But sociology does not explain everything: the failure was also a result of the *political* ideas and strategic choices of key actors.

Of the 1,548,836 foreigners below the age of 27 who lived in France in 1980, young Portuguese and young Algerians were almost equally numerous, accounting for 28.5 per cent and 27.4 per cent of the cohort respectively. They were followed by young Moroccans with 10.5 per cent, up by 53 per cent since 1975, while young Maghrebis added together made up 41.9 per cent of the total (38 per cent in 1975). The young Spanish and Italians' 6–7 per cent each of the age-group was roughly half their communities' shares of the foreign population as a whole, reflecting their long establishment in France and the operation of the nationality law which made their children French at birth if just one parent was born in France. Since the law also provided that all foreign children born in France might become French automatically at the age of majority (18), the authors of a specially commissioned 1982 report coined the category of '*jeunes d'origine étrangère*', immigrant-origin youth, estimated at some 2,300,000 individuals, of whom three-quarters were born in France and one-third had French nationality (Llaumett 1984, pp.19–27). Right up until the end of the 1990s there was no ethnic monitoring in France, so attempts at sociological analyses of ethnic mix had to be based on nationality, which necessarily underestimated overall numbers of those of immigrant origin and ignored also the more than 300,000 black citizens living in France but originating in the overseas departments of the West Indies or the Indian Ocean. Some idea of the evolving ethnic mix of the French population can nonetheless be gauged from the transformation in the sources of in-migration during the 1980s; Spanish, Italians and Portuguese represented only 3.4 per cent of all new immigrants in the year 1990, the Maghreb countries provided 35.4 per cent (half of them from Morocco) while immigrants from black Africa accounted for 10.8 per cent, Vietnamese 7.2 per cent and Turks 7.5 per cent (Festy 1993, p.39). In 1992–93, young Maghrebis represented just over 50 per cent of all foreign students in French secondary schools, the Portuguese just over 15 per cent, while students from black Africa and Turks accounted for around 7 per cent each (Bocquet 1994, p.76). In short, the share of non-Europeans among young foreigners living in France has been rising continuously for two decades, while young people of Maghreb origin remain numerically dominant.

School and work

In school, young foreigners are disproportionately concentrated in classes for less able students leading to earlier exit with low levels of qualification. Thus, in 1980–81, when foreign students were 7.9 per cent of the secondary school population, they accounted for 16 per cent of those in 'special' education (in theory reserved for those with 'slight intellectual deficiency'), 10.7 per cent of students in remedial or pre-vocational classes (CPPN and CPA), 8.4 per cent of students in vocational classes leading to manual or clerical professional qualifications (CEP, BEP or CAP), but they were only 3.2 per cent of students in the top streams leading to the *baccalauréat* (Llaumett 1984, pp.53–5). These figures should not be taken to confirm either the low ability of foreign students or racist attitudes by the school authorities. Quite simply, the French school system is highly selective in relation to social class and the streams in which foreign children are concentrated are those inhabited by children from the most disadvantaged social groups. In the 1980s 38 per cent of French students came from such a background, compared to more than 80 per cent of foreign students, whose parents, moreover, were concentrated in positions at the bottom of the hierarchy, a foreign worker being twice as likely to be unskilled as his French counterpart. Educational attainment also varies according to family size: only 16 per cent of French families, against two-thirds of foreign families, have four or more children (Bocquet 1994, p.80). Some studies have suggested that, once these variables are taken into account, foreign students, if anything, do better than their French peers (Hargreaves 1995, p.64).

Nonetheless the highly bureaucratised selection procedures operative in the French school system played a role in maintaining and reproducing this pattern of exclusion which necessarily limited foreign students' chances of integrating smoothly and successfully into the host society. Once a child had been excluded from streams leading to the *baccalauréat* or to one of the more sought-after vocational specialisms, via crucial decisions at ages 11, 14, and 15 when factors such as social background and family size might be taken into account, there was little or no chance of making up the ground or changing streams at a later date (Prost 1992).

Of those who survived into the last three years of secondary school at the turn of the 1980s, 60 per cent of French students avoided vocational courses by enrolling in the 'long' cycle, aiming for the *bac*, while 38–40 per cent of Italian and Spanish students did so, 27 per cent of Algerians (29.5 per cent of all Maghreb students) and only 23 per cent of Portuguese (Llaumett 1984, p.58). While Maghrebis and Portuguese, the most recently arrived of the groups cited here, were both massively disadvantaged compared to the others, Maghrebis' marginally superior performance reflects a different attitude to and experience of the job market. A 1988 study found evidence that young Maghrebis deliberately shunned the unskilled work, bad conditions and poor pay which had been their fathers' lot. When they were in work they earned more and were more highly qualified than young Portuguese; the latter were three times more likely to be workers, 45 per cent of them finding their first job in industry while only 22 per cent of Maghrebis did so (Lapeyronnie 1991, p.65).

Although the proportion of young foreigners out of work in the early 1980s (between 25 and 30 per cent) was only slightly higher than that among young French people, the jobless rate of young Algerians was two and a half times that of young Portuguese. And among young men the imbalance was even greater, for unemployed Algerians under 25 were more or less evenly divided between men and women, whereas among both young French and young Portuguese, the share was one-third men and two-thirds women (Jazouli 1986, p.23; Llaumett 1984, pp.81–2).

These differences can be explained partly by the strong community networks which encourage young Portuguese to leave school relatively early and find jobs with small-scale Portuguese owned firms, often in the building industry (Tribalat 1991, pp.24–5). In the absence of similar community support, young Maghrebis have had to contend with discriminatory attitudes among employers, which affect between a third and a half of all job offers, according to evidence collected by the High Council for Integration; by the end of the 1980s the likelihood of being unemployed was 39 per cent greater for a foreigner than for a French person of the same age, same education and qualifications and working in the same sector. While 29 per cent of all foreigners aged 15–24 were unemployed in 1990, 42 per cent of the same age group from non-EEC countries were (Zylberstein 1993, pp.161, 310–11). In short, the professional aspirations of young Maghrebis mirror those of young French, in contrast to the attitude of the Portuguese, who seem to accept their 'immigrant' status. Yet the young Maghrebis encounter much the more serious barriers in the way of their successful integration into French society.

Housing

Consigned to the least promising streams in school and distinctly second-class status in employment, foreigners in France have inevitably suffered an even more visible form of exclusion via the housing market. Until the mid-1970s they lodged mainly in circumstances characteristic of what were thought to be the 'temporary' needs of single male workers: hotels, hostels, transit camps, shanty towns and, for those who tried to settle their families decently, the oldest and most dilapidated privately rented flats in run-down city-centre areas where the owners had long ceased to carry out repairs and maintenance since rents were controlled in 1948 (Ginesy-Galano 1984). The atrocious conditions in which they had grown up, giving them a sense of stigmatisation and exclusion by the host society, were still sharp memories for young Maghrebis interviewed in the 1980s (Jazouli 1986, pp.48–9). From the mid-1970s foreigners began to move into the public rented sector as governments attempted to clean up the shanty towns and earmarked funds for cheap social housing (HLMs – *Habitations à loyer modéré*) intended to house their families, who were moving to France in increasing numbers. The percentage of foreign households lodged in HLMs increased from 15 in 1975 to 24 in 1982 and 28 in 1990; they were particularly popular among Maghrebis, providing shelter for 34.3 per cent of Algerian families in 1982 (37.6 per cent of Moroccans) rising to 43.4 per cent (44.3 per cent) by 1990 (Hargreaves 1987, p.12, 1995, p.71). At first sight, this seemed like a move out of the 'ghetto' into sharing the central heating, running water and inside toilets which the poorest French manual and clerical workers had begun to enjoy only in the late 1950s and the 1960s when flats in the new concrete towers and horizontal blocks were mass-produced as cheaply as possible at the rate of 500,000 a year (Menanteau 1994, p.54).

Yet even as the former outcasts began to enjoy the new comforts, the dream was turning sour. Many HLMs were built far from city centres, with which they were poorly connected by public transport, on the cheapest available land often sandwiched between motorway slip-roads and railway lines – areas bereft of the small shops, cafés and street markets which create the individual ambience of the French *quartier*. Surveys of the residents revealed that the place where most social contact occurred – when inadequate soundproofing had not yet turned relations with neighbours into a nightmare – was the lift shaft. The mainly French families housed in the first such estates suffered record levels of mental illness and divorce. Already by 1963 the rise of juvenile delinquency was being blamed on such an unnatural habitat, while surveys showed 80 per cent of French people wanted to live in individual houses like the Americans and the British (Menanteau 1994, pp.54–60).

Given all this it was hardly surprising that many of the first occupants moved out as soon as they could afford to, a phenomenon occurring in the private sector also when the original residents could escape by subletting their flats to others (Wieviorka 1992, pp.280–5). Aware that the law of the market unchecked meant a permanent tendency to decantment of upwardly mobile whites and the sucking-in of non-Europeans, policy makers began by the end of the 1960s to advise the adoption of ethnic quota systems in order to disperse foreigners as much as possible throughout the estates under public control (MacMaster 1991). From 1975 onwards each HLM authority was allocated a share of the proceeds of a special tax earmarked for the housing of immigrants in exchange for their promise to reserve a certain proportion of their stock for immigrant families. Inevitably, dispersal did not take place everywhere as planned. The condition or the location of some of the worst-built estates were so unappealing that European families simply refused to accept them, no matter how long it meant waiting for another offer. The most unscrupulous HLM authorities responded by shoving their 'quota' of foreigners into such estates or even one or two blocks of the same estate and leaving the rest empty (Weil 1995, pp.399–405). The quota policy was often interpreted to mean that a French family had to be replaced by French and a non-European by non-Europeans, thus barring access by the latter to the more sought-after locations. Soon run-down estates became identified with a high density of immigrants and European residents fled in ever-greater numbers. Although the proportion of foreigners in the public sector as a whole probably never exceeded 10 per cent, there were estates on the fringes of Paris said to house practically only immigrants (Gaspard and Servan-Schreiber 1985, pp.138–9); in Marseilles, government-funded dispersal of the Maghrebis crowded into the northern suburbs was prevented by the surrounding municipalities' refusal to allow new housing construction on their territory (Weil 1995, p.404); by 1981 in the eastern suburbs of Lyons, estates like the Grappinière in the commune of Vaulx-en-Velin or the Minguettes in Vénissieux typically had immigrant-origin concentrations of 35–80 per cent (Jazouli 1992, pp.19–20). To those who had to live in them, the concentration of immigrants seemed like a deliberate policy of exclusion:

> When you live there you're convinced that it has been done deliberately, that they've shoved you out on the extremity to make sure you stay there, that you never feel really at home, that you're there, close to the exit and at any moment they can kick you out altogether. (Malika, 25, from Marseilles, cited in Jazouli 1985, p.49)

In 1978 the average number of children per family was 3.1 for French and 4.6 for foreign HLM residents, of whom 47.2 per cent were said to be under the age of 20; 15 per cent of French, 49 per cent of Portuguese and 62 per cent of Maghrebi families were in flats too small for them (Llaumett 1984, pp.44–5). The consequences of this farrago of a housing policy did not take long to appear: children perpetually playing in the corridors and stairwells, exchanges of insults with the neighbours, adolescent males with time on their hands and no money to spend on amusements, the empty flats as tempting refuges for getting high on drugs or storing stolen goods – all the ingredients were present for explosions which detonated at regular intervals throughout the 1980s and 1990s.

Police and justice

The fact that a certain kind of crime – theft and resale of consumer goods – is concentrated among the social categories residing in dilapidated housing estates, where many foreigners also live, lends plausibility to the routine allegations of the NF and their sympathisers that all immigrants are criminals and that but for them crime would disappear. Immigrant-origin youth have certainly been on the receiving end of more severe treatment by the justice system. A study of 1200 convictions of young people in three courts in the Paris region in 1974–75 revealed that 35.5 per cent of cases concerned foreigners, when the latter made up only about 7–8 per cent of the population. But it was just as likely that this differential represented a 'super-conviction' rate as that it reflected 'super-criminality' by young foreigners. For one thing, an accurate comparison between two national groups would require samples identical in terms of the factors known to affect criminality: age, sex, social category and housing conditions. In the absence of such studies, part of the apparent 'super-criminality' of foreigners can be assumed to be linked to their concentration in 'at-risk' social categories. Another part can be attributed to the cumulative impact of prejudice which plays a role at each stage of the accusation-to-conviction chain. It is known that members of the public are more likely to complain if they suspect an offence has been committed by a foreigner. Immigrant-origin youth are kept under closer surveillance by the police; when charged they are more likely to be refused bail (since less likely to be solvent) than young French people; once in preventive detention, they wait longer for hearings which in turn are more likely to result in a prison sentence if the culprit has already been held in custody. All these factors would help explain why, in the study cited above, 32.6 per cent of the Maghrebi group received prison terms, whilst 23.1 per cent of the French did so, and why in the Lyons area in 1982, 58 per cent of minors in detention were of foreign origin (Llaumett 1984, pp.31–5; Gaspard and Servan-Schreiber 1985, pp.118–25; Lapeyronnie 1987, p.296).

While it is doubtful if immigrant-origin youth are bigger villains than French people who share their social status, there is no doubt that part of the immigrant population are unique *victims* of particular kinds of crime. The early 1980s saw a recrudescence of a pattern of racial terrorism present in France since the Algerian war of independence: a mosque destroyed by explosives in the Rhône valley in May 1982, a wave of shotgun attacks on individuals and premises in Corsica the same month; four murders in the Paris and Lyons regions from September to November; in March 1983, the murder of a child playing near a transit camp in a district of Marseilles by a bomb thrown from a passing car; a 17-year-old youth attacked by three assailants and stabbed in the stomach in June; in July a nine-year-old and a 15-year-old shot, one fatally, by bullets fired from the windows of high-rise blocks in La Courneuve and Tourcoing. The motives of these attacks vary. They may arise when trigger-happy individuals are pushed over the edge by some domestic incident. Sometimes they are the result of a *ratonnade*, a mini-pogrom in which a group of armed racists combine a pub-crawl with a tour of an Arab district in search of potential victims. They might be planned by a political organisation, like the series of attacks by the Parti Nationaliste Français et Européen on foreign workers' hostels in the Nice area in 1988. Often, of course, racist outrages are the deliberate or accidental result of over-zealous policing (Gaspard and Servan-Schreiber 1985, p.133; Wieviorka 1992, p.39; Jazouli 1992, pp.44–5; MacEwen 1995, pp.120–1). For its part the National Front officially deplores such actions while in private its members are very clear that their 'political' activity is partly geared to making them more acceptable. 'The genius of Le Pen', one of them told an undercover journalist when she quizzed him about the rifle he kept at home,

> ... is to have chosen the electoral strategy. By going easy, we'll get our ideas across better. Look, if you kill an Arab when Le Pen has only got 0.5 per cent there's straightaway an outcry, you're called a racist. When we've got 15 per cent, already there's less of an outcry. So we've just got to carry on, and you'll see, at 30 per cent there won't be any outcry at all. (Tristan 1987, p.251)

Quantification of the rate of racial murder and attempted murder a stigmatised group suffers is difficult because in many cases the assailants are never caught and in France, even when they are, it is difficult to secure convictions unless the attacker signifies clearly that the *reason* for the attack is racial difference. Not all assassins shout 'down with the Arabs' as they pull the trigger. The total of convictions which met these criteria from 1980 to 1992 was 289 woundings and 25 murders, 232 of the former and 23 of the latter suffered by Maghrebis alone. Although this official murder rate was lower than that in Britain (Costa-Lascoux 1994), the figures for actual attacks are clearly much higher; according to a list kept by Radio Beur there were nine murders in 1982, although there were no convictions at all in that year.

Immigrant-origin youths have developed a sense of solidarity and a deep sense of injustice founded on the perception of all immigrants as potential victims of racial violence and the 'double-standard' which sees racial murders uninvestigated, police outrages unpunished and themselves routinely harassed and severely condemned for minor offences:

> The cop arrests you, sometimes he insults you or smacks your head in, and after, you end up in front of the judge who finishes off the job by sending you for a rest-cure behind bars. For me, all that lot are working hand-in-hand to press us down even more, to smother us. (Karim, 21, from Marseilles, cited by Jazouli 1985, p.55)

It is striking how soon and how regularly their reactions to the murder of innocent youth or children are described by activists of the 1980s in their accounts of the formation of their political consciousness. For Bouzid, from Aix-en-Provence, who became one of the leaders of the 1983 March against Racism and for Equality:

> ... I had to go on this March to defuse the bomb of rage which was ticking away inside me ... The summer of 1983 was more than I could bear. To witness impotently all those murders ... One of the most odious crimes was the assassination of little Taoufik at La Courneuve. Because he was making a noise. After the heat, people's irritation, regrettable accidents, police blunders, here was someone taking a pot-shot at a child of nine and using as an excuse the noise he was making. (Bouzid 1984, pp.15, 27–8)

Harlem Désir, first president of *SOS Racisme*, has described how, one morning in the winter of 1977,

> ... when we arrived at school, our innocent little universe had been blown to bits. The night before, during a Peter Gabriel concert at the Porte de Pantin, which many of us had been to, a high school kid of 17 had been shot dead by one of the security guards. Lucien Mélion

was West Indian ... coffee-coloured, like me. Crazy about music, a *lycéen* and still a kid, like all of us. What had happened to him could have happened to any of us. Everyone felt concerned, shocked, by this murderous anti-youth, anti-black racism. (Désir 1985, p.20)

Youth and political mobilisation

Birth of the associations

Protest at racist violence was the motive for the foundation in 1980 of RAP, Rock Against Police, which spawned a network of local committees in the outskirts of Paris. The inaugural concert, organised by two brothers, Mogniss and Samir Abdallah, drew 3000 to commemorate the murder of Kader of Vitry by a security guard. During the next three years dozens of free concerts were held in the suburbs of Paris, Lyons, Marseilles and Geneva for youths tired of battling with bouncers to gain entry to mainstream concerts and clubs. Although the idea of free open-air rock concerts was borrowed from the example set by Rock Against Racism in the UK a couple of years previously, the more combative title (everyone claims to be against racism, but not everyone is against the police) signalled a desire to stay as close as possible to suburban youth, as did the decision to hold concerts in the suburbs themselves, at which the performers were always local bands, rather than in 'a neutral venue like Hyde Park where people simply turn up as consumers'. The association and its newsletter were wound up in 1983 after a rocky career during which the Abdallah brothers themselves were served expulsion orders but reprieved after a vigorous campaign; the impetus was not lost, however; those who had been involved with RAP turned to other issues and other campaigns (Bouamama 1994, pp.36–7; Jazouli 1992, pp.28–9; Boubeker and Beau 1986, pp.51–6).

During the 1980s, some 500 to 800 associations were founded every year by persons or groups of immigrant origin, with 5000 or so still in existence at the end of the decade (Zylberstein 1993, p.120). While the majority of these served the welfare or cultural needs of a particular ethno-cultural group rather than a broad audience of minorities (Hargreaves 1995, p.141) many hundreds were founded by and for the ethnically mixed youths of the suburbs. Most were less directly political than RAP. But even when they were cultural, like the theatre groups which toured their plays in suburban schools and community centres, or economic, like those which helped set up small businesses or organised training courses, they implicitly challenged the wider social and political context. The vast majority depended on public subsidies, which would in time foster a tendency for them to be sucked into conflict management on behalf of the state. A significant aspect of the suburban associations was the leadership role played by young Arabs. Largely absent from or occupying subordinate roles in school and workplace, it was the places where they lived which helped the more resilient of them achieve a sense of belonging (while giving a new word, *Beur*, to the French language) and a minimal sense of power. They took the lead in forming associations for solidarity with the victims of racist crimes or administrative sanctions, campaigns for the improvement of housing conditions, theatre groups, rock bands, sports clubs, associations running newsletters, literacy classes, outings and group holidays. Most associations were small, limiting their catchment area to the *quartier* or even the housing estate, and oriented on the local context in which they were founded, rather than on an ethnic dimension of identity. A detailed study in Marseilles found that almost every peripheral housing estate had its own association containing the word 'youth' in the title, along with the name of the block or the housing estate, mostly set up when groups of youths approached local social workers with a request for a meeting room. Effective as mobilising networks which could bring hundreds of youths together on special occasions, at the same time they jealously guarded their autonomy, preventing the emergence of stable federative structures (Zylberstein 1993, pp.120–7; Jazouli 1992, pp.49–50; Cesari 1993).

Youth in Lyons offered the sharpest example of the extremes of organisation and violent revolt. While young men were at the forefront of joy-riding and fighting with the police, the group Zaâma d'Banlieue was set up towards the end of the 1970s mainly by young women whose quest for personal liberation had led them to break with their Maghrebi backgrounds, adopting instead the libertarian-revolutionary ideas influential in the city-centre left. Their campaigns against the police and the justice system gained a large audience among young Arabs in the suburbs, culminating in 1984, in a demonstration against a visit to the city by Le Pen, and the foundation of a 'Youth Collective for the Lyons Region' (Jazouli 1992, pp.36, 78; Bouamama 1994, p.38).

In the absence of a federative structure the roles of communication channel and national focus fell to associations devoted to remedying the distortion or the simple silence to which immigrants were subject in the media. These were the monthly magazine *Sans Frontière* (1979), Radio Beur (1982), Radio Gazelle (in Marseilles) and the news agency Im'média (1983). Although dominated by young Maghrebis, they have not aimed at a specifically Beur audience or treated solely Maghreb or Arab issues, addressing themselves not only to other immigrant communities but also to French youth as a whole and not hesitating to criticise developments in their parents' home countries (Gaspard and Servan-Schreiber 1985, pp.192–5). One of their early tasks was to gain a national audience for a campaign for justice by the Residents' Association of the Gutenberg transit camp in Nanterre, west Paris, whose 20-year old Moroccan leader was shot dead in October 1982 by a local shop assistant who was subsequently sentenced to twelve years. Staffed by young Arabs with a university education or some experience of politics in the French left, the media organisations became in a sense the intellectual leadership of what some referred to as an emerging 'Beur movement', of which the suburban associations were the grassroots. As will be seen, relations between the summit and the base or the centre and the periphery would not always run smooth.

Dimensions of Beur identity

Although sociological and cultural convergence of Arab youth with their peers in France, Europe and north America who share a similar lifestyle is an important facet of Beur identity, one should not lose sight of Arab youths' resistance to unconditional identification with France or at least with French society as it is presently constituted. The very term Beur was coined as a defiant assertion of 'Arabness' in the face of the pejorative charge with which it is frequently invested. The product of a double Parisian back-slang (the two syllables of *Arabe* pronounced backwards give *Rebe* which, in turn, gives *eBeur*) the word

> … indicates something slightly different from our parents' identity but at the same time the affirmation of an Arab origin. More exactly, it expresses the emergence of a new aspect of French identity: the existence of *French* Arabs. Up until then, France had known only Arabs *in France*. (Bouamama 1994, p.69)

Attachment to an Arab identity could not be separated from emotional reaction to the bloody history shared by France and her former colonies. Those who grew up during the Algerian War in the shanty towns of the 1950s and 1960s long remembered the police raids and the massacre of October 1961 or a mother's accounts of the repression and torture she had suffered during the war (Jazouli 1986, pp.52–3; Bouamama 1994, p.25). Another recalled the 'Indian Reservation' set aside for his father, a former *harki* who had fought on the French side in Indochina and Algeria, commenting bitterly, 'I had been French for several generations but nobody, me first of all, had ever regarded me as such' (Bouzid 1984, p.33). In the same vein, young Arabs' automatic reflex of solidarity with the exiled Palestinians is clearly linked to a perception of their parents' home countries as occupying a subordinate position in the global power system, rather than being the 'paradox' which Roy wants to make of it (Roy 1994, p.62).

But this was not all. For the Parisian youth who invented it, the term Beur did not refer only to 'Arab' as an ethnic identity but also to 'Arab' as synonymous with 'the bottom of the heap'. It was not applied to or used exclusively by young Maghrebis, for young 'native' French as well as Africans and Portuguese referred to themselves in the same way. In this sense the shared experiences of suburban youths in terms of school, unemployment and their life on the estates were the basis of a sense of solidarity surpassing their separate 'ethnic' origins, even those who were less immediately exposed to the most violent forms of xenophobia feeling that, in the event things got worse, they would be its next victims (Bouamama 1994, p.69; do Céu Cunha 1988, p.57). Within this social group of excluded suburban youth, however, there was no question that young Arabs were seen as the 'driving force' (Cesari 1993, p.85), fulfilling a leadership role recognised by, for example, those young Portuguese who

... have a tendency, not to differentiate themselves from the Arabs but on the contrary to identify with this group, whose forms of struggle they imitate. (do Céu Cunha 1988, pp.66–7, n. 25)

The Beurs and political autonomy

The Beurs' involvement in protests and resistance against a wave of deportations of juvenile delinquents during the last years of the Giscard presidency led many of them to distrust the French left and favour Beur political and organisational autonomy. From 1978–81, in what seemed to be a deliberate policy of intimidation aimed at inducing immigrants to leave France voluntarily, between 5000 and 8000 youths per year, three-quarters of them Maghrebis, were deported to their parents' countries of origin on the grounds that petty thefts or other offences for which they had already served time, constituted an imminent threat to public order. Committees were formed all over France to campaign against what amounted to a double penalty for a single offence which in any case had occurred on average up to a year and a half previously (Weil 1995, pp.207–9). The government proving impervious to legal argument, the committees set about helping hundreds of the rootless youngsters to return to France clandestinely as soon as possible. This cloak-and-dagger routine was blown into a political issue of national prominence right in the middle of the 1981 election campaign by the Catholic priest Christian Delorme's cleverly organised three-man hunger strike staged in his native Lyons. The fast ended in victory when Prime Minister Barre agreed to suspend expulsions of Maghrebi youths for three months, a moratorium subsequently made permanent by the incoming government (Delorme 1985, pp.71–86). Although the campaign had remained decentralised, depending for its impact on the actions of local activists, those Beurs who took part got their first taste of the battles for hegemony between branches of the French and Algerian lefts and a motley collection of libertarians, Christians, social workers and 'third worldists'. The realisation that their problems might serve as no more than a convenient battleground for rival interests would lead many towards an insistence on the autonomy of Beur initiatives and strategies (Lapeyronnie 1987, p.303; Jazouli 1992, p.27), an attitude reinforced by the activities of the French Communist Party.

Towards the end of 1980, in preparation for the 1981 presidential election, the party launched a demagogic attempt to gain a few extra votes in the municipalities where most young Arabs lived by running campaigns against the concentration of immigrants in working-class suburbs. The Communists had a point, since many right-wing councils had for years refused to allow the construction of workers' hostels within their municipal boundaries. But using the argument that the mere presence of immigrant communities of a certain size necessarily provoked social problems and resentment by the local 'French' was hardly conducive to fighting racism or building solidarity with targeted groups. The campaign made national headlines during Christmas 1980, when the Communist Mayor of Vitry in Paris led an expedition to wreck a local hostel in a bid to prevent the imminent arrival of a group of Malian workers. Some commentators' enthusiasm for assigning to the Communists the major responsibility in legitimising the discourse of the National Front (Schain 1985, p.186; Grillo 1991, p.53) – as if government ministers had not already been saying for years that there were too many immigrants in France! – has led them to miss a far more significant point: the national notoriety of 'the bulldozer of Vitry' wrecked Communist anti-racist credentials with immigrant-origin youth all over France, deepening their suspicion of the French left and hardening their determination to rely on their own organisations (Bouamama 1994, pp.32–3).

Between Mitterrand and the Beurs there was no honeymoon: at best an uneasy courtship. The unquenched thirst for self-assertion and adventure of jobless youth found expression in the Minguettes rodeos of July–August 1981 even before the new Socialist government had had time to relax the rules governing family reunions, suspend aided repatriation, permit foreigners to form their own associations on the same terms as French people and organise an amnesty which eventually covered 130,000 undeclared foreign workers. While these measures and the efforts of community leaders and youth-workers like Delorme helped ensure a relatively quiet summer in 1982, the following year opened with a series of strikes in the car industry in which north African workers' prominent involvement was denounced by government leaders as the result of manipulation by external, possibly Islamic agitators, an accusation subsequently shown by a team of university researchers to be without foundation (Mouriaux and Wihtol de Wenden 1988). More seriously the Beurs' twin chief grievances, police racism and the non-elucidation and non-punishment of racist crimes (four murders in September and October 1982) just would not go away. Although Delorme defused a new crisis between police and youths in Lyons in the spring of 1983 with a new hunger strike which this time failed to evoke any political echo and was instead criticised for its pacifism and lack of concrete results, the summer saw a new rash of racist attacks all over France (Bouamama 1994, pp.52–3). Adding insults to these injuries, the hectoring and rasping voice of Le Pen was heard over the air-waves for the first time that autumn following his party's successes in the year's local government elections, especially and famously at Dreux.

In these circumstances Delorme and his circle in Lyons launched an ambitious initiative aimed at putting the Beurs' grievances on the national agenda. The 'March for Equality and Against Racism' was a watershed of enormous symbolic importance. The ten young Maghrebis who set off from Marseilles in October were greeted in Paris in December by a solidarity demonstration of between 60,000 and 100,000 people and an audience with the President of the Republic – a moving contrast with the murderous onslaught on men, women and children demonstrating for Algerian independence which had disfigured Paris in 1961. On the other hand Mitterrand did not keep his promise to the marchers to introduce a law punishing racial violence more severely and the one tangible result of the interview, the later introduction of a ten-year joint work and residency permit, was of little relevance to the Beurs, most of whom had French nationality (Bouamama 1994, p.67; Weil 1995, pp.278–80).

Furthermore the planning and carrying through of the march had revealed serious differences concerning its strategic orientation – was it against the National Front, was it about the specific grievances of the Beurs, especially the police and the justice system, or should it be the beginning of a social movement for equal rights with the potential and the ambition to involve *everyone* living in France, not just the Maghreb community? Linked to this was the question of autonomy. If mainstream French associations or parties – in this case Christians and pacifists – were allowed to join the march and the support committees, was there not a danger that they would attempt to take over, imposing their own slogans, and then take the credit for whatever the march managed to achieve? (Bouamama 1994, pp.56–61; Jazouli 1992, pp.56–9). Papered over while the march was on, these differences were hotly debated at what was intended to be the founding 'national conference' in Lyons in June 1984 of a movement linking the hundreds of Beur-led community organisations. Those who warned against the manipulative and self-interested tendencies of the French left were accused of proposing a purely 'ethnic' strategy, a *repli communautaire*, which would have little resonance for the thousands of Beurs whose cultural references were already mostly French and succeed only in condemning the 'community' to continued marginality and discrimination. On the other hand those who argued that the Beurs should take their place in a broader social movement were caricatured as giving in to the assimilationist republican tradition which rejects ethnic communities as illegitimate (Bouamama 1994, p.96; Jazouli 1992, pp.85–7). With the Parisian delegates taking a broadly multiculturalist approach and the Lyons organisers defending Beur autonomy, others admitted ruefully that the divisions ran through 'each collective, each association, even each person present' (Jazouli 1992, p.87). The conference's dispersal without result was later seen by two very different participants as a missed opportunity: in 1984 the movement was not mature or self-confident enough to adopt a strategy of alliance with the left, of which Beur autonomy could have been the pre-condition, not the negation (Jazouli 1992, pp.80–1; Bouamama 1994, p.96).

In this context a new national initiative, Convergences '84, failed to mobilise as much support as the March had done, despite a multiculturalist message that was an improvement on the vague humanism which had been the butt of so much criticism. The idea was to organise five columns of youngsters of diverse origins, representative of the African, Asian, Caribbean, Portuguese and French communities, travelling by moped from five different cities in order to converge on Paris where they would be met by a solidarity march and carnival with floats again underlining the multicultural theme. The slogan 'France is like a moped, to get anywhere you need mixture', deliberately challenged not only the 'isolationist' temptation of the minority communities but also the assimilationist French orthodoxy which says 'to be integrated you must do as we do'.

The welcoming carnival in December 1984 was attended by some 30,000 people – fewer than the year before but still an important achievement in the year that the National Front sent ten deputies to the European Parliament. But once again, behind the scenes, there had been discord. The idea of Convergences was that *all* communities should come together to tackle issues of inequality and discrimination. On the Marseilles–Lyons–Paris leg of the route the mopedders complained that the local councillors and dignitaries who made up the welcoming committees had neither taken this message to heart nor examined their own practice on such issues. At the official receptions they did all the talking, condemning the local Beurs to silence, if indeed they were present at all, for in many towns there appeared to be no contact between the European town-centre middle-class left and peripheral working-class Arab youth. This experience led the Convergences' inventor, Farida Belghoul, to reassess her former dismissal of the importance of Beur autonomy and to vent her spleen against the liberal 'do-gooders' in front of the 30,000 crowd at the Place de la République. Yet the experience of the other Convergences columns had not been identical to that of the Marseilles group and some of the mopedders, themselves Beurs, hastened to publicise their disagreements with Belghoul's new 'autonomist' position (Bouamama 1994, pp.98–111; Jazouli 1992, pp.88–94).

By the autumn of 1984, then, despite two dress rehearsals attracting a sizeable audience, a unified and autonomous Beur movement open to working with the mainstream left had failed to appear on cue. Efforts to repair the damage would continue but there were to be few second chances, for at national level centre-stage would be occupied for the next few years by two new organisations, each in different ways removed from the urban peripheries where racism was felt most keenly and hostile to the autonomous project.

France Plus and SOS Racisme

One of these, France Plus, symbolised in its own discourse and activities the schizophrenia of Beur political mobilisation, for it made real contributions to community affirmation and mobilisation while insisting at the same time that the best way to defend oneself against racism was to avoid behaviour drawing attention to differences from the French 'norm'. It marched for equal rights in 1985, campaigned on nationality law and for voter registration in 1986–87, and tried hard to bring together the descendants of the mutually hostile camps of Algerians who took opposite sides in the war of liberation (*Le Monde* 25 May 1987). In style it preferred discreet lobbying in the corridors of power, criticising the more public demonstration strategies of its publicity-hungry rival SOS Racisme (Wayland 1993, p.98). More or less ignoring the National Front it concentrated instead on persuading foreigners to apply for naturalisation and the Beurs to vote and run for election. In the 1989 city council elections it commissioned opinion polls to convince local politicians of both left and right that they ought to offer young Maghrebis places on their lists of candidates to improve their appeal to sizeable local immigrant-origin electorates (Poinsot 1993, pp.84–5).

Critics of France Plus in both minority and majority communities did not focus on the electoral strategy as such, since those favouring a more radical autonomous Beur self-affirmation had also long urged electoral registration and full use of civic rights (Jazouli 1992, p.48; Bouamama 1994, p.206; Poinsot 1993, p.86), but rather on its hypocritical use as a tool of upward social mobility by middle-class Maghrebis posing as 'whiter than white' by insisting that 'communities don't exist' (as France Plus leader Arezki Dahmani told *Le Monde* on 8 February 1991), while getting themselves elected on the basis of an 'ethnic vote' and an ethnic mobilisation strategy (Bouamama 1994, p.127; Geisser 1992). Worse even than that, France Plus was not accepted as a truly autonomous vehicle of community concerns, of whatever social class, since it was widely assumed to be in origin a tool of the Socialist Party (Jazouli 1992, p.106), even a tool of one faction of Socialists in their battle with another credited with using SOS Racisme for the same purpose (Bouamama 1994, p.126; Poinsot 1993, p.88). The association's audience in the suburbs was so narrow (Jazouli 1992, p.107) that its 500 or so candidates, once elected, were often no more than captive tokens of the political correctness of their patrons, with no power to influence policy (Geisser 1992, p.135; Bouamama 1994, p.208). These weaknesses likewise limited its capacity to fulfil what would seem to be its real vocation – to act as a partner for state and local governments in their variously defined battles to manage social conflict and 'integrate' rebellious suburban youth (Cesari 1993; Roy 1994; Leveau 1994).

Nonetheless, the political patrons of France Plus, like those of SOS, made sure that the association had a handsome income made up almost entirely of public subsidies of one kind or another, as well as plenty of media attention. It was able to use these to join SOS on centre stage at crucial moments such as during the 1985 march, the 1986/87 nationality campaign and again during the Headscarf Affair in 1989 when the more radical Beur associations were trying desperately to get an audience.

SOS Racisme was by its own account founded in a fit of moral outrage at the turn of 1984/85 by a multiracial group of friends revolted by an incident of racial harassment suffered by one of their black 'pals' (Désir 1985). It has also been represented as a stage in the personal career strategy of one of the original pals, the movement's behind-the-scenes leader, Julien Dray (Malik 1990), and as the machination of a group of backroom staff at the presidential palace (Weil 1995, p.292). All of these versions are consistent with the association's development down to 1988, although its character changed somewhat thereafter. Like Convergences '84, it was intended as the vehicle of a multiculturalist vision of France as a melting-pot, symbolised by the ubiquitous badge with its catchy message, 'Hands off my mate', and realised in a series of huge multicultural rock concerts. Its programme appeared to consist of no more than the urgent desire to record and publicise all racist attacks. The vaguely defined target audience of 'people, not bigwigs, the schools, the campuses, young people who are looking for a job or just starting work' responded in their thousands to the obvious sincerity and simple eloquence of its telegenic president, Harlem Désir, whose regular debating visits to 16–19-year-old schoolchildren in the *lycées* were conveniently facilitated by Socialist officials (Désir 1985, pp.26–30).

Strategy was based on the conviction that the most effective way of convincing someone that an idea is just is for a famous celebrity to endorse it on television. SOS was a mass organisation of an entirely new type, impossible before the audiovisual age, whose members were urged to organise locally but only as transmission belts for the latest national initiative. Julien Dray's disillusionment with a decade of activism in Trotskyist and student politics had led him to conceive a structure loose enough to obviate the eternal battles to 'take over the apparatus' by rival sects, and in which communication with the membership by television was ideal, for it allowed everyone to participate without having to go to meetings (Dray 1987, p.205)! Although in 1995 visitors to the SOS national office were still being regaled with the myth of the 'apolitical' founding pals, it had long since been known that the association owed its meteoric rise to help from the Socialist establishment, astutely aware of their need to widen their bases of support ahead of Mitterrand's campaign for re-election. The first concert, held in Paris' Place de la Concorde went ahead with a 2 million franc subsidy from the Ministry of Culture and the promise of 3 million francs' worth of advertising from commercial sponsors after the then state-owned television channel, TF1, guaranteed that it would be broadcast live. Performers gave their services free (Malik 1990, pp.98–104). Personal friends of Mitterrand, like the industrialist Pierre Bergé, and members of the Elysée staff, headed by Jean-

Louis Bianco, introduced other sponsors and big stars like Guy Bedos, Coluche and Simone Signoret who deliberately wore the SOS badge during TV appearances, soon joined by well known media pundits and supporters of leftist causes like Marek Halter and Bernard-Henry Lévy (Malik 1990, pp.78–85). During the spring of 1985 the association was said to have sold 300,000 of its badges to school students all over France, of whom a small army were employed to man the telephones and receive the donations flooding in to the national office (*Le Monde* 26 March 1985; *Le Point* 7 April 1985; Malik 1990, pp.49–52). SOS came to play a leading, perhaps the crucial role in the massive mobilisation of school students against the Devaquet bill extending selection in higher education in 1986, partly because it was the only national youth organisation present in many middle-sized towns which did not have universities (Dray 1987, pp.47, 66, 88). In doing so it helped the President to pose as the friendly uncle, protector of youth and minorities, and contributed to ruining Chirac's chances in the 1988 presidential election.

The President's media specialists were called in to mould the naively optimistic themes and slogans which would be launched by Harlem Désir and his friends on the airwaves. Their influence was evident in March 1985 when Désir and Socialist bigwigs joined a demonstration in Menton on the Côte d'Azur to protest at a racist killing. Albert Lévy, a leader of the MRAP, made a strong speech incriminating the extreme right and its propaganda and drawing attention to the fact that the murder had occurred near a bar where Le Pen's supporters' habitually gathered. In contrast, Harlem appeared apolitical, denouncing racism for undermining the *joie de vivre* of French youth (*Le Monde* 28 March 1985). The themes of youth, beauty and lost innocence were also present in posters and a press advertisement in which the image of a model with perfect skin was accompanied by the slogan, 'Am I not more beautiful than a Le Pen poster?', a clever way of effacing from the public's memory the dirty overalls and anxious faces of the car-workers from the spring of two years previously.

Dray failed, however, in an attempt to persuade Beur associations to join a kind of federation under SOS hegemony (Malik 1990, p.30), for Beur activists were suspicious of what they regarded as a vehicle of the mainstream left created by inexperienced people who had little contact with or knowledge of the existing Beur movement, a judgement confirmed by Désir's own account of the original pals' turning for advice to the nationally known Christian Delorme in Lyons, far from their own Parisian suburbs (Désir 1985, p.27). Those few Beurs who did join the association in the early days, swept along by the extraordinary *élan* with which it burst on the scene at the beginning of 1985, soon left again, unable to accept either the prominence of the Union of Jewish students, which they regarded as Zionist, and whose president became the SOS general secretary, or Dray's peremptory manner of dealing with critical voices in the 'fake' national bureau (Malik 1990, pp.58, 71–2; Bouamama 1994, p.120; Jazouli 1992, pp.103–4). They were especially infuriated by the SOS habit of responding to racial violence by 'parachuting' into trouble spots activists unknown in the locality, followed by a photo-opportunity and a quick retreat. The media then gave an exaggerated impression of SOS implantation, which was in fact inadequate for the type of detailed coalition-building and follow-up required (Malik 1990, pp.68–9, 84; Poinsot 1993, p.83).

SOS Racisme's lionisation by the media and its potential for dissipating rather than strengthening grassroots anti-racism were amply demonstrated at the end of 1985 when it unilaterally launched the so-called 'third march against racism', this time on scooters, from Bordeaux to Paris. Beur anger at this attempted takeover was so intense that a rival march was set up by a collective of Beur associations. This in turn split into rival factions after only four days, with the recently founded France Plus accused of trying to impose its own assimilationist vision by reducing the march to a simple campaign of electoral registration. The majority continued the march without France Plus on a platform of maximalist demands for equality of rights in residence, schooling, work, housing, family reunion, politics and the justice system as well as insisting, naturally, on the need to safeguard the autonomy of Beur anti-racist initiatives. The polemics arising from this double split necessarily undermined the efforts of the support committees, both en route and on the separate arrival dates in Paris when neither contingent attracted as many as the 30,000 mobilised by Convergences '84 (Bouamama 1994, pp.130–43).

While the SOS media bulldozer contributed to blocking the emergence of a radical but tentative and divided national Beur movement, it had little effect in countering the rise of the NF, a failure excused by Désir on the ground that the Front was already at the height of its power in 1984, when SOS had not yet been born (*Le Monde* 19 August 1987); at a press conference after Le Pen's 14.4 per cent share of the vote in 1988 he claimed that Mitterrand's re-election would bring the National Front 'to a halt' (*Le Monde* 18 June 1988). In truth, SOS Racisme's media strategy called for it to initiate anodyne activities with the potential to mobilise more or less unthinking assent among the passive television audience. A call to demonstrate against an NF meeting or an attempt to dispute territory on the streets with its paper sellers obviously did not fit this prescription;

a campaign against apartheid was much more acceptable, though hardly urgent since this theme had been well worked over for many years by the Communist Party and the MRAP. In the same vein, a rather farcical attempt was made at founding an international federation for which initial contacts were frequently supplied by Socialist notables or even Foreign Ministry officials, rather than grassroots activists (Malik 1990, p.136). In a move which appeared to illustrate a strategic orientation towards countering racism by defying its consequences rather than by political struggle, in 1987 the association produced a book, *SOS Désirs,* which, instead of stressing themes of racial and social exclusion, recounted in upbeat and optimistic style its collaboration with members of the Socialist business elite in developing job and business opportunities for the odd black or Beur success story (Désir 1987).

Slowly but surely SOS and its claimed 17,000 active members were evolving from what *Le Monde* called an 'anti-racist force' into a 'movement for equality and integration' (5 April 1988), an exhaustion of its potential to be a radical focus for autonomous youth mobilisation which seemed to be confirmed by Désir's public endorsement of Mitterrand's campaign for re-election and the presence of an SOS delegation at every one of his meetings (Malik 1990, p.156). In August 1987 Désir had told television viewers that if they really wanted to fight racism it was no use just shouting 'Le Pen, Le Pen, Le Pen!', but much better to set about repairing the lifts in the seedy tower blocks which were its breeding grounds (*Le Monde* 18 June 1988). The 1988 conference adopted a programme of six demands covering nationality, rights of entry, the right to vote, an independent police authority, housing and schools and simply 'submitted them to the government' (*Le Monde* 18 June 1988), rather than contemplating a militant campaign for their implementation. In a long interview shortly after the election, Désir commented with satisfaction on the association's role at local level as 'mediator' between the people and the authorities, explaining that they were increasingly being asked to give legal advice, find housing and organise children's holidays (*Le Monde* 18 June 1988). Paradoxically, SOS Racisme had evolved into a decentralised lobbying organisation sucked into a role of conflict management closely paralleling that played by many Beur associations which had been among its sharpest critics.

Meanwhile, among the Beur associations which had stood apart from both SOS and France Plus, the desire to create an autonomous national immigrant-based movement was still alive but carried by activists with different strategies, Texture of Lille favouring a movement open to all immigrant-origin communities, while the JALB (Young Arabs of Lyons and its Suburbs) preferred a more restrictive 'Young Arab' self-identification. After four planning meetings during 1986–87 a new convention took place in May 1988, attended by delegates from 130 associations from all parts of the country and by representatives of the older generation of activists as well as the Beur generation. Debates were less passionate and more consensual than in 1984 and agreement was reached on the creation of a new national peak organisation: 'Fertile Memory, action for a new citizenship'. The title expressed a protest at what many saw as the artificial, media-created barrier between a troublesome 'first generation' of immigrants, good only for kicking out once industry no longer needed them, and an 'assimilable' second generation which had grown up in France (Bouamama 1994, pp.83–5). The concept of a new citizenship referred to the movement's demand that political rights should not be restricted only to those able (or willing) to take on French nationality. After the founding conference voted overwhelmingly in favour of addressing the national political arena, the spring 1989 local elections revealed divergent strategies at work, affiliated associations in some areas willing to negotiate lists of candidates with the left and the Greens, while elsewhere a more strictly autonomous strategy was adopted: commenting from the sidelines or organising meetings at which all the main candidates were invited to answer questions about their attitude to immigration-related issues.

At the end of Mitterrand's first septennate, neither the situation of immigrant-origin youth nor that of grassroots anti-racism were very promising. As many as 4,375,000 French citizens had cast their votes for the leader of a party committed to racial discrimination and the outgoing government had shown signs of wanting to go down the same road. Meanwhile those who wanted to do something about the situation were being asked by the organisation which had briefly looked as if it might act as the focus for radical anti-racist campaigning to attend one of the three simultaneous live concerts in Paris, Dakar and New York, with which SOS celebrated Mitterrand's re-election, or to help repair the lifts in tower blocks in the hope that the resulting improvement in their residents' lifestyle would encourage them to adopt a more fraternal attitude to their neighbours.

Facing up to the Gulf War

But more serious trials now had to be faced. First the mainstream parties and the mass media joined in an intimidating campaign against a few Muslim girls' desire to wear a headscarf to school, paving the way for the victory of a National Front by-election candidate who had campaigned on just that issue (see Chapter 3). Next, the government sent French troops to fight in the US-led coalition to expel Iraq from Kuwait. Once hostilities began, on 17 January 1991, the gun shops in various southern cities were cleaned out by individuals frightened by constant press speculation about likely pro-Saddam terrorist activity at home in the event of French troops actually going into battle. As a result, hundreds of panicky Tunisian building and agricultural workers from the south-east and Corsica fled the country (*Le Monde* 22, 26 January 1991). Many Beur associations chose resigned silence rather than appear to support Saddam Hussein, butcher of the Kurds, but half a dozen of them met journalists in Lyons to denounce the *raison d'état* which was 'abolishing' the rights of man in Iraq and to explain how they felt like objects of suspicion, some even claiming that ten years of efforts to foster integration were in ruins. In contrast, France Plus, ever keen to avoid breaching the French 'norm', applauded the war effort, though its leader, like many others, spoke of the need to ensure that the unprecedented multinational operation really did lead to a new world order in which all the problems of the Middle East would be solved by negotiation (*Le Monde* 26 January 1991). Yet even members of the integrated socio-professional elite of Maghreb origin whom France Plus represented, most of them reluctantly approving the war, revealed in a series of interviews how they felt they had an unwelcome 'ethnic identity' thrust upon them by the reductionism of the media which lumped together 'Arabs', 'Muslims', 'Iraqis', and 'Maghrebis'. One found it difficult to accept,

> the way the French state looked on us as hostages by addressing the Algerian or Maghrebi or Arab 'community' in France. (cited in Rachedi 1994, p.72)

Another was despondent about the absence of French intellectuals from the many demonstrations against the war, and a third lamented the poor quality of journalism:

> There's been no solid, deeply researched documentary about Iraq. Iraq has simply been turned into the enemy to be destroyed, and along with Iraq, Arabs. (cited in Rachedi 1994, p.74)

Among SOS Racisme's founders, Julien Dray was one of the two deputies to vote against the war in Parliament, while Harlem Désir tried to steer a middle course, on the one hand drafting an appeal to end the conflict by peaceful means, which was signed by representatives of the League for the Rights of Man, the leftist students' union UNEF-ID, Radio Beur, the Greens and Christian pacifist organisations, on the other sending a letter of solidarity to the Israeli ambassador in Paris. But even this timid opposition to government policy, together with Désir's presence at an anti-war demonstration on 16 January, was enough to trigger the resignations from SOS of Pierre Bergé, Bernard Henri-Lévy and others of the Parisian intellectual set who had helped launch the association in 1985 and who now described Désir as 'irresponsible', a *'munichois'* appeaser and 'infantile'. Marek Halter weighed in the following day, deploring SOS' complicity with both the Communists and the NF (*Le Monde* 19, 20 January 1991). The rumour that the Union of Jewish Students had also broken with the movement proved unfounded, since their leader Eric Ghebali remained as SOS general secretary, but the impossibility of the association serving as a possible rallying point for its supporters was confirmed when a hurriedly arranged national council agreed that, for the duration of the war, members would be free to take any initiative in a personal capacity (*Le Monde* 24 January 1991).

While SOS was thus weakened, France Plus' support for the coalition was gratefully accepted and its hopes for the future of the Palestinians cynically ignored. Fertile Memory, which never managed to develop into a structure able to carry a nationally agreed discoure or strategy independently of the sum of its parts, rapidly fell apart, its leadership confessing their neglect of mundane organisational and financial matters in favour of the intense debates stimulated by these new challenges (Bouamama 1994, pp.212–19; Poinsot 1993, p.86). Meanwhile the National Front continued its menacing progress, but now confronted by two new anti-racist organisations which emerged from the extreme left.

Trying to target the fascists

By the end of the 1980s, after Mitterrand's statement that there were now too many immigrants in France (see Chapter 3) and Cresson's adoption of a muscular anti-immigrant discourse, the Socialists had moved so far to the right that they were leaving space for the development of new grassroots anti-racist movements. Looking back, those who became activists in this period identified Le Pen's 14.4 per cent score in the 1988 presidential election as a watershed which alerted them to the feeble impact of the moralistic anti-racism propounded by SOS Racisme and to the realisation that the NF successes in 1983–88 represented more than just a mood of frustrated protest around which no solid organisation could be built (interview with Eric Osmond, 9 April 1996). This new context offered a growing audience to initiatives by two small Trotskyist currents. The first was developed by a tiny faction called Convergence Socialiste, led by former student leader Jean-Christophe Cambadélis, which had recently broken away from the International Communist Party (PCI) to join the Socialist Party. In June 1987 Cambadélis launched the 'Manifesto of the 122' which called for the left to mount an anti-racist campaign specifically targeted on the NF in a way which SOS never was. The group successfully appealed to French mayors in June 1990, at the height of the Carpentras affair, to use all possible means to avoid allowing Le Pen or the NF the use of municipal halls for their meetings. Shortly after Cresson's replacement of Rocard, a 'National Convention of the Manifesto' brought together 200 delegates in June 1991, followed up in the autumn by a well organised media launch of the Manifesto at a 3000-strong meeting at the Mutualité on 27 November. At a weekend conference ten days later a wide range of associations met to share anti-NF ideas and strategies and endorse the Manifesto group's plan for a permanent co-ordinating structure.

That same autumn, after the summer in which Cresson, Chirac and Giscard had outdone each other in parading their anti-immigrant credentials, saw the parallel launch of a separate text, the 'Appeal of the 250', brainchild of the Ligue Communiste Révolutionnaire (LCR) but piloted on the intellectual and show-biz circuit by the radical freelance writer and LCR sympathiser Gilles Perrault. Ahead of the spring regional elections, these two new campaigns brought tens of thousands of people on to the streets of Paris on 25 January 1992 for a demonstration which sparked a wave of protests hampering the Front's ability to hold meetings throughout France. The momentum was fuelled by press features which gave details of the war-time collaborationist activities of two of the Front's candidates, Roland Gaucher and Paul Malaguti (*Le Canard Enchaîné* 26 February 1992). On 28 February 500 Corsican nationalists, having held up Le Pen's plane when it attempted to land at Bastia airport, fought a pitched battle with police outside the conference hall where Le Pen was due to speak, prompting the local prefect to ban the meeting (*Le Monde* 1–2 March 1992). Other NF meetings were banned in Caen, Marseilles and Lyons. On 2 March 300 people occupied the runway at Limoges airport, forcing Bruno Mégret's plane to land elsewhere, before surrounding his hotel (*Le Monde* 4 March 1992). Other demonstrations took place in Grenoble, Nîmes, Dijon, Perpignan, Bayonne, Toulon, Nice, Nantes, Lille, Rouen and Brest, where up to 8000 people protested against the arrival of Le Pen (*Le Figaro* 5 March 1992). In response, several dozen National Front sympathisers attacked opposing demonstrators with baseball bats and bottles in Chartres (*Le Monde* 17 March 1992) and in the southern town of Bagnols-sur-Cèze a protestor was seriously wounded after being shot, according to the police, by a member of the Front's security force (*Le Monde* 21 March 1992).

Spurred by these events, the 'Appeal of the 250' transformed itself into Ras l'Front, a nationwide structure rooted in 30 or so decentralised collectives, with a monthly paper of the same name.[1] Clearly, it and the Manifesto had radically changed the atmosphere in which the Front was operating. Whereas in the 1980s many had tried to laugh off the free publicity generated by Le Pen's televised ramblings, now at last people began to realise that the NF and what it stood for were no joke. But this belated appearance of serious opposition could hardly be expected to stop the Front in its tracks so soon after the indirect endorsements it had received from all and sundry in 1991. In fact it was on a roll, its momentum maintained by a sequence of elections similar to those which had assisted its breakthrough in 1983–86 and its appeal heightened by the corruption scandals dogging the Socialists' last two years in power and the atmosphere of *fin de règne* attending Mitterrand's illness and decline, while the emergence of issues like closer European Union and globalisation blurred the edges of the traditional left–right political divide. (We discuss these issues in the next chapter.) In the regional elections, as we saw in Chapter 3, the party made a significant advance, winning 13.6 per cent of the vote and returning over 200 councillors. The following year its 12.5 per cent in the parliamentary election was up by a quarter over the 1988 mark and opened up clear water between itself and the Communists who could only manage 9.2 per cent. No FN candidate was elected but more than a hundred of them passed the 12.5 per cent threshold allowing them to stand in the run-off in their constituencies, a feat managed in only 30 constituencies five years before. June 1994 saw another European election, in which commentators again underestimated the Front, expecting it to suffer from competition with the rival anti-Brussels right-wing list, the Majorité pour l'autre Europe, led by the maverick UDF deputy, Philippe de Villiers. The NF won 10.51 per cent of the vote and eleven seats; de Villiers and his friends had a higher share of the poll, 12.33 per cent, but were unable significantly to erode the NF vote (which was only slightly down on its 1989 and 1984 showings), eating instead into support for the RPR–UDF. Finally, in his 1995 presidential bid, Le Pen achieved his best score to date (15 per cent), trouncing de Villiers (4.7 per cent) and the Communist Robert Hue (8.7 per cent) and coming narrowly behind

1. Based on the colloquial phrase *ras-le-bol*, expressing the idea of being extremely fed up with something.

the two mainstream conservative candidates Balladur (18.6 per cent) and Chirac (20.8 per cent). On the fringes of the NF campaign its activists again met opposition with violence. In February they shot and killed a Comorean youth who disturbed them while they were putting up Le Pen's posters; in March the NF youth leader Samuel Maréchal was arrested after two school students were attacked by members of his organisation, and in May 15,000 to 20,000 people joined a demonstration against racism in Paris after a Moroccan youth drowned in the Seine, having been set upon by skinheads who had earlier taken part in the Front's annual march in honour of Joan of Arc.

This bulldozing progress by the Front corresponded to a nadir in the popularity of the Socialists and in the fortunes of the Manifesto campaign, whose leaders later admitted that membership fell to a 'few hundred' in 1994 (*Le Monde* 29 March 1997). The Manifesto was distinctly hampered by its close association with the Socialists, a party of government. From the beginning it linked the fight against the NF to the task of asserting its own leadership on the left fringe of the Socialist Party, reflecting the founders' conviction that the only way to be rid of the NF was through the ballot box and that this in turn required the 'renovation' of the Socialist Party. The Manifesto backed the government's war on Iraq and endorsed the Maastricht treaty on European Union, while Ras l'Front and its audience took the respective opposite views. If Ras l'Front's prominent features on issues like the Holocaust or the Nazi attitude to women and the family had the merit of explicitly stressing the link between the NF and the fascism of the 1930s, the Manifesto downplayed it. Following the lead of a prominent intellectual who consistently denigrated this 'commemorative anti-racism', Pierre-André Taguieff, they described the NF as 'national-populist', comparing it to re-emergent nationalism in central and eastern Europe, frequently lacing their analyses with references to other 'national populists' such as Jaruzelsky, Zhirinovsky or the Bosnian Serbs. However impeccably internationalist, this was a strategy in which the general obscured the particular, diverting attention from the tasks of anti-racists in France, and standing little chance of creating an audience among the Beurs, for whom Vénissieux and Sartrouville were more immediate concerns than Vukovar or Sarajevo. The Manifesto's chances of linking up with associations founded by Beurs or other immigrant-origin youths was further weakened by their militantly 'Republican' attitude which deprecated outward signs of cultural difference, refusing for example to defend Muslim girls stigmatised for wearing the headscarf. In general, the Manifesto's close association with the Socialist Party necessarily repelled those who were disgusted by the evidence of Socialist Party corruption or felt it had not done enough to combat racism.

In the long run, Ras l'Front would fare rather better than the Manifesto, using a different strategy and appealing to a more anti-establishment sensibility within the French left. It adopted a flexible and open structure with no centralised administration or prescriptions, leaving the initiative to a network of local collectives. During 1993 there were no more than 35 of these, nearly half of them in the Paris region. But by 1997 they had increased to 90, with about 30 members in each, while the paper's circulation reached 15,000. By then the Manifesto also had recovered its strength to 1800 members, 80 per cent of them in the Socialist Party (*Le Monde* 29 March 1997). In that year they and thousands of other anti-racists crowned several years' hard campaigning with a strong demonstration against the National Front congress, held in Strasbourg, which was not without effects on the NF's confidence and cohesion. In order fully to explain how the tide was turned and the NF was put on the defensive, we need to situate the associations' efforts in a more global context, showing how they formed part of a wider surge in 'unofficial politics', in which thousands of activists were sucked into campaigns against the effects of globalisation and against the aggressive neo-liberal policies of a conservative government elected in 1993.

7
New Contexts for Racism and Anti-Racism, 1992–2002

The political conditions in which anti-racists were at last to experience some success in their attempts to roll back the National Front were initially set by the change of government which had occurred in 1993. The Socialists' crushing defeat, the circumstances of which we describe in Chapter 9, gave the RPR–UDF an incredible 485 seats out of 577 in the National Assembly. The size of the landslide was partly owed to the fact that over 13 million people chose either not to vote or spoilt their ballot papers, double the number who voted Socialist, and more even than voted for the conservative majority. After his experience in 1986–88, Chirac, leader of the conservative camp, had no wish to repeat his role of Prime Minister in a second cohabitation administration in which Mitterrand would remain for another two years at the Elysée. Edouard Balladur, his former Finance Minister, therefore took over the premiership with Chirac expecting to prepare his presidential bid free from the cares of office. When Chirac in due course achieved his life's ambition and became President in 1995, it was only after a dramatic and uncertain campaign in which his chief rival had been none other than Balladur, his 'friend of thirty years'. Paying the price of his betrayal, Balladur was replaced as Prime Minister by Alain Juppé and some of his chief ministers were in turn thrown overboard to be replaced by Chirac loyalists of dubious ability, among them, as we shall see, the preposterous Jean-Louis Debré. Despite their differences, the Balladur and Juppé governments added up to something we have not so far encountered in this book: four years of uninterrupted right-wing government urged on by a massive parliamentary majority with the National Front breathing down its neck. It produced attacks on immigrants and minorities as vicious and farcical as could be expected. Naturally they did not satisfy the Front which appeared to go from strength to strength, provoking a public debate about the 'Lepenisation' of society (*Le Monde* 11 March 1997), and for a while anti-racists appeared to have their backs to the wall. But the situation was transformed when Alain Juppé undertook a sweeping reform of the social security system, with precious little prior consultation and in flagrant breach of Chirac's campaign promises. Juppé provoked the emergence of a powerful and multifaceted 'social movement' which launched a series of struggles against homelessness, redundancies, unemployment, global inequalities between rich and poor, and sprang to the defence of the most vulnerable of all, foreigners not legally settled in France. Anti-racists were provided a more favourable context to operate in, and their realisation that the conservatives and the fascists would spur each other on to further excesses made them as determined to resist the former as the latter. When Juppé persuaded Chirac to hold a snap election in 1997, the right found itself once again sandwiched between an ever stronger Front and a revived left which took power and held it for the next five years, adopting, as we shall see in the next chapter, what in some respects was a radically new approach to problems of integration and racial discrimination.

On the face of it, the Front had adapted more successfully than any other party to the so-called New World Order post-1989 by integrating a critique of the free market into an anti-'mondialist' perspective in which familiar anti-semitic references to cosmopolitanism sat alongside a new and trenchant anti-Americanism. In quick succession it won 15 per cent in the 1995 presidential election, a similar score in the 1997 parliamentary poll, several hundred local councillors, the control of four towns and, in 1995, a higher proportion of working-class votes than any other party. By 1998 leading intellectuals like Pierre Bourdieu were warning about the 'fascisation of French society' (*Le Monde* 8 April 1998) while commentators like Jérôme Jaffré, having characterised the FN vote during the 1980s as an apolitical cry of despair, were now asking, 'How could anyone be so naive as to think that the Frontist phenomenon is transitory when it has relentlessly rooted itself over eleven years and when a generation is now ready to succeed JM Le Pen?' (cited in Dély 1999, p.81). 'Ominously,' one academic was moved to write by the end of the decade, 'the future does indeed belong to the National Front' (Declair 1999, p.224).

How, then, to account for the dramatic turn of events as 1998 drew to a close, when the FN suddenly and acrimoniously fell apart, with Le Pen's most brilliant lieutenant, Bruno Mégret, leaving the party along with the majority of the organisation's leading cadre? The second half of this chapter offers an explanation for the split which draws on our analysis, outlined in Chapter 5, of the strategy developed by the organisation since its formation. But we begin with an examination of how the context within which the Front was attempting to operate this strategy changed dramatically in the mid-1990s with the rise of a new and unpredictable 'unofficial' politics which was to have profound implications for mainstream parties, the anti-racist movement and the extreme right.

The rise of 'unofficial politics'

During the 1990s the social inequalities which had marked the previous decade continued to make themselves felt. In the early 1990s unemployment hit the 3 million mark for the first time, generating renewed concerns about the extent of social deprivation in France. Yet while the average rate of pay had remained virtually unchanged between 1981 and 1993, France's gross national product had risen by over a third, the equivalent of a £50 a week increase in the entire population's wages (Frémeaux 1994). During the same period the proportion of workers on very low wages, equivalent to less than half the average wage, rose to 10 per cent (Ponthieux 1998, p.150). By the middle of the decade two in five of all those without jobs were long-term unemployed while social security payments, the sole source of income for 6 million people, had fallen below the poverty line (*Le Monde* 19 January 1998). Such figures were no longer an embarrassment to the Socialist Party, which had long since ceased referring to the abandonment of its reform programme as a 'parenthesis' and appeared content, like the right, to embrace the neo-liberal agenda shared by 'responsible' governments across the world. For a brief period in the late 1990s it looked as if the plural left coalition led by Lionel Jospin might try and buck the trend by reviving the Keynesian model of state-directed reform, but nobody in his coalition seemed to have much stomach for such a fight. In any case by this time mainstream politics had sacrificed political debate in the pursuit of consensus (Ysmal 1998, p.464) and dismantled, through financial deregulation and integration into the European monetary system, many of the tools which facilitated state direction of the economy (Bensaïd 1998; Hincker 1997). In the late 1980s and early 1990s growing concerns about social inequality combined with frustration at the shortcomings of the left to give rise to a new political culture. Small but significant currents began to emerge alongside or within established organisations as activists concluded that if change was to take place it would have to be fought for outside the mainstream.

The co-ordination and *sans* movements

A number of strikes in the late 1980s, by railway and motor industry workers, students, postal workers, nurses and teachers, saw the emergence of a rank-and-file movement in the trade unions around the strike committees or 'co-ordinations' which had bypassed the trade union bureaucracy and led the disputes. Some of these became fully fledged and combative independent unions offering a commitment to democratic rank-and-file participation in union activity, and proving particularly attractive to young and previously non-unionised workers, the latter making up 40 per cent of the independent postal workers' union, Solidaire, Unitaire, Démocratique (SUD). By the mid-1990s levels of support for SUD among Post Office staff (15 per cent) and France-Télécom employees (27 per cent) in workplace elections were reflecting a widespread desire for grassroots democracy. Other examples of this process included Act Up, a dynamic and highly visible AIDS awareness group formed in 1989; Droit au Logement (DAL), a homeless association founded in 1990, notable for its high-profile 1995 occupation of a squat in the Rue du Dragon, central Paris; Droits Devant!!, campaigning on broader civil rights issues, formed during this occupation; Agir Ensemble contre le Chômage (AC!) and Association pour l'Emploi, l'Information et la Solidarité (APEIS), associations emanating, respectively, from the CFDT and CGT trade unions, which organised a wave of occupations in defence of the rights of the unemployed in the late 1990s. Such currents were a reaction against the institutionalisation of existing associations, while the accompanying militancy was motivated, as Robert Castel has noted, not so much by demands for 'always more' as the fears of 'always less' (Castel 1999 p.717), experienced by a generation whose conditions of work were inferior to those of its parents. The first to act were Air France pilots and bank workers, who struck successfully in 1993 over concerns about job security, pay and working conditions, and school students, who forced the Balladur government to back down on its plans to introduce a cheap youth employment scheme. By 1994 *Le Monde* was describing France's social climate as poised 'between resignation and explosion' (10 February 1994).

December 1995 and anti-capitalism

At the end of the following year, the explosion occurred. Prime Minister Juppé's draconian programme of cuts for the social security system enraged those who still remembered Chirac's presidential campaign slogan of a 'France for All'. Two million strikers and their supporters took part in the biggest demonstrations seen since May 1968. Like the co-ordination movement, the 1995 strikes were characterised by a desire for unity and democracy, expressed in the joint union banners, previously a rarity, which appeared on all the demonstrations, and the disappearance of separate, sectional union contingents by the end of November. '[W]e are no longer fighting for ourselves,' one railway worker remarked a week into the strikes, 'we are on strike for all wage earners. To start with I was on strike as a train driver, then as a railway worker, then as a public sector worker, and now it's as a wage earner that I'm on strike' (Barets 1996, p.12). In virtually every workplace rank-and-file concern to retain control over union representatives meant that mass meetings, often open to other workers, replaced behind-closed-doors negotiations as the focal point for the strikes. The constant refrain of every demonstration, '*Tous ensemble!*' (All together!) stood in direct contradiction to the values propagated for over a decade by the NF and signalled an end to the period of resignation opened up in the 1980s. New hopes and expectations generated a 'latent combativity' (Dubois 1996, p.106) which gave rise initially to the so-called 'social movement' and, as the decade wore on, a vibrant anti-capitalist current. Links began to be made between the labour movement and various other groups involved in struggle, from students and the unemployed to immigrants and gays. The occupation tactic of the *sans papiers*, immigrants made 'illegal' by legislation introduced by the Balladur government, was adopted by unemployed workers who took over job centres, the Bank of France, the Ecole Normale Supérieure and the Socialist Party headquarters in the winter of 1997/98. The 'die-in', popularised by Act Up, became a regular feature of demonstrations against redundancies planned by Moulinex, Alstom, Seita and Akaï. By the turn of the century the influence of a developing anti-capitalist movement could be seen in the presence of contingents from Attac and other anti-globalisation groups on demonstrations in defence of jobs at Marks and Spencer's and at Danone, and in the controversial internet campaign to boycott Danone's products which provocatively targeted and subverted the company logo.

A notable feature of these years was the establishment of the *sans* groups as actors rather than just victims. The *sans papiers* became a *cause célèbre* following their high-profile occupation of a church in central Paris. The unemployed associations' campaign for more state aid for those out of work had a similar effect. Television news pictures showed angry demonstrators striding into well-to-do restaurants and demanding to be given food. When one group was offered out-of-the-way tables in the basement they stood firm until they were seated alongside the other diners. 'Don't you think', Lionel Jospin was asked as Prime Minister on the evening news at the height of these protests, 'that there's a whiff of a pre-May 1968, or a pre-revolutionary situation in the air?' (TF1 21 January 1998). In October 1998 more than a million students staged protests about conditions in secondary schools in over 350 towns. Governments of left and right faced strikes by tramworkers, truckers, teachers, medical staff and pilots. The neo-liberal orthodoxy which had dominated politics for the previous decade was suddenly confronted by activists newly confident in their ability to effect change and resolute in their opposition to the scapegoating of immigrants and the stigmatising of the unemployed. The challenge to this orthodoxy was relayed into the intellectual arena by the sociologist Pierre Bourdieu. His response to a petition issued in defence of the Juppé reforms by a group of leading academics linked to the journal *Esprit* sparked an often acrimonious public debate during the course of which Bourdieu dismissed his opponents as 'lackeys' of the establishment (Wolfreys 2000a). 'This crisis', he argued, 'is a historic opportunity for France and all those who refuse the new alternative: liberalism or barbarism' (*Le Monde* 14 December 1995).

A thriving counter-culture began to develop, reflected in the popularity of a number of books critical of the free market, notably Viviane Forrester's *L'Horreur Economique*, Bourdieu's own *La Misère du Monde* and the range of cheap, accessible publications produced for the emerging movement by his publishing house, Liber/Raisons d'Agir. Other developments included the return of class as a subject for French cinema in the late 1990s and the success of the music and arts magazine *Les Inrockuptibles*, along with that of the more highbrow *Le Monde Diplomatique*, which recast itself as an anti-globalisation review and played a leading role in the formation of Attac, which called for financial speculation to be liable to a Tobin tax, or 'global solidarity tax', with the money raised funding sustainable development. Within two years of its formation over 100 local committees with over 40,000 members and an international network covering around 20 countries had been set up as the association began to occupy a political space fast being vacated by French social democracy.

Along with Bourdieu, the figure who came to be most associated with anti-capitalism in France was José Bové. The campaign by his Confédération Paysanne against '*la malbouffe*' – mass-produced processed food and its threat to health, environment and artisanal production alike – became a powerful symbol in the developing anti-globalisation movement. The presence of various *sans* groups, Attac, the Ligue Communiste Révolutionnaire, the Groupe des dix federation of independent trade unions, the CGT and the opposition within the CFDT, at the 50,000-strong demonstration at Bové's June 2000 trial in Millau, were an indication of the breadth and depth of the movement. Activists campaigning on one issue were increasingly being drawn into wider struggles, and this applied to anti-racism along with the rest, the subject to which we now turn.

Pasqua, Debré, Le Pen ... one struggle

The confidence with which Juppé had embarked on his social security plan might have looked like reckless arrogance in the wake of the strikes but derived at the time from the ease with which the right had been able to implement its revision of nationality and immigration law between 1993 and 1995. So smooth was the passage of these measures that Balladur's Education Minister, a leader of the UDF's centrist faction, François Bayrou, even felt able to revive the controversy over the wearing of the Muslim headscarf in school when in 1994 he issued a circular to head teachers inviting them to be vigilant in supervising the everyday dress of their pupils, without actually mentioning the scarf. Five years previously the conflict had ended with the Conseil d'Etat, France's highest administrative court, deciding that the wearing of the scarf was not in itself an offence against secular principles, but it would be if it could be interpreted as flaunting a religious affiliation or as an attempt to convert others. Legally, therefore, toleration of the scarf depended on the interpretation of individual head teachers, based on their knowledge of their pupils and local conditions, and a number of them proceeded to carry out a series of expulsions of Muslim students. This time some of the expelled pupils were indeed supported by demonstrations originating among their family and neighbourhood, with a group of youths creating a disturbance in a school in Lille and a 300-strong demonstration supporting a score or so expellees in Mantes-la-Jolie, where they chose to march behind a banner inscribed with the republican slogan, 'Liberty, equality, fraternity'. In due course legal appeals led to panels of judges sorting out the 'innocent' scarf wearers from those judged to be deliberately provocative (Hargreaves 1995, pp.130–1). But on this occasion the stigmatised girls were even more isolated than had been the case in 1989, for not only did France Plus but also SOS Racisme refuse to support them. For reasons we explore in Chapter 8, SOS abandoned its multiculturalist position of 1989 to demand that a law be passed banning the wearing of all religious symbols in schools.

Since, as we know, many schoolteachers and left-wing intellectuals were themselves hostile to the headscarf, much greater attention and opprobrium were heaped on Bayrou's cabinet colleague, Charles Pasqua, Minister of the Interior, whom we encountered in 1988 trying to convince National Front voters that they and Chirac's RPR shared the same values. Within weeks of taking power in 1993 he introduced three measures relating to nationality, identity checks and immigration which explicitly targeted France's immigrant population, while he announced, 'France has been a country of immigration, it no longer wishes to be one' (*Le Monde* 2 June 1993). The Nationality Code was revised in a way which required children born in France to non-French parents to apply for nationality at some time between the ages of 16 and 21, instead of gaining it automatically by reason of their birth and residence in France. Acceptance would depend on a probationary period during which the candidate would have to desist from all political activity. Foreigners who married a French partner would have to wait a year between the marriage and permission to apply for French nationality instead of six months. Rights of entry were tightened by making family reunion with an immigrant worker conditional on two years' residence rather than one. Finally, greater powers were given to the police to carry out identity checks on foreigners suspected of 'threatening public order'. These measures, collectively known as the Pasqua Laws, would make little difference to the overall numbers gaining French nationality every year, and were accepted by France Plus (interview with Arezki Dahmani, 19 April 1995). But they would plunge thousands of people effectively settled in France into agonising uncertainty about their status, including many teenagers born there but of foreign parents and, in the case of marriages involving at least one French spouse, many others who were not themselves legally permitted to reside in France but were parents of a French child. For all these reasons the Pasqua Laws were bitterly criticised by all the other immigrant support organisations as pure vindictiveness with little real impact on the 'problem' he claimed to be addressing. In the face of a government freshly and massively legitimised at the polls, however, they were not able to mobilise much opposition on the streets. Indeed in April 1996 a parliamentary committee proposed a series of new measures designed to make the deportation of immigrant children easier and to restrict access to schools and hospitals by immigrants whose papers were not in order. Of the 30 members of the committee, 22 were from constituencies with a high NF vote (*Le Monde* 19 April 1996).

When Juppé took over the reins of government, new Interior Minister Jean-Louis Debré established his get-tough credentials in what had become the traditional fashion by deporting two planeloads of illegals, before rapidly falling into the trap gratuitously prepared for him by his predecessor, Pasqua. Throughout his term of office he was increasingly embarrassed by mounting support for the plight of several thousand immigrants, many of them parents of children enjoying French nationality, who had fallen foul of the 1993 Pasqua Laws and were facing deportation. In June 1996 demonstrations took place in several towns demanding that these *sans papiers* be granted residence permits. A number of churches were subsequently occupied by the immigrants and their families and in July 1996 some of those facing deportation began a hunger strike. In August when riot police took axes to the doors of the Saint-Bernard church in Paris and evicted the 200 or so *sans papiers* and their supporters, the brutality of their operation was widely condemned and, although a small proportion of those concerned were 'regularised', that is given papers which allowed them to stay in the country, the issue remained the focus of determined resistance by anti-racists. While demonstrations calling for the repeal of the Pasqua Laws rumbled on for months, a series of opinion polls showed that a majority of the public condemned the police attack on the church.

The polarisation of immigration-related issues was intensified by the fact that the National Front had won control of three southern towns, Marignane, Orange and France's ninth largest city, Toulon, in the 1995 local elections, followed by a fourth, Vitrolles, in a local by-election in 1997. Having made its first steps towards the 'recapture' of France (Mégret, cited in Soudais 1996, p.15), the Front was able for the first time to translate the party programme into practical action in a way which would affect peoples' lives, giving the lie to all those who had dismissed it as archaic and unelectable. In October 1995 Le Pen reminded his mayors that they were not like other mayors, that it was the Front, not them, which was running their towns, and that their task was not to 'manage decadence' but to implement their political programme as far as was legally possible (*Le Monde* 1 November 1995). This meant that immigrants and minorities suffered systematic discrimination. Not a single request for temporary visas was granted during Jean-Marie Le Chevallier's first year as mayor of Toulon; in Marignane school canteens were ordered to stop serving kosher and halal food; and all NF towns rigorously implemented Le Pen's directive that subsidies to associations which 'favoured immigration' should be scrapped (*Le Monde* 1 November 1995). The increasingly authoritarian atmosphere pervading these towns was typified by the decision of a local court in Toulon to sentence two members of the rap group NTM to three months in prison for insulting the police during a concert (*Le Monde* 16 November 1996).

Immigrants were not the sole targets of the NF administrations. From the day of their election, in the face of widespread calls for an artistic boycott of NF towns, culture became a major battleground for the Front's mayors. In Toulon, Le Chevallier tried to impose the participation of the Catholic fundamentalist daily *Présent* in 1995 on the popular annual Book Fair (*Le Monde* 7 November 1995). When his opponents decided to honour the achievements of the Jewish writer Marek Halter the following year, Le Chevallier announced that the town hall would take over the running of the fair, provoking a boycott of the event (*Le Monde* 24, 25 November 1996). He also tried to close down the world famous Châteauvallon dance theatre (*Le Monde* 4 April 1997), sacking its director Gérard Paquet and having him arrested on corruption charges, of which he was later found innocent. The new administrations' belligerent attitudes to their opponents were illustrated in Orange, where the harassment of a local union official drove him to suicide, and in Toulon by the treatment meted out to Ahmed Touati, a former leading member of SOS Racisme and aide to a prominent member of the previous administration. After the NF victory he asked to be moved to a non-political post in the city's archives but was instead offered a job in the cleaning services (Soudais 1996, pp.20–6). In Vitrolles, the municipal cinema manager was sacked for 'promotion of homosexuality' after organising an evening discussion on the theme 'Love in the age of AIDS'. She was one of a total of 150 municipal employees made redundant or replaced in a purge which closed down two of the town's theatres and all eight of its local community centres within six months (*Nouvel Observateur* 31 July 1997).

The brutal scapegoating by these administrations and their ruthless elimination of political opponents were a shocking confirmation of many people's worst fears about the Front. When Le Pen chose in June 1996 to question the patriotism of France's black footballers, and in August to advertise his belief in racial inequality, reiterating the message at every available opportunity, Juppé publicly condemned the Front (*Le Monde* 21 September 1996) and Justice Minister Jacques Toubon announced new measures designed to outlaw such verbal racism (*Le Monde* 22, 23 September 1996). After more than a decade of watching its vote being eroded by its extremist rival, the RPR commissioned one of its more progressive deputies, Jean-Pierre Delalande, to develop anti-NF arguments for a glossy brochure distributed to party members. For many people, however, the Front's actions were evidence that the Front carried with it the threat not just of xenophobia and intolerance, but of fascism. An explosion of anger at Le Pen's remarks and at the treatment meted out to the *sans papiers* started brewing on the left. September saw the creation of a National Committee of Vigilance against the Extreme Right which united 43 different left-wing and ecologist parties, trade unions and anti-racist associations who agreed to meet once a fortnight to plan their activities. By December virtually every public appearance by a National Front leader was being met by protesters: on 9 December 20,000 responded to an appeal by 76 different associations to demonstrate against Le Pen in Grenoble; other protests followed in Annecy, Le Havre and Toulouse. The demonstrations were fuelled also by the antics of Jean-Louis Debré who appeared to think his office required him to carry the persecution of immigrants to a farcical level. Just before Christmas he provoked derisive protests from the artistic and intellectual community by bringing forward a bill which required anyone acting as a host to a foreigner to apply for a residence permit on their behalf and then to report his or her guest's departure to the town hall or face a ban on extending hospitality to foreign friends in the future. With the parliamentary arithmetic so overwhelmingly in Debré's favour, Julien Dray fought a virtually lone battle in parliament while the real opposition was on the streets. In March 10,000 demonstrated against Bruno Mégret in St Etienne and on the same day in Marseilles 5000 took part in a day-long discussion on the defence of republican values (*Libération* 24 March 1997).

A new milestone was reached in February 1997 with a run-off between the Socialists and the National Front in a municipal by-election in Vitrolles, a town of 40,000 people near Marseilles. Until then, whenever the mainstream parties had sunk their differences and jointly called on voters to defeat the Front, the tactic had usually worked, as it had indeed in a recent by-election in Dreux. This time, despite conservative support, the beleaguered Socialist candidate for mayor, embroiled in a corruption scandal, was defeated by Catherine Mégret, wife of the NF chairman, himself barred from office for having exceeded the permitted campaign budget in the previous election. The unexpected realisation that the combined forces of the mainstream were unable to halt the Front, coming on top of disquiet about the so-called 'Lepenisation' of government policy and the Socialists' failure to oppose it, served to raise the level of grassroots resistance by several notches, producing the largest and most dynamic burst of anti-racist campaigning since the 1980s.

Within two days of the Mégret victory, 59 film directors launched an appeal for civil disobedience against Debré's bill requiring citizens to inform the authorities of the presence of foreign visitors in their homes. In Paris a national demonstration against the bill called by artists and other professional groups was attended by 100,000 people. The march set off from the Gare de l'Est, from where the Vichy regime had despatched Jews to Auschwitz, and many demonstrators turned up with suitcases to evoke the similarity between Debré's measures and Vichy legislation on the harbouring of Jews. The verve of this imaginative protest, organised independently of the political establishment, whose failure to stand up to racism was derided (*Le Nouvel Observateur* 20–26 February 1997), prompted the *Nouvel Observateur* magazine to comment, 'Suddenly, nothing is the same any more' (27 February–5 March 1997). The following month the streets of Strasbourg, where 50,000 marched in protest against the presence of the National Front congress in the town, echoed to the cries of 'Le Pen, we're on our way!' Once defensive, bitter affairs (Shields 1994), anti-racist protests towards the end of the decade had become a heady mix of combativity and optimism.

Naturally, it would have been unrealistic to expect these events to translate into an early decline in NF support. People who have grown accustomed to voting for a certain party do not stop just because opponents have grown in confidence. Later that spring, when Chirac dissolved parliament, gambling on a snap election which was supposed to catch the opposition off guard, the Front scored 15 per cent, its best ever parliamentary score, over 50 per cent up on its 1988 performance. The Front was given a final helpful leg-up by Interior Minister Jean-Louis Debré who embellished his campaign with a vintage Le Pen turn of phrase to ask his audience what they would think of immigrants 'coming to your home, settling in, opening your fridge and helping themselves?' (*Le Monde* 30 April 1997).

But during and after the campaign there was evidence that the NF leaders were divided about the image they ought to present, a sure sign that they were debating among themselves how to respond to the more systematic campaigning against the party. While Mégret confidently asserted that the Front's strategic aim was to force the mainstream conservatives to collaborate with it, Le Pen's antics were deliberately aimed at reinforcing the party's outsider status and rendering unlikely any possibility of a deal. In his final campaign meeting he indulged in a gruesome charade at the expense of Catherine Trautman, the Socialist mayor of Strasbourg who had been present on the March demonstration, having an effigy of her head served up to him on a plate. The next day, canvassing for his daughter, a candidate in Mantes-la-Jolie, Le Pen physically attacked the local Socialist candidate, Annette Peulvast-Bergeal, attempting to rip the republican sash from around her body, before lunging at the hostile demonstrators who had surrounded him.

Although it returned only one deputy, Jean-Marie Le Chevallier in Toulon, the party felt strong enough to declare open war on the conservatives, maintaining all 132 of its candidates eligible to go into the second round, 69 of them in three-way contests against sitting RPR–UDF deputies, the resulting split in the right-wing vote emphasising the Front's potential role as an arbiter. Meanwhile, Chirac's manoeuvre backfired hopelessly. Lionel Jospin, now the undisputed master of the Socialists, campaigned on a left-wing programme, promising to reduce the working week from 39 hours to 35 and create 750,000 jobs. His hastily formed alliance with the Communists and Greens snatched an unexpected victory, sending the Socialist leader to Matignon at the head of a red–green coalition including Communist and Green ministers.

The National Front in a new context: towards the split of 1999

In Chapters 4 and 5 we spelled out the dilemma faced by a revolutionary fascist party which wants to gain an audience and recruits by working in the parliamentary arena. If it shows its revolutionary ambitions and its contempt for democracy too openly it will never grow beyond the fringe. If it is too successful in having its members elected to office, there is a danger that its councillors, mayors or deputies will become so attached to the pleasures and perks of office, or so engrossed in managing affairs, that they become detached from the revolutionary strategy. Worse, if the party is seen to become part of the establishment, and especially if it is drawn into alliances with the previously vilified 'old elites', its electoral appeal will collapse. The problem for the National Front in the context of heightened social struggle after 1995 and the weakening of the mainstream right after 1997 was that it ran all these risks at the same time. On the one hand, as we shall see, the powerful anti-NF demonstrations tended to provoke elements within the party into potentially embarrassing outbursts of violence. On the other, the catastrophic loss of authority suffered by Juppé and Chirac after they clumsily gave up power to the left in 1997 led straight to a regional election contest in 1998 in which the NF emerged as powerful enough in five of the 22 regions to become *de facto* part of the right-wing majority which elected the regional presidents. Thus, for the NF, the period which opened in 1995 with their historic capture of four municipalities, and led to their split in 1999, was one in which unprecedented opportunities to break out of the *cordon sanitaire* which the mainstream wanted to wrap around it were accompanied simultaneously by the risks of incorporation into the 'system', and unprecedented opposition welling up from the grassroots activists of the left. Necessarily, the Front's navigation of these challenges and difficulties sparked sharp internal discussions. Objectively, the crisis was probably not serious enough to force it towards a split. What made the split inevitable was that the discussions became overlaid by and took the form of a leadership contest.

The conflict between Mégret and Le Pen, more than a simple personality clash but less than a fundamental difference in outlook, involved elements of sincerity and elements of opportunism. For example, Le Pen undoubtedly thought that Mégret carried with him the danger that the fascist project would succumb to some or all of the comforts of office, the blandishments of the mainstream and the temptations of technocratic managerialism. Certainly these dangers would indeed be greater with Mégret at the helm than Le Pen, the bombastic and domineering veteran of post-war fascism's struggle for survival. But it would be wrong to say that the leadership crisis came about because Mégret, in the changed context of 1995–99, became the spokesman of a strategic option markedly different from Le Pen's. Undoubtedly, Mégret thought he would make a more effective leader of the NF than Le Pen did and wanted to replace him. Once again, in some respects, as we shall see, he was probably right. But that did not mean that his lust for power drove the party into a conflict which otherwise would not have occurred. In other words, there were two problems in a dialectical relationship. The dual strategy of the fascist party which took the parliamentary road of course produced arguments over short- and medium-term tactics and goals. Was Le Pen right to launch a physical attack on a female Socialist candidate half his size under the eye of the television cameras? Should the National Front mayors go all out to implement the programme of 'national preference' in their towns, at the risk of being prosecuted for breaking the law, or should they go more carefully in order to convince the electorate of their seriousness? These were questions to which there were no easy answers, even for the most sophisticated proponents of the dual strategy, and they would have exercised the minds of all the party's activists. But these arguments were exacerbated because they were taken up and used against each other by the camps of two leaders who did indeed differ in temperament and abilities and who, crucially, were at different stages of their careers. In 1999, Le Pen was 71, Mégret barely 50. The succession would have to occur some time soon. So why not now? In a moment we show how the crisis came to a head around a number of themes. Mégret's managerial skills made him the favourite of much of the party cadre, if not actually their spokesman. This gave him the temerity to attack Le Pen for his own and his coterie's organisational failures. Le Pen responded with a display of tyrannical behaviour and the time-honoured strategy of divide and rule, setting up internal offices to block Mégret's influence. But he failed to carry all the leadership with him and when he began the expulsion of the Mégret camp many leading members defected to set up a new party under Mégret. Throughout this process Le Pen kept up the sort of provocative public behaviour which was bound to maintain the party's image as an anti-system outsider, just as it reassured the Front's fascist hard-core that he remained faithful to them and to the common cause. Before we describe these manouevres in more detail, we outline some episodes which underlined the atmosphere of hope and anxiety in which the Front feverishly launched itself on a path to self-destruction.

Hope and anxiety, 1997–98

Chirac's loss of authority, which began with the 1995 strikes and was confirmed by the self-inflicted defeat in 1997, meant that basic survival instincts increasingly dominated the attitude of conservative politicians to the question of electoral alliances with the National Front. After the regional elections of March 1998 the NF emerged holding the balance between right and left. It gleefully decided to vote for the mainstream right candidates who stood for the regional presidency. When five members of the UDF were elected in this way, a debate once more broke out within the mainstream about what attitude should be taken. Some of the newly elected presidents resigned immediately when faced with charges from the left of collusion with the fascists, but others saw no reason to sacrifice the chance of office. In the most notorious case the former Defence Minister Charles Millon laced his speech with so many nods and winks to the National Front's programme that his election was annulled some months later by a court ruling, on the grounds that the election of the regional presidents was meant to take place without a debate. In the immediate aftermath of the 1997 parliamentary election, *Le Figaro*'s chief political columnist, the former Gaullist minister Alain Peyrefitte, had already argued that alliances with the NF should be considered, although not while Le Pen remained leader (*Le Figaro* 2 June 1997). Now two veteran employers' leaders, Ambroise Roux (*Le Monde* 10 March 1998) and Jacques Calvet (*Le Monde* 11 April 1998) backed his stance, while Edouard Balladur proposed setting up a commission, open to the far-right, which would publicly debate the NF's ideas on 'national preference' (*Le Monde* 2 June 1998). With such influential voices preaching collaborationism, the UDF coalition was brought to the brink of collapse, Alain Madelin, leader of Démocratie Libérale (DL), supporting collusion in the five regions, and François Bayrou, leader of the party's social catholic wing, opposing it. By May, Madelin and Démocratie Libérale had left the UDF, blowing away a major pillar supporting the representational structure of democratic French conservatism. To those who took elections as the principal gauge of a party's strength, the National Front appeared in a virtually unassailable position (see Declair 1999).

However, for the National Front activists, the hopes raised by this evidence of their growing influence on the political elite must have been matched by anxiety at the rise of opposition from the grassroots. This took two forms, direct and indirect. The latter manifested itself in a general shift in attitudes on immigration-related issues. When the multiracial French football team, once a target of Le Pen's derision, won the 1998 World Cup, various politicians in pursuit of reflected glory trumpeted their 'tolerance'. Charles Pasqua, of all people, declared himself in favour of granting residence papers to the *sans papiers*, a call backed by 45 per cent of the population before the year was out (*Le Monde* 12 December 1998). At the close of the decade, for the first time ever, a majority of the population (52 per cent) were in favour of granting immigrants the right to vote in local elections, while 60 per cent saw immigration as a 'source of cultural enrichment', up 18 per cent on the early 1990s (*Le Monde* 25 March 1999). Direct opposition to the Front, in the form of the unrelenting wave of demonstrations, forced out the culture of violence at its heart. In October 1996 an anti-racist demonstration in Monceau-les-Mines was attacked by an armed and helmeted branch of the Front's security force, a 'secret' unit of former marines, one of whom boasted to the press that they were capable of overthrowing a government within 48 hours (*Libération* 13 November 1997). Le Pen then made his call to the party's youth wing, which we noted in Chapter 5, to prepare for revolution. At the 1997 Strasbourg congress the Front chose to present its legal face, revising its constitution and proclaiming its fidelity to the 'institutions of the Republic and democratic pluralism' (Darmon and Rosso 1998, pp.94–5). The presence of 50,000 anti-NF demonstrators in the town proved too much for some to bear, however. Party veteran Roger Holeindre blurted out before the congress his vow that the anti-fascist organisations Scalp and Ras l'Front would cry tears of blood when the NF came to power. Outside the hall, meanwhile, several of the organisation's security force were arrested for impersonating riot police and carrying out bogus identity checks on the demonstrators. In Mégret-run Vitrolles during the truckers' strike of December 1997, NF members led by the head of the municipal police force attacked a picket line, seriously injuring a striker (*Le Monde* 19 December 1997). These outbursts were evidence of frustration within the party at the Front's apparent inability to match its electoral success by building on the organisational bases which it had established since its emergence as a major political force. Party membership stood at around 40,000 (Perrineau 1999), significantly down on the leadership's no doubt exaggerated claims of 80,000 members in the early 1990s (Marcus 1995, p.41) and certainly not any higher than at the start of the decade. Membership of the party youth wing, the Front National de la

Jeunesse (FNJ), however, had slumped from the 15,000 members it once claimed to below 2000 in 1998 (*Le Monde* 12 December 1998).

Bruno Mégret: the emergence of a challenger

While its ability to recruit appeared to be stalling, the Front could boast around 1500 elected representatives by the mid-1990s. Between 1995 and 1997 the number of full-time party functionaries had risen to nearly a hundred and expenditure on salaries from £780,000 to £1.78 million (*Libération* 3 May 1999). This expanding party apparatus was gradually coming under Mégret's control. Widely credited with the modernisation of Le Pen's image and the professionalisation of the party since joining in the mid-1980s, and always ready to remind anyone who listened that he was the inspiration and author of the party programme (interview with Bruno Mégret, 28 May 1993), Mégret's influence on the education, training and theoretical orientation of party members through the National Training Institute and the Editions Nationales was beyond dispute. His popularity with party activists grew such that he came top in the central committee elections at the March 1997 congress, closely followed in the popularity stakes by four of his closest supporters. Mégret was seen by the younger cadre as best able to oversee and profit from the alliances with the mainstream which they saw as the key to the Front's further advance, not least because sections of the traditional right were only prepared to contemplate such a move under his leadership. Mégret was positioning himself as the natural successor to the 70-year-old Le Pen, derided in a 1994 Mégretist bulletin as a 'tyrannical has-been geriatric' (*Les Dossiers du Canard Enchaîné* October 1998, p.64). Despite their growing influence within the party the Mégretists were far from satisfied with its organisational health. Their frustration was forced into the open in the run-up to the 1999 European election campaign when Le Pen, barred from office following his 1997 attack on a Socialist Party candidate, chose to nominate his wife as his replacement, a move which appeared to confirm that a process of 'demégretisation' was under way. This charge was made in an internal document circulated by Mégret's supporters in December 1998 which pinpointed three underlying problems faced by the NF: the party's activist base was diminishing, its satellite organisations were little more than empty shells, and the party cadre was weak and inexperienced. Several leading Le Pen allies were singled out as barriers to growth. All were criticised for their personal failure to retain members and build effective local party organisations (*Le Monde* 12 December 1998).

'Neither right nor left'?

Some observers of the Front have claimed that the party's leadership conflict was caused by a clash between the revolutionary culture of the activists, loyal to Le Pen, and the more pragmatic interests of the party's elected representatives, who identified with Mégret (Perrineau 1999). Although this was an element in the struggle for control of the party, however, relations between the two leaders and the rest of the party were not this clear cut. Since the early 1990s Mégret and Le Pen had both fought to impose an anti-'mondialist' perspective on the organisation in place of its traditional anti-communist outlook. After 1989 the shift from an ultra-liberal agenda (the 1985 programme had called for a 'liberal revolution') to one which placed greater emphasis on social policy and protectionism had become a priority for the top party leadership. So much so that it was prepared to go against the instincts of the Front's predominantly middle-class cadre. It was in this context that Le Pen's son-in-law Samuel Maréchal, frequently used as a stalking horse for Le Pen's own ideas, proclaimed the party 'neither right nor left', in a deliberate echo of Jacques Doriot's definition of the Parti Populaire Français in the 1930s. The 1995 strikes put this strategy to the test. Having won a record score in working-class areas in the spring presidential election, the NF's claims to represent ordinary workers were soon at odds with the leadership's attitude to the strikes, characterised by Le Pen as an 'archaic and ruinous' (*L'Humanité* 8 December 1995) 'revolt of the privileged' (*France-Inter* 20 December 1995). Since opinion polls showed that 71 per cent of the Front's electorate supported the strikes (Darmon and Rosso 1998, pp.48–9), *National Hebdo* was soon publishing letters from readers 'absolutely scandalised' by the party line (*Les Idées en Mouvement* March 1996).

If the Front's long-term aim had been 'to capture the energy of social protest and link it to the power of nationalism and xenophobia built on fear' (Monzat 1996), the strikes underlined how labour militancy could undermine this agenda and leave the organisation isolated. Le Pen attempted to win back lost ground in 1996, choosing to use his speech in honour of Joan of Arc in May to salute the 'long struggle of workers and trade unions for more justice, security and more freedom at work' and paying tribute the following year to 'workers' struggles'. But the strikes had exposed the lack of social influence wielded by the Front via its satellite organisations, a concern which prompted Le Pen, as an internal party bulletin revealed, to instruct general secretary Gollnisch to 'reduce the shocking disproportion which exists between the 50,000 official members of the Front and its five million electors'. With Maréchal's assistance Gollnisch would be setting up associations to act as transmission belts into the Front with the aim of establishing it as a 'genuine mass party' (*La Lettre du Magazine Hebdo* 12 December 1996). Up to this point it was Mégret who appeared to be making the more serious effort to strengthen the party's base in the working class, turning up in October 1996 to distribute leaflets outside a Moulinex factory threatened with closure in the town of Mamers in the Sarthe and repeating the gesture to France-Télécom workers threatened with privatisation the following September. He also set up an NF trade union for Paris Métro workers and ensured that the Front stood candidates for election to council housing committees.

Divide and misrule?

Because of the brewing leadership crisis the Front was unable to resolve the problems posed by 1995, its attempts to build a 'mass base' hampered by the multiplication of structures whose existence derived as much from internal conflict as the need to turn the party outward. Gradually Mégret's activities threatened to put Le Pen in the shade. Already the Mégrets' success in winning the town of Vitrolles in 1997 had convinced Le Pen not to stand as a candidate in either the parliamentary or local elections later that year for fear of being overshadowed by his chairman. For the first time since its electoral breakthrough the Front went into a national election without its leader as a candidate. Further blows to Le Pen's prestige came between the two rounds of the 1997 election, when both Mégret and Gollnisch publicly distanced themselves from his stated preference for a Socialist majority, and again in March 1998 when the *bureau politique* rejected his demand that the endorsement of the principle of national preference be made a condition of electoral alliances with other right-wing parties (*Le Monde* 18 March 1998). Le Pen's ability to continue as NF president was now openly questioned in the press, forcing him to assert his leadership by differentiating himself from Mégret, who for his part knew that leading the NF into the European elections would give irresistible impetus to his prospects of leading the party permanently.

For 20 years, the federative strategy which we described in Chapter 5 had artificially bound the different components of the National Front around the personality of Le Pen. Political cohesion had been assured, on the one hand, by the different factions' willingness to participate in the Le Pen personality cult, and, on the other, by a system of parallel internal structures which allowed the different factions a zone of power within the organisation. In the 1980s Le Pen's main rival, Jean-Pierre Stirbois, had his influence as national secretary checked by the creation of the post of chairman filled by Mégret. In the 1990s Mégret's increasing predominance was countered by Bruno Gollnisch, appointed by Le Pen to the beefed-up post of general secretary. Now that he was under threat, Le Pen turned to an even more exaggerated use of parallel structures in an attempt to block his rival's influence, even to the extent of deliberately undermining Mégret's efforts to build NF influence in the unions. Thus Gollnisch, acting, as we have seen, on Le Pen's instruction, set up a rival transport union in Lyons, and Maréchal established the National Circle of Unionised Workers to federate NF members in the unions. Mégret's supporters, who ran the Front's Renouveau Etudiant student organisation, were severely critical of Maréchal for his leadership of a rival youth wing, the FNJ, whose membership had plummeted to below 2000 despite an annual budget of over 1 million francs and a permanent staff of nine (*Le Monde* 12 December 1998). Following the victory of Mégret's supporters in the 1997 central committee elections, Le Pen allowed Jean-Claude Martinez to set up yet another counterweight to Mégret's influence, in the form of a shadow cabinet, or government in waiting. Mégret, in turn, formed his own security force to prevent the NF's official security unit from keeping track of his movements. Le Pen's strategy of creating parallel structures to house rival factions was now spiralling out of control. The multiplication of structures was attacked by Mégret, who accused Le Pen of wasting party funds on them with the sole aim of reducing his influence. Further evidence, he argued, that Le Pen's leadership, 'contested', 'isolated' and surrounded by courtesans, had become 'bunkerised' and was incapable of building a party of government. The nomination of Le Pen's new (and very rich) wife Jany to head the party's list in his place was the final straw. Having only recently joined the organisation she was rejected by the Mégretists as someone whose 'temperament, attitude, standard of living, all added up to a bourgeois candidate cut off from our most popular electorate' (*Le Monde* 12 December 1998).

In or against the system?

Irrespective of Mégret's talents or activities, the most ideologically committed fascists in the party, Le Pen included, were aware that electoral success might exert its own influence on the NF, creating the potential for the bureaucratisation of a layer of the organisation's cadre and generating a culture of managerialism which was at odds with the more anti-system attitudes of much of the membership (Perrineau 1999). But those who wanted to ward off this tendency had no qualms about pinpointing Mégret, whom they despised as an *arriviste* technocrat, as its chief exponent. In 1997 the Le Pen acolyte Jean-Claude Martinez contrasted the 'warmth' of the current around Le Pen to the Mégretist faction, described as 'technocratic, cold', and, revealingly, 'Juppéist' (*Le Monde* 16 June 1997). Once frustration with the difficulty of the choices facing the organisation escalated into a fight for control of the party the conflict took on a different dimension. Each side was obliged to appeal to those it could count on in terms that polarised the dispute. For Le Pen this meant appealing to the old guard by stressing the Front's outsider status and his own streetfighting credentials. This was the context for his attacks on Trautmann and Peulvast-Bergeal between the two rounds of the 1997 election. He drew attention to what many saw as Mégret's principal weakness, his distant manner and effete technocratic style, and contrasted his own rough and ready populist image to Mégret's lack of 'popular fibre' ('Mégret–Le Pen. Le combat des chiefs', in 'Mégret. Facho deviant!', *Les Dossiers du Canard Enchaîné* October 1998, p.63). At the end of the same year, at a joint press conference in Munich alongside the former Waffen SS officer and Republikaner Party leader Franz Schönhuber, Le Pen declared that the Germans 'were the martyred people of Europe' and went on to reiterate his belief that the Holocaust was a minor detail of World War II (*Le Monde* 9 January 1998). Prior to the 1998 regional elections Le Pen decided to lead the annual ceremony to mark Duprat's death six days early, so that the Front's anti-establishment credentials could be paraded in advance of the election. As far as the Le Pen camp was concerned, the NF must at all costs 'embody the alternative to the system', as Samuel Maréchal put it (*Libération* 14 June 1997), if it were to benefit from the demise of the mainstream parties.

Ever since the Front had become established as a major electoral force Le Pen had been constantly preoccupied with countering the bureau-cratisation or incorporation of the organisation. He ensured that anyone elected on an NF ticket must pay a sizeable proportion of their salary to the Front. The detail and Durafour affairs, coming in the wake of the successful election campaigns of 1986 and 1988, were calculated, by making the Front an object of scandal, to offset the temptations of office among the party's elected representatives. That the message was heard by its intended recipients was shown by the resignations of MEP Olivier d'Ormesson after the detail remark and of parliamentary deputy Yann Piat following the Durafour scandal. Similar considerations were behind Le Pen's insistence on the implementation of national preference in NF controlled towns in 1995 and his comments on racial inequality in the summer of 1996: the Front's desire to prove its capacity to become a party of government had to be accompanied by reinforcement of the outsider status which allowed it to attract votes from the disillusioned and to remain the force of 'last resort' should the political and social system undergo some sort of serious breakdown. Nothing threatened this outsider status more than the possibility that the Front should be seen to compromise with the mainstream right by making electoral or managerial alliances with it, and it is no surprise the question of alliances was hotly debated in the party and became a key issue in the battle for power. Mégret made no secret of his belief that the medium term strategy for the Front should centre on inducing some fraction of the mainstream right into joining the Front first locally and even eventually nationally in implementing part of the Front's programme. No doubt his aim would have been to use such an alliance to build the party's strength and then set new conditions for collaboration which the hapless fellow-travellers would find difficult to resist. Le Pen was less sure that the time was ripe for such manouevres. He enjoyed nothing more than an opportunity for the Front to demonstrate that the right was unable to outvote the left without its help, as happened in the 1998 regional presidents embroglio, when his ally Gollnisch publicly supported Millon in Lyon in order to embarrass him. But that Le Pen was not ready to sacrifice the party's outsider status for a mess of potage may have been behind his attempt to prevent any formal alliances being agreed by setting the impossible condition that the mainstream parties should agree to implement national preference before the Front would agree to get into bed with them. His vision of the 'last resort' which the NF represented, which must not be compromised, was spelled out in 1996. If the goal of such alliances was to ensure the return of proportional representation, giving the NF 60 deputies and five ministers, 'it's totally useless. I'd even say it would be harmful. That would kill the only hope the French have left' (Darmon and Rosso 1998, p.135). A year later, when Le Pen loyalist Carl Lang warned of the danger of alliances with the traditional right by invoking a maxim attributed to Lenin, 'Unity at the top, never! Unity at the base, always!' (*Libération* 14 June 1997), there is no doubt that he was attempting to undermine Mégret. Such attacks were probably unfair. Responding to claims that alliances would soften the Front's image, Mégret replied:

The strategy I am putting forward has nothing to do with Gianfranco Fini's in Italy, who renounced his programme and turned his movement into something totally bland so that it might gain acceptance from the establishment.

With some justice he defended his record:

> I who have put into action the policy of national preference in Vitrolles ... I will never accept that the movement compromises itself and abandons any aspect of its values or programme. (*Présent* 16 October 1998)

But by this time the die was cast. When things finally came to a head towards the end of 1998, Le Pen acted decisively, knowing that his status as leader figure depended on maintaining the illusion that he was the all-powerful presence driving the NF forward. In November he informed staff at the party headquarters that only his portrait could appear on its walls (*Le Monde* 12 December 1998). Having nominated his wife to head the Front's European election list, thus avoiding the possibility of a Mégret bandwagon threatening his own chances of remaining the Front's candidate for the 2002 presidential election, Le Pen then expelled two Mégret supporters for having circulated an internal document critical of him. Following his own expulsion Mégret founded the Front National-Mouvement National, a name he was forced to change to the Mouvement National Républicain once Le Pen won the legal battle for control of the party name and finances. Neither organisation did particularly well in the first electoral test following the split, the European campaign of 1999. Le Pen had to contend with rumblings of discontent within the NF party after polling only 5.69 per cent, and Mégret, having scored 3.28 per cent, and with his party in severe financial straits, had to apply for readmission into the public service post he had left when he went into politics.

In some ways, then, the story of the National Front appeared, in 1999, to have become a story of its rise and fall. Having risen to prominence on the back of disaffection with a Socialist government in the context of rising unemployment, a demoralised labour force and an increasingly ineffective anti-racist movement, the wheel seemed to have come full circle. The labour movement was reviving, anti-racism had sprung back to life and the left had returned to office to oversee a fall in unemployment. But the story has a sting in the tail. In 2002 Le Pen won the biggest ever vote for a fascist party in the post-war period. In Chapter 9 we explain how he appeared to come back from the dead.

8
The Republican Model in Question

In previous chapters we have shown how French political and intellectual elites have buttressed their belief that French society is not particularly racist on the abstract rights enshrined in a republican constitution. Often they have argued that the abstract citizenship model recognising only the individual, stripped of any communitarian identifying markers, is more effective in integrating newcomers than the so-called 'Anglo-Saxon' model accepting of diverse communities. Remarkably, our scepticism about these claims is now less controversial than it used to be, for in the last five years of the twentieth century the model was either increasingly ignored in practice, or more and more consciously called into question as a diverse range of actors discovered the category of 'race' as a major structuring factor affecting the life chances of immigrants and immigrant-origin youth. Both policy-makers and anti-racist associations were increasingly drawn towards formerly decried Anglo-Saxon methods in their attempts to combat racism. We begin this chapter by taking stock of anti-racism in the 1980s and early nineties, when the influence of Pierre-André Taguieff, the most prolific prophet of the republican model, was at its height. Next we examine what happened when the 1997–2002 plural left government tried to supplement colour-blind territorially organised integration policies with an explicit campaign against 'racial' discrimination. Then we look at the return of SOS Racisme, which we saw in Chapter 6 abandoning the showbiz and media antics of its early days in favour of day-to-day campaigning in the deprived suburbs, a sojourn which led it to focus more and more on the fact that the single biggest factor structuring the social exclusion of its members and supporters was the colour of their skin. We conclude by tracing the plural left's attempts to deal with the legislative and humanitarian consequences of their predecessors in office.

Anti-racism and the Republic: taking stock

On one level the patchy record of anti-racism from 1981 could be explained by the community diversity which hindered ethnic mobilisation, and the class divisions which offered certain routes out of exclusion to some members of the discriminated minority which were not available to others. It also owed something to the opportunist manipulation which turned many Beurs away from SOS Racisme. But on a third level the failing was ideological. On four or five occasions when populations of Maghreb origin or Islamic religion were isolated and stigmatised, anti-racist organisations retreated from their previous defence of the stigmatised groups as the political environment became more hostile. In 1993 France Plus abandoned its former opposition to government plans to abolish automatic citizenship at 18 for the children of Maghrebi parents, on the grounds that only potential wrongdoers could object to constant identity checks (interview with Areski Dahmani, 19 April 1995). Whereas in 1989 the MRAP, the League of the Rights of Man and SOS Racisme defended the Creil schoolgirls' right to wear the Muslim headscarf, five years later when it was again made an object of suspicion and rejection, SOS joined the anti-scarf coalition, demanding that it be banned, along with other religious signs, because of the growth of Islamic fundamentalism in the suburbs (*Le Monde* 27 October 1994). In fact the demand for a law which simultaneously banned the scarf, the *yarmulke* and the crucifix was a clear sign of adherence to the lay left-republican tradition of uniformity; both its 1989 and its 1994 positions on the scarf were compatible with SOS Racisme's vague vision of the non-racist society as a melting-pot which eventually succeeds in obliterating all cultural differences. Yet in a situation in which the National Front was in the forefront of a campaign to stigmatise and attack members of a minority, then the first duty of anti-racists was surely to defend the targeted groups. SOS' failure to do that in the wake of the massive conservative victory of 1993 was an example of anti-racism undermined by adherence to the republican model.

The Trotskyist groups which helped kick-start the revival of anti-racism in the 1990s did not use the Headscarf Affair as an occasion for springing to the defence of a stigmatised minority either, though for slightly different reasons. The rather one-dimensional Marxism of the LCR, inspirers of Ras l'Front, led them instinctively to avoid seeming to endorse a 'communitarian' practice which could be a brake on class mobilisation (interview with Christian Picquet, 17 April 1996). But it was the Manifesto against the National Front which provided the most striking example of the hazards of attempting to run an anti-racist movement on the abstract basis of equality of all citizens before the law. Asked whether minority community associations had been systematically invited to its 1991 co-ordinating conference – a step which would be axiomatic to the initiators of a broad anti-racist campaign in the UK – the group's spokesman justified the fact that no such initiative had been taken by a lengthy statement of the orthodox republican deprecation of 'communities' as structures which prevent individuals enjoying the social and political equality supposedly guaranteed by republican principles (interview with Eric Osmond, 9 April 1996). The Manifesto was influenced by the National Front's pretence that it was cultural not racial difference which made it impossible to assimilate Maghreb-origin immigrants into French society. The Manifesto leaders were far from taken in by this 'non-racist' justification of repatriation and the NF doctrine of 'national-preference', treating it for what it was, a smoke-screen which hid the authentically racist intentions of the NF. But, following their mentor, Pierre-André Taguieff, they concluded that, since the NF defended (however hypocritically) the right to be different, it would be a mistake for anti-racists to do the same, since this would contribute to strengthening the NF's position (interview with Eric Osmond, 9 April 1996). In a voluminous corpus of writing, Taguieff attacked not only the notion of the right to be different, but also those left-wing journalists and part of the political left (mainly the Communist Party and Ras l'Front) who tried to discredit Le Pen by stressing his links with the personalities and ideas of 1930s fascism, dismissing such campaigns as 'commemorative anti-racism'. Taguieff also developed the view that the rise in support for the extreme right could be explained partly by the abandonment by the political mainstream of the idea of the nation as a focus of community identity and solidarity. This led him to call on the opponents of the Front to compete with it in endorsing nationalist sentiment on certain issues like the institutional evolution of the European Union (Taguieff 1996). So, according to Taguieff, one should *not* defend the right to be different because Le Pen defended it, but one *should* defend national sentiment, because Le Pen defended it and he might otherwise have a monopoly of it! The contradiction in this muddled thinking could hardly be starker or illustrate more crisply the negative influence of the republican model on anti-racism. Within a few years the Manifesto against the National Front had collapsed while Ras l'Front, which ignored Taguieff, survived and prospered. Nothing underlined the declining influence of Taguieff's ideas more than the intellectuals' defence of the *sans papiers*, many of whom had stayed in France illegally, often as adults, to eke out a living in the black economy and who were arguably less likely to integrate easily than the suburban youths who defended their Beur identity.

The discovery of 'race'

The rise of this more generous form of anti-racism was paralleled by the emergence of signs that aspects of the republican model of citizenship were no longer being respected by the state itself. First among these was the principle of colour-blindness in the administration of social policy. As part of its drive against youth unemployment in the suburbs the new left government elected in 1997 created thousands of low-paid public-sector auxiliary posts such as learning partners in schools, monitors on school buses and special constables. Researchers found that, in a form of unavowed positive discrimination, those recruiting to these jobs 'spontaneously matched the ethnic characteristics of those hired to the ethnic composition of the client community' (Calvès 2000, p.77). Further, a scheme, in existence since 1993, to pair unemployed youths with an older, usually retired, person who would advise and guide them in preparation of their CV, interviews and training strategy, in order to help them find jobs, was specifically reoriented towards immigrant-origin youth when its charter was rewritten in 1999 and the use of ethnic categories in monitoring its success was openly planned (Calvès 2000, p.79). Civil servants were increasingly encouraged in this direction by their political bosses. Jean-Pierre Chevènement, Minister of the Interior and one of the most fervent defenders of the republican model held a meeting with all his prefects in February 1999, at which he set out the long term aim of making sure that the police service reflected the 'image' of the population, and invited them to make sure that plenty of immigrant-origin youth found their way into the ranks. Later the Paris police authority published a communiqué in which it expressed its satisfaction that 35 per cent of the auxiliaries hired to help in mediating suburban conflicts were 'immigrant-origin youth', even though to compile such a statistic was illegal (Hargreaves 2000, p.94). Chevènement's example was followed by the head of the state railway SNCF, and by Catherine Tasca, Minister of Culture, who asked the state television companies France 2 and France 3 to remedy the under-representation of black, brown and Asiatic faces on their screens (Calvès 2000, p.82).

Ministers' new willingness to think in terms of ethnic categories, previously 'unnamed and unnameable' (Calvès 2000, p.79) reflected their awareness of the failures of the republican model increasingly reported in academic studies and incorporated into official reports landing on their desks. In one ground-breaking study, the use of ethnic categories demonstrated that, at 40 per cent, the unemployment rate of young men of Algerian origin in the 1990s was twice that of their Portuguese-origin peers, a difference which must have been largely explained by racial discrimination in hiring practices (Tribalat 1995, cited in Hargreaves 2000, p.89), yet there was on average in the same decade only one conviction per year for racial discrimination at work. In another startling break with the old thinking the High Council for Integration proposed its own replacement by a more powerful body modelled on the British Commission for Racial Equality, which would have the power to investigate individual complaints of racism and support victims in taking their cases to the courts (Hargreaves 2000, p.85). When the Minister of Employment, Martine Aubry, asked for a special report on the working of the administration over the whole field of integration policy, its author, Jean-Michel Belorgey, in turn proposed a virtual catalogue of previously demonised 'Anglo-Saxon' practices, endorsing the idea of an independent authority buttressed by ethnic monitoring and charged with negotiating codes of good practice and action programmes with unions, employers, the civil service and public bodies such as housing authorities. Stressing the need for a serious attack on racial discrimination he took a sideswipe at the 'astringent framework of republican integration', insisting that minorities 'shouldn't have to efface the traces of their previous life' in order to win acceptance in France (*Le Monde* 7 April 1999). Belorgey's report was warmly received by *Le Monde*, which itself supported the new mood by running an interview with Sukhdev Sharma, former executive director of the CRE (*Le Monde* 26 August 1998), as well as introducing its readers to the concepts of 'racial' discrimination and 'institutionalised racism', previously unknown to the general public but which it admitted was rife in schools, work and housing allocation (*Le Monde* 17 December 1999). There was evidence also that the current of public opinion was turning in favour of more liberal integration policies. A 1998 survey found that 73 per cent of respondents had a fairly open attitude to asylum seekers (against 61 per cent in 1992). Immigration was thought to be of 'positive benefit' to France by 42 per cent, as against 45 per cent who thought it was a 'burden' (they had split 27:60 on the same questions in 1990–91); 52 per cent thought that giving foreigners the right to vote in local elections (a measure urged by Belorgey) was a good tactic in the fight against racism. Only 33 per cent had thought so in 1991 (*Le Monde* 25 March 1999). Even Alain Juppé announced that he was in favour of a CRE-type institution and that he regretted his government's 'clumsy' handling of the *sans papiers* (*Le Monde* 1 October 1999).

An action plan against racial discrimination

In this relatively favourable environment, the government brought into being, in chaotic and piecemeal fashion, what it would eventually call its 'Action Plan Against Racial Discrimination'. In January 1999 the Interior Ministry instructed all prefectures to set up Commissions for Access to Citizenship (CODAC in its French abbreviation) whose overall mission was 'to help young people of immigrant origin to find a job and a place in society and to reduce the discriminations which they suffer, in work, housing and leisure activities'. They would do this by publicising notices of entrance exams for candidates for the public service, by 'sensitising' employers and encouraging the partnership scheme between individual youths and an older advisor. The CODACs would also receive and investigate complaints of racial discrimination from official sources or from 'simple citizens' (*Le Monde* 28 January 1999). They would not necessarily automatically refer all complaints to the courts. The aim would be to proceed by mediation to highlight and change unsatisfactory practices. Sceptics warned that the CODACs didn't seem to have been given enough resources to do the job and that it would be uphill work securing more convictions for racial discrimination unless the burden of proof was shifted from plaintiff to defendant. The government seemed to have a problem co-ordinating its policy, moreover, for in acting in the area of integration policy Chevènement was trespassing on the territory of Aubry's Ministry of Labour and Solidarity, and she had previously discounted the idea of an organism open to individual complaints (*Le Monde* 28 January 1999). There was dissonance on other issues as well. Justice Minister Elisabeth Guigou had publicly favoured a CRE-type institution as early as October 1998; Aubry did set up an 'observatory' to research the incidence of discrimination (the GED – Groupe d'Etudes sur la Discrimination) but Belorgey's key proposal was never implemented, as both unions and employers flatly rejected the idea of an independent authority, while Aubry herself decided that such a body might serve as an alibi that would let other actors abandon their responsibilities (*Le Monde* 13 May 1999). Chevènement and his chief collaborator at the Ministry of the Interior, Karim Zeribi, a fellow member of the ultra-Republican MDC, rejected the authority on the ground that it would be taken as a sign of weakness on the part of the Republic, 'as if it were somehow incapable or disinclined to act against discrimination' (Hargreaves 2000, p.95). There were arguments also about changing the law, which was already tougher than in other countries, for racial discrimination could be punished by jail in France, not just by fines. It was for this reason that the unions, among others, opposed shifting the burden of proof entirely on to the defendant, which seemed to them to infringe natural justice. Instead, a compromise was reached, which allowed plaintiff and defendant each to present their case and the judge to form his own opinion on the basis of the evidence. The unions argued for and won, however, the right to take cases to court on behalf of their members, while the powers of the factory inspectorate were increased to allow them to investigate and issue formal warnings, as was already the case on health and safety issues. All of these changes finally reached the statute book in November 2001 (*Le Monde* 9 November 2001).

The government attempted to boost the impact of its policies by holding a rally of a thousand delegates from associations representing minorities and anti-racists in March 2000. In truth it had precious little to offer. It was on this occasion that Jospin announced that there would definitely be no independent authority while Aubry turned down proposals to open up millions of jobs in the public sector which were by tradition reserved for French citizens only. She tried to reassure those disappointed by the weak impact of the CODACs by announcing that there would soon be an anonymous telephone line on which those afraid of approaching the commissions (in which the police were active participants in some cases) could register their complaints (*Le Monde* 20 March 2000). Alas! At the end of the year an internal government report on the functioning of this system was so devastating that it was kept secret and not discovered by the press until March 2001. The setting up of the CODACs and the discrimination hotline were both condemned as 'precipitate' and inadequately publicised. Local councillors, the police and the education service were found to be insufficiently involved and the commitment of other parts of the administration was uneven. Of the 715,000 calls received from May to November 2000, only 15,000 were actually studied (this was the job of the GED), and only 4900 led to a referral to a CODAC. Although the telephone had certainly increased the number of referrals to CODACs, it could do nothing to alleviate the bottleneck which they represented. The panels which decided how complaints were to be followed up were made up entirely of civil servants, 'insufficiently critical' of their own employer, while the associations' offers of help were ignored. If the victims were contacted at all it was generally much too late and the collaboration with prosecutors' offices was too 'timid'. They too often took no action on cases referred to them. All in all, the proportion of useful calls was 4 or 5 out of every 10,000 (*Le Monde* 9 March 2001). Elisabeth Guigou, who had by now taken over as Employment Minister, tried to patch things up by meeting the secretaries of the hundred or so CODACs and organising a new round table with the associations, unions and employers (*Le Monde* 21 April 2001). Deep down, she must have known that, with the necessary legal changes due to come into effect only a few months before presidential election, the government's showpiece anti-discrimination policy was in tatters.

Tested and found wanting

If the government's 'fight against discrimination' was a failure in its own terms it nonetheless turned the media spotlight on the whole question, which SOS Racisme made use of with some vigorous campaigning. During 1998, employing yet another technique borrowed from British and American practice, the association began to mount 'testing' operations against nightclubs which had the reputation of barring entry to immigrant-origin youths. In the presence of court officials and other witnesses, using two or sometimes three different couples, white, black and Beur, they recorded refusals to allow entry to the non-white youths and immediately launched court cases against the offenders. In March 2000 an evening of co-ordinated testing of clubs all over France took place, at which court officials witnessed black or Beur youths being told that they were 'not the right style', or the 'quota of blacks' was full, or they had to be a 'regular client'. They recorded 45 flagrant breaches of the law in the 88 establishments visited. In Paris, 60 per cent of clubs were at fault, with other racist hotspots in Lille, Reims, Montpellier and Bordeaux (*Le Monde* 20 March 1999). The following December, 78 more clubs were tested on the same night in Paris and 20 other cities, netting 31 flagrant breaches of the law. A sharp drop in the proportion of offences in Paris allowed SOS to conclude that its campaign was bearing fruit, while on this occasion Clermont-Ferrand, St Etienne, Grenoble and Marseille were the worst offending cities (*Le Monde* 12 December 2000). The SOS campaign had the effect of galvanising more official actors to follow suit. The Bouches-du-Rhône CODAC successfully exposed a bar in Marseille (*Le Monde* 26 November 1999), and the Minister for Urban Affairs, Claude Bartolone, personally took part in an operation mounted by young Socialists in the Pas-de-Calais (*Le Monde* 5 June 2000). Seeking a consensual way of mediating the exclusion which for young people starkly symbolised their exclusion from the whole of society, Bartolone induced two trade associations in the field of hotels and entertainment to sign a 'National Convention against discrimination in the access to leisure' with his own ministry and the Minister for Tourism. The convention provided for a commission which would produce quarterly reports on cases brought to light especially by the (ineffectual) CODACs. But SOS refused to take part in the commission, its president believing that 'the only reason they have signed is to escape the court cases we have launched against them' (*Le Monde* 19 July 2000). At intervals during 2000 SOS was alerted by clients of a number of public housing bodies to irregularities such as the illegal recording on their personal files of their 'country of origin' or even details about their style of dress. Once again the assistance of court officials was enlisted in checking the entire files of the incriminated authorities, an operation which led the association to launch a court action against 22 authorities it suspected of deliberately parking foreign or immigrant-origin clients in the most run-down or inconvenient estates (*Le Monde* 25 September 2000). In the private sector, SOS joined other associations in securing the convictions of two landlords who openly refused to let their property to immigrant-origin French citizens in Compiègne (*Le Monde* 4 February 2000) and the Paris suburbs (*Le Monde* 7 April 2001). But a more insidious form of abuse was revealed in two smaller and more provincial locations: in Wasselonne, in Alsace, and Haumont in the Sambre, estate agents habitually refused to sell properties to immigrant-origin families, explaining that the local mayor did not want them to settle in the town centre and that he would exercise the council's right to compulsory purchase in order to prevent it. In the latter case the League of the Rights of Man established a dossier of 14 separate occasions when the mayor and RPR Senator, Jospeh Osterman, had abused purchase orders 'for the good of the commune' (*Le Monde* 4 August 2000, 9 January 2001). The largest proportion of discrimination cases dealt with by the associations, however, concerned hiring policies. Their informants enabled them to mount a campaign against temporary employment agencies who were complicit in the racist requirements of their clients. For example, the ADECCO agency in Paris habitually used a racialised code for recording their job-seekers' appearance in which PR1 (=*bonne présentation*) corresponded to the highest level of grooming, and 'not PR4' meant 'no coloureds'. BBR (=*bleu blanc rouge*) was used if the client – usually a hotel or a directors' club or a 'big house' – insisted on whites only. Braving the taboo which kept agencies' complicity with client racism a guilty secret, more politically aware staff, some of them themselves of ethnic origin, began to make use of the telephone loudspeaker in order to catch the clients *in flagrante* before witnesses. One hotel which suddenly invented competence in English and Spanish as a condition for hiring a Martiniquais as a waiter, earned itself a visit from the factory inspectorate (*Le Monde* 6 February 2001). The adverse publicity which the associations were able to generate played a role, along with the imminent change in the law relating to the burden of proof, in forcing employers to re-examine their practice. The furniture company IKEA, convicted after one of its employees had sent an email telling branches not to recruit 'coloured' people to distribute their catalogues door to door (*Le Monde* 6, 7 February 2001), announced that it had instituted an outside 'audit' of its compliance with equality law and was setting up an anti-discrimination committee. ADECCO, much more at risk than its clients because temporary agencies are in law the direct employers of labour, subjected itself to study by a management consultant, sent a letter to all its big clients explaining that discrimination was contrary to its working methods and instituted a new training module with an explanation of the law and guidance on how to deal with racist requests for labour. VediarBis, another employment agency with 700 branches undertook similar actions, including identifying a senior staff member to whom breaches of the anti-racist code could be notified (*Le Monde* 4 September 2001). Manpower adopted a more minimal approach, involving no more than a system of internal emails reminding staff of the law. Its Bordeaux branch was prosecuted by SOS Racisme after it found that all 41 temporary staff it had sent to a local fish-processing firm were of French or European nationality (*Le Monde* 21 March 2001).

The plural left and the *sans papiers*

If the plural left's action plan against discrimination had turned out to be something of a damp squib, they disappointed the associations also in not replacing the Pasqua and Debré Laws with a big new text which would rewrite both the nationality law and the law on rights of entry and residence. Instead they reversed some of the worst abuses enacted by their predecessors, rather as the left had done on two previous occasions, in 1981 and 1988. But the world had changed a lot in two decades and the government found itself under attack from the associations on grounds far to the left of that which most of them had occupied when Mitterrand first entered the Elysée palace. The Loi Guigou concerning the acquisition of French nationality abolished the provision of Pasqua's 1993 law which had required all children born in France of foreign parents to make a declaration of their wish to become French citizens some time between their 16th and 21st birthdays. French citizenship was again to be automatic at 18, and it could be applied for at 16 by young people acting alone, or at 13 with the support of their parents. But Guigou had not restored a pre-1993 clause which allowed foreign parents who had lived in France for a minimum of five years to ask for French nationality for their children. She was therefore under attack from all those who favoured restoration of that right, or the even more sweeping principle of the '*droit du sol intégral*': anyone born on French soil is French at birth. Her critics included not only the MRAP and SOS Racisme, but also many of her Communist and Green allies, who abstained when the measure went through Parliament. The law was finally passed in March 1998. A more complex package of legislation covering entry and residence rights was sponsored by Chevènement and effective from May. Many aspects represented a clear liberal reform of the Pasqua Laws and as such were welcomed by the associations. Among those to benefit were asylum seekers, students, retired workers, welfare claimants and those wishing to bring their families to join them in France. Debré's famous *certificat d'hébergement*, which had so incensed the artistic community was replaced by a differently named certificate which could be obtained from other offices than the town hall, so obviating the possible obstruction of right-wing mayors. The obligation to inform the authorities of the departure of one's guest was abolished. A major innovation of the Chevènement law was a one-year residence permit to be made available to those with personal or family links in France, to those needing medical treatment, to scientists and artists, and to those who could prove ten years' residence in France. The foreign partner or spouse of a French citizen would be able to obtain a residence permit immediately instead of having to wait a year, on condition that he or she had not entered France illegally. This last clause was a clue to understanding the hostile reaction to the law, for Chevènement continued to make many of the benefits he was conferring conditional on the person having entered France legally in the first place. He and Jospin also refused to reform the 'double penalty' afflicting those offenders who had first to serve a prison term before being deported (*Le Monde* 5 September 1997). These were the causes of the passionate attacks launched by many associations against the new law, which they saw as reproducing the same 'logic of suspicion' as the Pasqua Laws, and against Jospin, who they said had reneged on his promise to repeal them (*Le Monde* 28 August 1997). The League of the Rights of Man, the CIMADE and the MRAP, like the CNCDH of which they were members, criticised the discriminatory nature of a measure which (like all those it was replacing) made access to visas and to the right to family reunion completely unfettered for some nationalities, but not for others. However they stopped short of proposing a completely unrestricted right to settle in France, in other words a policy of open borders, which was defended by another group of associations including the GISTI, Droits Devant!!, Act Up and one of the magistrates' unions. These groups maintained that border controls could never be completely hermetic, and their drawbacks were that they discouraged exits by those who feared that they might not be able to get back in, and, by nourishing a climate of suspicion against some foreigners, harmed the chances of integration of foreigners who were legally settled, and even of their children who were born in France. In an age of free global movement of goods and capital, why not of people too? (*Le Monde* 23 August 1997).

All these points of view were aired even before the law was debated in Parliament, as part of a series of protests over the last part of the Pasqua–Debré legacy which we will deal with here: the *sans papiers*. Soon after coming into office, on 27 June 1997, Chevènement issued a circular containing details of the criteria he would use in granting 'regularisation', effectively an amnesty and the right to stay in France to the estimated 250,000 who were illegally present on French territory. By September the associations had organised a 2000-strong demonstration of solidarity with those who were unlikely to meet the criteria (mainly single men who could not prove that they had lived in France for more than ten years, students, or those who had been refused asylum). On 2 October an appeal calling on the government to grant papers to all those illegal residents who asked for them was signed by 1300 artists and intellectuals. Chevènement set the tone for his exchanges with his critics by replying caustically that if the African politicians he dealt with could understand the difference between legal and illegal entry, then surely 'eminent French intellectuals' should be able to as well. There then began a painful and long drawn-out 'case by case' examination of 142,000 requests for regularisation, which went on until the end of 1998, by which time about 80,000 residence permits had been issued. Administratively there was little logic in Chevènement's attitude. Those illegals who were not regularised were issued with a notice telling them to quit French territory, but were not deported, just allowed to go home. Together with the estimated 100,000 or so illegals who had not come forward at all, there were therefore still nearly 200,000 people walking the streets in a state of limbo, who could be stopped at any time, asked for their papers, and deported. The problem was that no government in recent times had succeeded in deporting more than 12,000 in a single year (*Le Monde* 2 April 1998) – so why add to the numbers of those who, by the government's own logic, were vulnerable to the temptation of the black economy or other and worse illegal ways of making a living, when the whole operation was supposed to reduce them?

The political situation was hardly better for the plural left. By the autumn, small groups of those who had been refused permits, supported mostly by the extreme left, had occupied churches or other public meeting places in Orléans, Nantes, Clermont-Ferrand, and the Paris suburbs; in Créteil and Limeil-Brévannes (Val-de-Marne), Le Havre and Bordeaux they were on hunger strike; by mid-November twelve of the strikers had been hospitalised. While the bulk of the Socialist deputies remained loyal to their leaders, they were well on the way to losing contact with their activist base; at Le Havre the support committee was jointly led by a Socialist; in the Val-de-Marne a group of Communist local councillors were involved; at Bordeaux activists from SUD and Agir Ensemble contre le Chômage had joined the immigrant-support associations (*Le Monde* 25 September 1998). The ramshackle unity of the plural left did not completely break down, though it came under severe strain in mid-November when the Greens' Dominique Voynet made known her 'disagreement' with the government of which she was the Environment Minister, while the Communist Party seemed to be in complete disarray; its leader announced he was for the 'case by case' approach while the party's immigration department was for blanket regularisation (*Le Monde* 19 November 1998). As the European elections approached Green and Communist candidates called for blanket regularisation. Meeting for the nth time with Jospin's flat refusal to meet a delegation of hunger strikers, Professor Léon Schwartzenberg, a venerable pillar of the League of the Rights of Man, announced that he was going to vote for the Trotskyists of Lutte Ouvrière (*Le Monde* 20 March 1999). The rift between Chevènement and those supporting the *sans papiers* both in and outside the government must have been complete when they learned at the end of 1999 of a secret circular sent to prefects calling for a significant increase in the number of deportations in the last months of the year, encouraging them to organise (illegal) targeted identity checks in areas where foreigners were known to congregate and instructing them to set up a fingerprint register of those who had asked for a residence permit (*Le Monde* 2 November 1999). Jospin and his Interior Minister eventually toughed it out long enough to see a decline in the number of those willing to take part in full-scale demonstrations in favour of blanket regularisation. In November 1998 only 3000 marched in Paris and 6000 in the whole of France.

And what in the end, after so much argument and suffering, was the nature of the prize won by the lucky ones, the 80,000 who *had* been granted the right to remain on French territory? They had not been issued with the ten-year permit which was the fruit of Mitterrand's reform of 1981–82, but with a one-year permit which had to be renewed every year for five years, after which it would be upgraded to the ten years. By the end of 1999, when many of the newly issued permits were due for their first renewal, shocking details emerged of the scarcely improved conditions of existence of their holders. Many, believing that their new status would allow them to escape from undeclared employment, found themselves sacked as soon as they asked for a contract or official pay slips. They were now worse off than before, since they could not renew their permit if unemployed or with no evidence of employment. Others were given false pay slips showing that they had worked 169 hours for the legal minimum, when in fact they habitually worked up to 250 or 280 hours a month. With a one-year permit there was no hope of getting a bank loan or an overdraft or a three-year tenancy on a flat, and no right to the Revenu Minimum d'Insertion, the social security safety net. And to obtain *this*, people had been willing to starve themselves to death? To prevent people having *this*, ministers had been willing to sacrifice political support and see themselves portrayed as heartless tyrants? Of course, the prefectures behaved with their customary indolence and insolence in dealing with the renewals. Once their first permit had expired, people frequently found themselves holding no more than a receipt for their renewal application, or an invitation to an interview in two or three months' time, and these documents were not accepted as valid by the social services. In these circumstances a score or more associations found themselves once again inundated by a new wave of clients in distress (*Le Monde* 7 April 2000). The lucky ones.

9
The Collapse of Official Politics

In 2002 Jean-Marie Le Pen, leader of a party that was all but extinct in 1999, made headlines all round the world by apparently coming back from the dead to eliminate Lionel Jospin, the outgoing Prime Minister, from the presidential election before contesting the second round with Jacques Chirac, the President of the Republic. The role of this chapter is to ask what it was that was so bad about all the other parties that enabled the National Front not only to pull off this exploit, but indeed to have remained such a durable part of the political landscape throughout the 1990s, seeing its vote fall only when it suffered a disastrous internal conflict. There were a number of factors which seem to justify us speaking of the 'collapse of official politics'. One was the blurring of the left–right divide, which itself could be broken into two aspects: firstly, adherence to the neo-liberal consensus was such that it was increasingly difficult for the elector to see any clear blue water between the main left and right groupings, especially on redistributive issues (which we dealt with in Chapter 7) but also on issues like European union; secondly, the more the major parties were equally and flagrantly seen up to their necks in corruption, the more the voters condemned indiscriminately all politics as the enterprise of lining one's own pockets. But in another sense the collapse of politics was all too concrete as steadily rising levels of abstention in important elections provided clear evidence of popular disaffection with parties and institutions alike. One of the effects of widespread abstention was to produce results which did not seem fairly to represent the spread of opinion in the electorate by giving landslide victories to parties winning elections on a declining share of the vote. This crisis of representation soon extended to the institutions of the Fifth Republic itself, initially as the phenomenon of cohabitation between a president and a prime minister of opposing tendencies seemed to deprive elections of their function of choosing between alternatives, and later, when the role of the presidency itself, now a much weaker institution than when it was established in 1958, began to be questioned, giving rise to calls for a new constitution.

The crisis of the left

In the first half of the 1990s, the crisis of the left was illustrated by the dramatic collapse of the vote for its main component, the Socialist Party, in a context of rising corruption and internal conflict. After the record sums of money spent in the 1988 presidential election, Parliament had passed limiting legislation in 1988 and 1990. At the same time it amnestied those who had previously extorted money from firms who bid for municipal contracts, submitting bills for non-existent services 'provided' by 'consultants' who were in fact no more than party fundraisers. The first time it was applied, the amnesty law served to free from jail Christian Nucci, the pre-1986 Minister of Overseas Development, who had diverted part of his department's budget into the party's accounts, enriching himself in the process (Chalier 1991). In October 1990 a former fraud squad inspector published a book recounting in minute detail the system of extortion operated by the Socialists in the south of France and for good measure accusing the Ministry of Justice of doing its utmost to prevent the truth coming out by removing him and an investigating judge from delicate cases (Gaudino 1990). By the end of the year, the UDF actually took a decision to stop attacking the Socialists on corruption issues, realising that the most likely beneficiaries from the resulting generalised discredit of politics were Jean-Marie Le Pen and the National Front. But they did not speak for the press, which interpreted the amnesty legislation as prime evidence of cronyism, and for several years corruption stories were rarely out of the headlines.

Mitterrand tried to counter-attack after Edith Cresson had led the Socialists to a historic defeat in the 1992 regional elections, by replacing her with the man who appeared to be the Socialists' last card, the unassuming Pierre Bérégovoy, son of Ukrainian immigrants, a life-long Socialist militant who had worked his way up through the national gas utility to be a long-serving and orthodox Finance Minister in the 1980s. Although the new Prime Minister tried to live up to his reputation as a 'Mr Clean' by immediately announcing the creation of a parliamentary committee of enquiry into party financing, the choice of Bernard Tapie as Minister for Urban Affairs seemed an odd one. A 'self-made' millionaire from a humble background, Tapie specialised in buying up ailing companies, closing down the unprofitable parts, sacking a proportion of the workforce and selling on what was left. Tapie's need of friends in high places to grease his business deals made him a natural ally of the Mitterrand clique, for whom he served as a handy token of popular credentials. For all his faults, Tapie was the one figure of national standing prepared to adopt an openly hostile attitude to Le Pen and his supporters, producing a number of bruising encounters between the two men. Yet nothing symbolised the bankruptcy of the Socialists' commitment to anti-racism more than the increasingly prominent role afforded to Tapie, whose reign as minister lasted no more than 50 days before he was forced to take an ignominious sabbatical to answer corruption charges. His political career finally hit the buffers in 1997 when he was convicted in five separate court cases and sentenced to a total of more than nine years in prison (*Le Monde* 5 July 1997). But Tapie was not the only skeleton in the PS cupboard. In September 1992 Henri Emmanuelli, a vice-secretary and a former party treasurer, was charged with extortion in the matter of party fundraising. Next it was the turn of the new party secretary, Laurent Fabius. During his premiership in 1984–86 he had delayed the registration of an American company's system for detecting the AIDS virus in donated blood. When hundreds of haemophiliacs in France were later infected with the disease and it was revealed that Fabius' decision had been partly motivated by the desire to protect the commercial position of the Pasteur Institute, which was developing a rival screening process, he and his former Health Ministers were not unnaturally the target of an emotional campaign which accused them of having knowingly circulated contaminated blood (Bettati 1993) and dragged on for the rest of the decade (Wolfreys 2000b). As if all this were not bad enough, the spotlight next fell on Bérégovoy, the man who was supposed to clear up the mess. It was discovered that he had bought a flat in Paris using an interest-free loan of 1 million francs supplied by Mitterrand's close friend, Roger-Patrice Pelat, who later died of a heart attack while under investigation for having allegedly made a vast profit from inside knowledge about the price of shares in the privatisation of the aluminium multinational, Péchiney. Bérégovoy floundered helplessly, failing to clear his name. On May 1st 1993, shortly after the election had deprived the Socialists of four-fifths of their deputies, reducing the combined left-wing vote to the lowest recorded under the Fifth Republic, Bérégovoy took a revolver from his chauffeur's glove compartment, walked along a deserted canal and shot himself, his suicide a powerful symbol of the extinction of the ideals which had shone so brightly in 1981.

Europe: blurring the divide between right and left

The main event of Bérégovoy's premiership had been the debate on ratification of the Maastricht Treaty on European Union, which illustrated the blurring of the distinction between left- and right-wing alliances. On the left, the Socialists campaigned in favour, as befitted the party of government condemned to the permanent search for consensus with its European partners. The Communists were against, sticking to their line that the Europe of the single market was a ploy to force down wages for the sake of more efficient production and sharper competition, while small farmers and small businesses were driven to the wall. The Greens split in two, with one faction broadly endorsing the Communists' interpretation, and the other favouring the treaty. On the right, an anti-Maastricht campaign was led from within RPR ranks by Philippe Séguin and Charles Pasqua on the grounds of preserving French sovereignty, while other party leaders favoured abstention; but the Chirac–Juppé leadership endorsed the treaty for the same reasons as the Socialists and for the sake of coalition unity with the pro-European UDF, while allowing the Gaullist deputies a free vote. The National Front therefore found itself campaigning against ratification alongside not only the Communists and the RPR dissidents, but also the right-wing catholic UDF deputy Philippe de Villiers. The Front's campaign against the 'mondialist plot' represented by Maastricht was overshadowed, in particular by Séguin, who was granted an auspicious televised debate with Mitterrand, forced to intervene at the eleventh hour as polls began to contradict earlier predictions of an easy victory for the pro-Maastricht camp. The marginalisation of the Front prompted various commentators to claim that with its room for manoeuvre hampered by rivals (*Le Monde* 25 August 1992), it was experiencing an 'identity crisis' (*L'Express* 13 August 1992). As the rather low-key campaign came to end, however, it became clear that a significant number of voters were going to use the referendum as a chance to thumb their noses, not just at the President, but at the entire political elite. When the 'Yes' camp achieved a narrow victory by 51.1 per cent to 48.9 per cent, it was the Front, rather than the dissident leaders of the established parties, who took comfort from the fact that nearly half the electorate had chosen to ally themselves with an anti-system vote.

Searching for the left electorate

The sequence which went through the 1992 regional elections, the 1993 parliamentaries and the 1994 Europeans well illustrated the collapse of the Socialist Party's electoral credibility. In the 1992 vote which finished Cresson's career, their 18.2 per cent share of the vote was the party's lowest score since its formation in 1971. Evidence that only 58 per cent of Socialist sympathisers had actually voted for the party, against 76 per cent in 1984, when its score had slumped almost as badly to 20.8 per cent, indicated that many of their own supporters had deliberately switched to one of the two available ecologist lists as a protest (Jaffré 1992), bumping the combined Green vote up to 14.7 per cent. In the parliamentary contest the following year, the Socialists plumbed even lower depths; at 17.2 per cent their first-round vote was half what it had been in 1981 and 1988, one commentator calling this the biggest electoral collapse of the Fifth Republic (Hanley 1993). After a vote like this and with the disappearance of Bérégovoy, the stage was set for a leadership battle. Rocard ousted Fabius as party secretary and took first place on the party's list for the 1994 Europeans, only to find that his party's candidates were rivalled by Bernard Tapie's 'Energie Radicale' list, openly favoured by Mitterrand. The results illustrated the potential for this type of 'risk-free' election, run under proportional rules and with little apparently at stake to contribute to the splintering of parties and electorates, with the mainstream reduced to a similar electoral status as challengers like the National Front, which won 10.51 per cent. Tapie won 12.03 per cent, reducing the Socialists to a lamentable 14.5 per cent and wiping out the presidential ambitions of Michel Rocard, who immediately resigned his party post and was replaced by Henri Emmanuelli. With Bérégovoy dead, Mitterrand frail and ill, seemingly more concerned with preparing his retirement by publicly settling private issues which were troubling his conscience than with the fortunes of the movement he had once led, Cresson and Rocard rejected at the polls, and Fabius and Emmanuelli both facing court cases, the Socialist crisis was such that they were hard put to find a credible figure for the 1995 presidential election, let alone one able to defeat a conservative opponent. When the outgoing president of the European commission, Jacques Delors, finally decided not to stand, the Socialists adopted Lionel Jospin as their candidate in March 1995 shortly before the poll. Ironically, he went on to top the poll in the first round (perhaps helped by a period of illness which had kept him out of the bloodletting and the public eye) before losing to Chirac on the second.

The results of the other left parties during these years evinced a degree of volatility which showed that there was yet to emerge any viable electoral alternative to a social democratic type party committed to managing capitalism. The Communists were in historic decline, virtually alone of west European Communist parties in not changing their name since the collapse of the iron curtain, though this was not for want of trying by various dissidents who had tended to split off in separate waves instead of uniting to reform the party. In three parliamentary elections from 1988 to 1997 their vote hovered between 9 per cent and 11 per cent but this deceptively overstated the consistency of their support, for the Socialists increasingly adopted the practice of not standing a candidate against sitting Communist deputies in order to help the Communists maintain a parliamentary group of 20 deputies, source of important material benefits. A more accurate measure was Communist support in proportional elections such as the Europeans (6.7 per cent in 1999) or the first round of the presidential elections, which slipped from 15 per cent in 1981 to between 6 per cent and 7 per cent in 1988 and 1995 before crashing to 3.4 per cent in 2002. The party leader's failure to pass the 5 per cent barrier in 2002 had potentially catastrophic financial consequences for the party, disqualifying it from reimbursement of its campaign expenses. It was customary for a while for political commentators to remark that the decline of the Communists was compensated by the rise of the Greens. It is true that during the 1990s this party anchored itself firmly on the left, championing causes such as a shorter working week, solidarity with immigrant workers and scepticism about the neo-liberal direction of the European Union. But after their breakthrough vote of 10.7 per cent in the 1989 European elections their expected challenge did not materialise, their vote slumping to just over 3 per cent in both the 1995 presidential and the 1997 parliamentary elections. Led by the charismatic Dany Cohn-Bendit, they registered 9.71 per cent in the 1999 Europeans before falling back to 5.3 per cent in the 2002 presidentials.

The motley forces of Socialists, Communists and Greens were joined by two others in the electoral pact they signed in 1997 before the surprising victory which left them in charge of the government between 1997 and 2002. These were the Radical Party, so small it is not worth dwelling on, and the so-called Citizens' Movement (Mouvement des Citoyens), founded and dominated by Jean-Pierre Chevènement, which defined its place on the political chessboard by its defence of 'republican' nationalist values which made it oppose closer European union, pursue the fight against crime by strengthening the police and fight to the last breath against any semblance of home rule for Corsica. But any hopes of a departure from the neo-liberal orthodoxy proved short-lived. Within days of taking office Jospin had signed up to the Amsterdam stability pact which he had only weeks earlier denounced as a 'super-Maastricht' (*Le Monde* 21 May 1999). A few weeks later, when Renault confirmed that it was to close the Vilvorde car plant in Belgium, the government, a major shareholder in the company, went back on Jospin's earlier promises to make sackings harder for employers (*Le Monde* 26 June 1996, 15 September 1999). Later, when Michelin threatened similar action, his response appeared to confirm the Socialists' impotence before market forces: 'I do not think', he told a television audience, 'our role is to administer the economy' (*Le Monde* 15 September 1999). State intervention was at the heart of government policy when it came to law and order, however. A high-profile conference was organised in October 1997 where Jean-Pierre Chevènement led an attempt to convince the electorate that 'security' was a left-wing concept (*Le Monde* 28 October 1997). So strenuously did the government insist that law and order was its priority that it ended up as the electorate's priority too. Jospin's problem, as he was to find out to his cost, was that on this question, as with immigration, voters tended to reject those who copied Le Pen's ideas in favour of the original. Job insecurity, meanwhile, continued to grow during the plural left's five-year term, despite a fall in unemployment. This was partly because the number of contracts issued on a short-term basis continued to rise, but also because the government's flagship reform, the 35-hour week, had allowed employers to impose flexibility in the workplace. By the end of the 1990s almost a third of all workers felt that their jobs were in danger (Filoche 1999, p.127).

As for the Greens and the Communists, despite intermittent protestations about their commitment to meeting the needs of the social movement (Wolfreys 1999) neither maintained a convincing stance on the issue. The PCF, visibly in disarray, allowed its Transport Minister Jean-Claude Gayssot to oversee the freeing up of shares in Air France to private capital, an important element in Jospin's achievement of carrying out more privatisations than all his right-wing predecessors put together. The attitude of the Greens was no more consistent, the former student radical Daniel Cohn-Bendit summing up the plural left's loss of patience with the relentless protests against the lack of government reform in an interview given after fronting the Greens 1999 European election slate: '[I]n France, there's something that complicates everything; it's the legacy of the strikes of 1995. It's time to go beyond all that' (*Libération* 17 June 1999).

In practice the plural left functioned as a cartel more than an alliance committed to a common programme: they helped each other get into power and then gave the impression of squabbling about what to do with it. The Greens were permanently at loggerheads with Chevènement over the *sans papiers*; Chevènement criticised the Communists for refusing to join him in a 'republican pole' against the Europe of Maastricht, and the Communists criticised the Socialists for not preventing factory closures. The antics of the Communist leader Robert Hue in particular put many onlookers in two minds. Putting together a list of candidates for the 1999 European elections in which a clutch of non-Communist media personalities alternated with party members, was bad enough. Inviting Mitterrand crony Pierre Bergé and the owner of the chic intellectuals' café, the Flore, to its launch was worse. But when he organised a fashion show in the party's headquarters, those who remembered the significance of its location at Place du Colonel Fabien didn't know whether to laugh or cry. Real life soon showed that the tactics were not clever. The electoral territory deserted by the Communists was occupied by two parties of the extreme left, Lutte Ouvrière and the Ligue Communiste Révolutionnaire, whose joint slate polled 5.18 per cent to Hue's 6.7 per cent, reducing the Communists, the would-be party of government, to the same status as the Trotskyists it had always contemptuously dismissed as an irrelevance (Amar and Chemin 2002). It was a result which tellingly prefigured the fate of the plural left in 2002 when each of its constituent parts insisted on presenting its own presidential candidate. Beyond the fact that Chevènement and the Radical candidate between them took enough votes from Jospin to make him slip behind Le Pen on the first round, the mainstream left camp as a whole suffered a loss of 1.5 million votes in comparison with its 1995 performance. Meanwhile the Trotskyists advanced by 1,358,000. Despite Jospin's humiliating defeat, the number of voters who chose a left or extreme left candidate had declined only marginally. The 2002 result seen against the background of electoral volatility in the left camp during the previous decade painted a picture of unhappy voters in search of a secure home. Official left politics was clearly not working. That must be a source of alarm to anyone regarding the rising tide of National Front votes as a temporary aberration which in 'normal' times could subside and flow back to the mainstream.

The crisis of the right

Although the mainstream right scored a stunning parliamentary victory in 1993 they were not in very much better shape than the left. Their winning share of the vote was less than their losing score of 1981, and they had still not resolved the two or three major strategic problems which had dogged them throughout the 1980s: the historic rivalry between the Gaullists and Giscardians, the fact that the Gaullist leadership is in a minority in its own party on the key issue of European integration, and how to stop the National Front eating into their votes. They compounded these strategic problems by indulging in a display of personal bickering, rivalry and betrayal which added to the general discredit of politics, playing into Le Pen's hands. The end result of all this was the collapse of the centre-right, the fragmentation of the UDF coalition marking the demise of that part of the right most hostile to the NF, and the degeneration of the Gaullist RPR into an empty shell in which various notables contended for the leadership.

Jacques Chirac, lame duck

Jacques Chirac's personal contribution to the collapse of official politics was great. Confronted by the betrayal of Edouard Balladur, who decided to use his office as Prime Minister as a springboard from which he ran for president on a liberal economic programme, Chirac, himself the arch liberal of 1988, defeated Balladur and then Jospin on a promise to heal France's 'social fracture'. Yet the mandate given Chirac in 1995, like that given Balladur's government in 1993, was far from enthusiastic. In a first round which saw the mainstream parties rivalled by an unprecedented array of minor candidates, one of whom, the Trotskyist Arlette Laguiller, won over 1.5 million votes, Chirac was elected President with the lowest first-round score of any victorious candidate in the Fifth Republic. Within months, his betrayal of his redistributory campaign promises and stubbornness in supporting Juppé's attempted reforms provoked the strike movement we described in Chapter 7. In the spring of 1997, with five years of his mandate left, Chirac dissolved Parliament, gambling on a snap election which was supposed to catch the opposition off guard but which instead brought to power Jospin's plural left coalition. Having devoted his political life to achieving high office he was forced to retreat to the role of receiving foreign delegations and signing the legislation prepared by his Socialist opponents. He became the first president of the Fifth Republic to spend not the twilight of his mandate but a full parliamentary term as a lame duck.

During the last years of the twentieth century it was the turn of conservative politicians to feel the long arm of the law taking a grip on their collars as judges extended to them the investigations into party financing which had brought the Socialists low. Balladur, during his premiership, had already lost two cabinet ministers, forced to resign when they came under investigation. Chirac did his best to prove that anything the Socialists could do in the way of corruption, he could do better. No sooner was he appointed than it emerged that Prime Minister Juppé and his family were benefiting from cheap deals on municipal apartments in Chirac's former fiefdom, the city of Paris, as was the family of the President's ally, Jean Tibéri, who had replaced him as mayor. These revelations ensured Chirac the lowest approval rating of any new president (*L'Express* 14 September 1995). The Tibéri family, meanwhile, would not go away. When an over-zealous public prosecutor had the temerity to begin an investigation into why Mme Tibéri had been paid around £20,000 by an RPR-controlled local authority for a report on a subject she knew little about the government frantically tried to track down the prosecutor's superior, on holiday at the time, so that the affair could be hushed up. But since this involved chartering a helicopter to find him in the Himalayas it had the opposite effect (*Le Monde* 9 November 1996). Concerns about corruption now extended to political interference in the justice system by politicians anxious to cover their tracks (Wolfreys 2000b). By the time the 2002 presidential election came around, Chirac had been cited in no less than six ongoing investigations, in which he himself could not be charged, thanks to a ruling by the Constitutional Council in January 1999 on the immunity conferred by the office of President of the Republic. The Council was at that time presided over by Roland Dumas, himself under investigation for pocketing millions of francs during the Elf affair, which revealed that for several decades the state-owned company had been used as a slush fund for the illegal financing of political parties. Dumas was later found to have pocketed huge sums of public money to bankroll his extravagant lifestyle and went to prison. Chirac, despite a campaign to bring him to justice led by the Socialist deputy Arnaud Montebourg, not only escaped trial but even avoided questioning. The bulk of the charges against him stemmed from the supposition that, during his tenure as Mayor of Paris, which lasted from 1977 until 1995, he used the time-honoured method of extorting money from construction firms in exchange for the offer of contracts. This and the practice of giving fictitious job titles at the Paris city hall for party workers so that their salaries were picked up by the municipality, was estimated to have brought tens of millions of pounds into RPR coffers every year (Wolfreys 2001). Other charges alleged personal enrichment and featured fantastical sums in cash alleged to have been spent by Chirac and family on their personal holidays (*Le Monde* 31 May 2002).

Europe and the right

The slow progress towards European union played a major role in fracturing the right-wing parties. One problem was the room for manoeuvre the issue gave the National Front; another was that the xenophobic tendencies of part of the Gaullist electorate and leadership resisted a seamless alliance with the Giscardian UDF on this question. In 1984 the National Front made its breakthrough when the RPR and UDF ran a joint list headed by the Euro-friendly Simone Veil. Five years later Veil fell out with her former colleagues (represented on this occasion by Giscard) and ran a dissident pro-European list, which polled badly and was indeed outvoted by the NF's list. In 1994, when the Maastricht issues of national sovereignty and the deflation required by monetary union were again debated, the mainstream partners attempted to put their house in order and again ran a joint list, headed by Dominique Baudis. They were challenged by a dissident list, 'La Majorité pour l'Autre Europe', run by the right-wing Catholic nationalist Philippe de Villiers, nominally a member of the UDF. To confuse the voters even more Charles Pasqua, at the time occupying the post of Minister of the Interior in Balladur's government, suggested publicly that he was tempted to vote for the de Villiers list. Although many commentators confidently expected that de Villiers would put the NF in difficulty, in fact Le Pen's list won 10.51 per cent of the vote and eleven seats. De Villiers had a higher share of the poll, 12.33 per cent, but was unable significantly to erode the NF vote (which was only slightly down on its 1989 and 1984 showings), eating instead into support for the RPR–UDF. Five years later, in 1999, the right was represented by no less than five lists. Of these two were the 'official' joint RRP–Démocratie Libérale list (DL was a component of the UDF in the process of breaking from the federation), led by Nicholas Sarkzoy, and a dissident pro-European UDF list led by François Bayrou. Pasqua, meanwhile, now out of office and shunned by Chirac, launched a joint anti-Brussels list with de Villiers under the abbreviation RPF, Rassemblement pour la France. The other two were the two rival National Front lists. It was lucky for the mainstream that the election had occurred so soon after the split, seriously damaging the NF's performance, for the 'official' list only narrowly beat off Bayrou's challenge, with 12.2 per cent of the vote to his 9.3 per cent, while both of them had been surpassed by the anti-Maastricht and therefore anti-government alliance of Pasqua and de Villiers, who took 13 per cent. The biggest party in France in that particular vote were the Socialists, by a street, with 22 per cent (Cathala and Prédali 2002, pp.93–102).

Personal squabbles and party rivalries: the collapse of the centre

The rivalry within the RPR between Chirac and Balladur in 1995 (which owed nothing to policy) and the failed gamble of the dissolution in 1997 both contributed to a phase of destabilisation and personal squabbling inside the RPR, which went through three leaders in four years. When party president Juppé stood down after the 1997 fiasco he was replaced by the heavyweight Philippe Séguin, who made no secret of his belief that both Chirac and Juppé were a pair of incompetents. But Séguin himself then suffered a defeat when the arch Chirac loyalist, Jean-Louis Debré, narrowly beat off his preferred candidate to become leader of the RPR parliamentary group. Séguin remained as president but resigned in a fit of pique in April 1999 after months of sniping and backbiting by Chirac's supporters. After something approaching a real political contest, Michèle Alliot-Marie was elected president in his stead, but the fact that Chirac had supported an alternative candidate, an obscure senator from the north, underlined the crisis of Gaullism, historically based on unconditional loyalty to its leader. This was further demonstrated in 2001 when Séguin and Tibéri fought each other for the mayoral nomination in the Paris municipal elections. Their rivalry allowed the Socialists to capture the city hall after 24 years of unbroken right-wing control. Chirac, as he lost control of the party, lost interest in it too, relying more and more on his kitchen cabinet centred on his daughter Claude and a retired businessman Jérôme Monod (Angeli and Mesnier 2000).

This was not the only bout of bickering which weakened the right at the end of the 1990s. The blurring of distinction between the RPR and the UDF, combined with the UDF's lack of credible presidential candidates, led some of its leaders to throw in their lot with Chirac, as Alain Madelin did in 1995, later carrying this step to a logical conclusion by withdrawing his party, Démocratie Libérale, from the UDF altogether. François Bayrou responded to this by persuading the remaining components of the UDF to fuse into a single party, which took the old confederation's name in the autumn of 1998 (Cathala and Prédali 2002, p.69). But Bayrou was undermined from within the party by his dapper and ambitious rival Philippe Douste-Blazy who, like Madelin, had by now decided to stake his political future on Chirac. The UDF had entered the three presidential elections prior to 2002 with a good chance of their candidate emerging as the principal challenger to the left. Before that, under Giscard d'Estaing, the party had held the presidency. Nothing better symbolised its demise by 2002 than the expression of delight on Bayrou's face at having achieved a 6.8 per cent share of the first-round presidential poll, a quarter of what the party had achieved before going on to lose in 1981.

Winners and losers of the NF split

Prior to the 2002 election, the one consolation for the RPR and UDF during their upheavals was that the NF appeared to be in an even worse state than them. If Le Pen thought that expelling Mégret would be like lancing a boil, the experience proved more painful than he perhaps imagined, with over half the Front's 100 or so departmental secretaries defecting to Mégret, along with a third of the organisation's political bureau and half its 1500 elected representatives, including three of its eleven MEPs.

Mégret also won the support of most of the NF's youth wing, the Front National de la Jeunesse, its entire student organisation, the Renouveau Etudiant, and some of the groups operating in its orbit, such as the notoriously violent GUD (Groupe Union Droite) and the openly fascist Jeune Résistance. Longstanding Mégret allies, like Yvan Blot and Jean-Yves Le Gallou, took with them a number of 'historic' far right figures like founder NF members Jean-François Galvaire and the *National Hebdo* journalist François Brigneau, along with the paper's editor Martin Peltier and the head of the Front's DPS security force, Bernard Courcelle. Frank Timmermans, once heralded as a leading representative of the so-called 'Le Pen generation', also decided the future now belonged to Mégret. To compound his humiliation, one of Le Pen's own daughters, Marie-Caroline, followed her husband Philippe Olivier into the Mégret camp, where they stayed until May 2000 (*Le Monde* 2 June 2000). Le Pen was left with a faithful band of old lags – Bruno Gollnisch, Jean-Claude Martinez, Martine Lehideux, Roger Holeindre, Bernard Antony and Marie-France Stirbois. None of them were particularly charismatic or innovative, while the only young face among them, Le Pen's son-in-law Samuel Maréchal, was soon to divide his time between the NF and a job in public relations (*Le Monde* 30 October 1999). The Front also had to contend with the scandal-ridden administration of Toulon, its only remaining town, where the mayor Jean-Marie Le Chevallier resigned from the party in the face of Le Pen's refusal to defend him against charges of corruption. Le Pen's own fall from grace was highlighted at the March 1999 party convention when his closing speech was accompanied by the French football team's anthem, Gloria Gaynor's camp disco hit 'I Will Survive'. Whether Le Pen intended this as an uncommon and rather bizarre exercise in self-deprecating irony or not, his subsequent plea to each of those present for a 5000-franc loan was enough to convey the image of a party in serious difficulty (*Le Point* 3 April 1999).

Not that Mégret had things any easier. His plan was simple. Figuring that when Le Pen eventually left the scene he would be the leading figure on the extreme right, Mégret played a waiting game. But his chances of building an organisation to rival the NF were dealt a severe blow by the decision of the courts to allow Le Pen to retain the party name and finances, including the 41 million francs of state aid the NF was entitled to under new laws governing the public financing of political parties, putting Mégret's Mouvement National Républicain (MNR) in severe financial difficulty. The June 1999 European elections made the situation worse since the MNR's score of 3.28 per cent meant that it missed out on the reimbursement of its campaign expenses granted to parties crossing the 5 per cent threshold, something which Le Pen's slate just managed with 5.69 per cent. Mégret was obliged to seek reinstatement in his old public service post, as was Jean-Yves Le Gallou. Their former colleague Yvan Blot returned to the Interior Ministry. Having left Le Pen for Mégret and gone back again, Blot summed up the demoralisation felt by many on the far right when he confessed in January 2000 that, 'I thought politics could bring about change in society. Now I'm sceptical' (*Le Monde* 5 January 2000). The sense that things were falling apart was reinforced by the crisis of the far right press. The long-standing far-right publication *Minute* went bankrupt. *National Hebdo*, which backed Le Pen, also suffered severe financial difficulties, as did the Catholic fundamentalist newspaper *Présent* which pleased nobody by taking a neutral stance on the split and was forced to reduce its number of pages by half (*Le Monde* 19 December 1998).

Picking up the pieces

Both the NF and the MNR remained faithful to essentially the same programme, often unveiling identical proposals on issues like law and order and taking the same position on questions like NATO's 1999 intervention in the Balkans, which each opposed. But while they each also sought to pursue the familiar strategy of legitimacy and radicalisation, they did so in different ways which betrayed contrasting readings of the political situation. Over time Le Pen's superior political instincts were to win out. The Mégret faithful retained a strident tone on immigration and often went further in publicly expressing racist sentiments than they ever had as members of the NF. In January 1999 Mégret turned up uninvited outside a school in northern France to lend his support to teachers protesting about the wearing of headscarves (*Le Monde* 11 January 1999) while Jean-François Galvaire regaled the first MNR convention by referring to the history of the 'white man' as that of the conquering 'superman' (*Le Monde* 23 March 1999). The following year the views of Pierre Vial provoked a number of resignations when Mégret refused to condemn either his references to mosques as symbols of 'ethnic colonisation' by non-European populations or his assertion that 'the true cultural revolution is the ethnic revolution' (*Le Monde* 30 May 2000). The MNR believed its stance on the immigration question would distinguish it from Pasqua and de Villiers. At the same time Mégret, who dismissed Le Pen's outbursts and 'provocations' as evidence of 'wallowing in opposition' (*Le Monde* 19 May 1999), was anxious to affirm the MNR's identification with the 'institutional principles of the Republic' (*Le Monde* 19 May

1999). The 'Republican' label attached to the movement's name was justified by the argument that in a period when 'soft ideas' were dominant, it was necessary to take such concepts from 'the enemy' and use them against it (*Le Monde* 4 October 1999).

Mégret had for some time been uneasy about Le Pen's stance on Islam, citing his willingness to offer support to fundamentalist movements in Iran as evidence of the 'talibanisation' of the NF (*Le Monde* 12 December 1998). The immigration issue was seen by the MNR as its 'nuclear heart' (Jean-Yves Le Gallou, *Le Monde* 4 October 1999), the best way of engaging with the mainstream. Le Pen used a very different approach to rebuild the Front. He recruited Charles de Gaulle, grandson of the general, from the de Villiers camp, to front the European election campaign with him, and gave Sid Hamed Yahiaoui, an Algerian Muslim, a prominent place on the NF slate. With the NF's anti-immigration credentials long established, Le Pen, aware that the prevailing mood had diminished the centrality of the debate, was now prepared to flag up the organisation's 'moderate' stance on immigration issues, even to the extent of adopting Samuel Maréchal's reference to France as a 'multi-faith' society during his son-in-law's unsuccessful attempt to modify the Front's hostile attitude to Islam (*Libération* 25 September 1999). Le Pen's attitude to the issue was in line with the conciliatory tone he adopted towards mainstream opponents like Pasqua, de Villiers and Chevènement (Le Pen 1999). Alongside this new tack Le Pen embarked on a concerted campaign to reinforce the image of the Front as a 'last resort'. The party's mission, he told *France-Inter*, was to act as the nation's 'lifebelt' when everything went wrong. 'When France's existence is threatened, its liberties, its security, perhaps she will rally to the proposals I make. It is, I think, the only time when we will mobilise the majority of French people around us' (19 March 1999). The same theme cropped up time and again. In May he told the party's central committee that he had never been under any illusion about the Front's mission. Like 'firefighters or paramedics' the NF would be called to power 'when there was nobody else around' (*Le Monde* 4 May 1999). The following year he complained to *Le Parisien* that the democratic path which he had mapped out for the extreme right had led to the Front's isolation and that his followers would 'draw their own conclusions' from this (29 April 2000). Perhaps aware that the 58 per cent abstention level recorded among NF voters in the 1999 European election (*Le Monde* 15 June 1999) reflected not just frustration with the state of the far right but wider disaffection with the political process, Le Pen thus remained true to his function, identified by Pascal Perrineau, of politicising a movement based on a rejection of politics (Perrineau 1997, p.115). This approach was apparent in Le Pen's reaction to the 11 September attacks on the World Trade Center and the subsequent 'war on terror'. Rather than use the events simply to whip up anti-Muslim sentiment Le Pen declared that the 11 September attacks had shown that 'ultra-liberalism and ultra-free exchangism, the twin ideological towers which shone down on the economic globe, can themselves also crumble' (*National Hebdo* 27 September–3 October 2001) and took a position on the intervention in Afghanistan similar to that adopted during the Gulf War, refusing to offer support to the US.

Between 1999 and 2002 the far right embarked on what Le Pen termed a period of 'convalescence' following the split. A number of indications nevertheless gave reason to believe that it was far from finished as a political force. The combined NF–MNR European score in 1999 of 8.97 per cent, although down on the NF's 1994 total of 10.52 per cent, demonstrated the far right's capacity to maintain a significant electoral base. This was further illustrated in the 2001 municipal and cantonal elections when, despite losing Toulon, it held on to all its other towns (Orange, Marignane and Vitrolles) and the NF, despite its difficulties, managed to stand more candidates (1703) than any other party. The Front now turned its attention to the state of the mainstream right. After the European elections an editorial in *National Hebdo* noted that of the 87 deputies representing France at the European Parliament, only four were from the RPR; proof that the establishment parties were 'in ruins'. The Front, having avoided becoming 'a party like the others' was now in a position to take advantage of a situation where 'everything has to be rebuilt' (*National Hebdo* 17 June 1999). On the eve of the 2002 presidential election campaign the far right was in a weaker position, both electorally and organisationally, than at any time for at least a decade. But when Chirac, his credibility shredded by public perceptions of him as a thief without principles, managed to make it past the first round only to find that Le Pen had emerged as his principal challenger, the collapse of official politics was complete.

The Fifth Republic in crisis: the 2002 elections

In the two decades leading up to 2002 the seeping away of popular support from the established parties of government had often been reflected in parliamentary elections. Voters had rejected every outgoing administration since 1978 each time they were given the chance to do so. As we have seen, the landslide majority won by the right in 1993 was achieved with a lower share of the first round vote than when it lost in 1981, while the left's victory in 1997 came with a far smaller share of the vote than when it lost in 1986. Both the 1993 and the 1997 elections resulted in a period of cohabitation between president and prime minister of opposing tendencies. This arrangement had once been held up as an example of the maturity of France's political institutions, evidence that the political cleavages of the past had given way to moderation and compromise. By the year 2000, however, cohabitation had been identified as a nuisance, preventing effective government and dissolving the left–right divide. One of the benefits of the proposal to reduce the president's time in power from seven to five years, then, was that it would make cohabitation less likely by synchronising the presidential and parliamentary terms of office. But although the proposal was approved by a referendum in September 2000, the unprecedented abstention rate of 69.3 per cent did little to produce the hoped-for boost to the credibility of the presidency.

This was brought home by the presidential election itself, when Chirac won the fewest votes of any outgoing president, and achieved a lower first-round score than any candidate who had ever gone on to lose the second round. When his votes were added to those of Jospin, the outgoing Prime Minister, they were still outnumbered by the 11 million abstentions, which included 40 per cent of young people (http://www.2002.sofres.com/histo1997) and, as in the previous parliamentary election, proved by far the most popular choice of registered voters. Jospin, with the lowest score of any Socialist presidential candidate since the party's formation in 1971, won his highest level of support from voters in their sixties while Chirac's came from those aged over 70 (www.ipsos.fr/CanalIpsos/poll/7549.asp). More generally, France's leading mainstream parties (the Socialists, Communists, Gaullists and the UDF coalition), once able to command three-quarters of the vote on a regular basis, saw their share of the poll fall below 50 per cent.

With three-quarters of voters claiming to see no difference between the two principal candidates, the stage was set for an outsider to emerge. Much of the media speculation during the campaign focused on who the 'third man' would be. That the first round would see Chirac and Jospin at the top of the poll was presented as a foregone conclusion. So Le Pen's 16.86 per cent share of the votes cast, representing 4.8 million people, which put him through to the second round run-off with Chirac, understandably caused a sensation. But close examination of the results shows that Le Pen's feat was caused not by a dramatic swing to the far right but by a crushing defeat for the parties of the mainstream. When Mégret's 2.34 per cent (667,026 votes) were factored in the total far-right score came very close to Chirac's 5,665,855. Indeed, if the vote from the overseas territories is taken out of the equation, the combined Mégret and Le Pen total was higher than for any other candidate in metropolitan France. But Le Pen's score represented an advance of around a quarter of a million votes on his 1995 performance. And it was not on the far right that the biggest surge in support occurred, but on the far left, whose score was up by almost 1.4 million at around 3 million votes, compared to a total rise of under 1 million for the far right.

The shock of Le Pen's defeat of Jospin sparked a remarkable wave of spontaneous demonstrations, underway from the moment the results were declared, proving that if the Front was still a player, then so was the social movement. Schools, universities, workplaces, housing estates, associations and trade unions held meetings and mobilised for the protests. Thousands turned up with slogans written on anything they could find – bits of cardboard, pieces of carpet, old sheets and scraps of paper: 'Vote for the crook not the fascist', 'I'd rather be screwed by Chirac than raped by Le Pen', 'Zero tolerance for fascists'. Students were particularly active, with entire schools marching together. On May Day 2002, 3 million demonstrated across France, with huge protests not just in Paris, Marseilles (100,000) or Lyons, where 50,000 marched in torrential rain, but also in many smaller towns – Perpignan (15,000), Caen (35,000), Rennes (20,000) and Clermont-Ferrand (20,000) – which experienced their biggest demonstrations since 1968. Far from an inward looking, defensive reaction against fascism, this was a vigorous, confident movement mixing anger, humour, solemnity and irreverence (Wolfreys 2002). The low profile maintained by the NF between the two rounds – Le Pen held only one poorly attended campaign meeting in Marseilles, no doubt partly due to continuing organisational weaknesses – further indicated that France was not on the verge of fascism.

Despite the verve of the protests, however, the candidate representing the biggest threat to democracy, Le Pen, still managed to win over 5.5 million second-round votes against the candidate who for many epitomised everything that was rotten in official Fifth Republic politics. Le Pen's first reaction to the result, having seen the entire political establishment line up to call for a vote for Chirac between the two rounds of the election, from the Communists, as he put it, to the employers' association, was to declare himself 'the only alternative to the system'. His defeat was nevertheless greeted with a degree of triumphalism, reinforced by the victory of Chirac's Union pour la Majorité Présidentielle (UMP) in the parliamentary elections that followed in June. But this election merely underlined the crisis of official politics exposed so spectacularly in April. Record abstention rates, rising to four in ten of registered voters on the second round, meant that the UMP's mandate was based on the support of less than a quarter of registered voters on the first round. The NF's score, although substantially down on the presidential result at 11.34 per cent (2.8 million votes), was roughly on a par with its 1993 performance once Mégret's quarter of a million votes were taken into account.

The events of the two weeks between the first and second rounds of the presidential election highlighted once again the stalemate arising from the changed political conditions of the 1990s. On the one hand, alongside an appalling electoral performance by all the mainstream candidates, the NF demonstrated once again its resilience and durability. On the other hand, the explosion of a vibrant and youthful anti-fascist movement and the stalled momentum of Le Pen's campaign between the rounds were reminders both of the strength of opposition to the Front and of the damage the party had sustained in recent years. But the fact that the grassroots movement subsided immediately following Chirac's re-election, along with the Front's strong showing in the subsequent parliamentary elections, underlined the grim fact that, for millions of voters, Le Pen and the National Front remained the only alternative to the discredited mainstream.

10
Where Do We Go From Here?

Shock at the electoral achievements of the National Front has been a recurrent, almost permanent feature of the reaction by mainstream commentators to its success (Wolfreys 1997). The reason for this is simple. The Front has generally been viewed by political scientists and media pundits alike as essentially an electoral organisation, with its performance at the polls seen as the principal gauge of the party's standing. One of France's most prominent political commentators, Alain Duhamel, for example, reacted to the comparatively poor vote picked up by the post-split extreme right in the 1999 European elections by declaring the Front 'if not politically dead, politically *moribund*' (*Le Figaro* 26 April 2000). By contrast Edward Declair's judgement in the study of the NF he completed just prior to the split was that, 'Ominously, the future does indeed belong to the Front National' (Declair 1999, p.224). Both views derive from the same belief that the Front's strategic aims begin and end in the electoral arena. So while Declair was right, on one level, to argue that by the late 1990s the Front had 'become the only thriving political force in French politics today' (Declair 1999, p.10), in other respects, as we saw in Chapter 7, the Front was struggling to come to term with the new context created by the emergence of the 'social movement' from 1995. The analysis we have developed, which relates doctrinal and programmatic features of the organisation to other elements, such as the party's origins and structure and the context in which it was operating, allows for an understanding of how the Front was torn apart at the very moment when it seemed about to establish its integration into mainstream politics.

Others have also attempted to place the Front in a historical perspective, relating it to the traditions of the French extreme right we encountered in Chapter 4. In France, most of those to have adopted this approach have seen the Front as the re-edition of a national populist tradition, part of the rich tapestry of a history dominated by republicanism but incorporating its polar opposite, a would-be nemesis resurfacing to threaten the Republic every so often and then, the futility of its mission confirmed, fading away again (Milza 1987; Winock 1990). The durability of the Front as it went from strength to strength in the 1990s appeared to confound this perspective, meaning that either, as Ariane Chebel d'Appollonia, a devotee of the 'national-populist' school, argued, the Front was an 'anomaly' (*Le Monde* 24 January 1999) or, more plausibly, that national-populism provided an inadequate theoretical framework within which to understand the NF. As with the studies which adopted an electoral focus, historians could see 'only two possible alternatives for the extreme right': integration into the mainstream, or a return to marginalisation (*Le Monde* 24 January 1999). The split of 1999 appeared to confirm this view, hence the widespread surprise at finding Le Pen apparently back from the dead in 2002.

Our argument, illustrated in Chapter 4, is that political traditions cannot remain static. The reactionary movements which emerged at the time of the Dreyfus Affair did not simply resurface in the same form after World War I; those who wanted to overthrow the Republic had to adapt to their environment if they were to shape events, while those like Maurras who refused to change found their slogans appearing increasingly anachronistic and their movements condemned to terminal decline. Le Pen's movement is not simply a replica of inter-war fascism, any more than it is a passing phenomenon. As we have shown in some detail, the NF is the product of a deliberate attempt to revive fascism precisely by adapting it to a post-Vichy, post-Holocaust world. The first step taken on the road to renewal was to ditch any public reference to Vichy, Hitler, Mussolini or anything else that might invite association with fascism; the second step was to cultivate an image of respectability by embracing legal forms of struggle; and the third, as we saw in Chapter 5, was to find a new way of expressing old racist ideas.

This book has focused on four key elements of the organisation which eventually emerged from this process: its origins, strategy, doctrine and party structures. In itself, the dominant role played by people such as François Duprat and Victor Barthelémy during the period of the Front's gestation, birth and incubation is not sufficient proof of the party's fascist character, although we believe that the presence over the years of so many individuals in the Front's ranks who identify with the Nazis, some intellectually, others to the extent that they were prepared to die defending Hitler's bunker, is hardly a coincidence. Our analysis of the NF doctrine in Chapter 5 shows that its core ideas – anti-egalitarianism, elitism, racial hierarchy, natural selection, the domination of the individual by the 'community of destiny' – are fundamentally the same as the ideas which inspired the Nazis' attempt to wipe out various classes of people and make war on their neighbours. This can hardly be overlooked on the grounds that the Front has also at times pragmatically adopted certain themes, such as economic liberalism, previously untypical of the extreme right.

Even a group of faithful acolytes keeping the ideas alive does not amount, however, to a fascist *party*. What distinguishes the Front from those members of the 'new' right who choose to confine their activities to the cultural sphere, or for that matter, from a Nazi sect whose main ambition is to firebomb immigrant or anti-racist premises, is its use of mainstream politics as a platform from which it can make itself known to potential sympathisers and create a climate of opinion favourable to some of its objectives. During the 1990s the Front moved into a third dimension of practical politics, taking power in local government.

We have also shown that the Front leaders have a particular idea of what kind of party should be the vehicle for this political struggle. They are not interested in simply trying to develop a popular electoral clientèle with demagogic slogans, like Boulanger. If winning votes were the Front's principal aim, as it is for conventional parties, then belittling the Holocaust, indulging in anti-semitic diatribes and even opposing the Gulf War would be gross mistakes. But the Front has never balked at alienating its more timorous supporters or opportunist 'notables' seeking to build their careers, by forcing them to choose whether they want to remain in a party which believes in Jewish conspiracies and racial inequality. It wants to build a movement on its own terms and with its own ideas of how to win power. The Front leaders understand that this requires constant training and education, ensuring that the strategy laid down by Ordre Nouveau, of reaching broad layers of the population and 'transforming them in our image', has been followed with remarkable success. As former politbureau member Roland Gaucher has written, winning influence requires an 'extremely hierarchical structure ... and an iron will to maintain the line' (*National Hebdo* 4–10 February 1993). Given the NF leadership's apocalyptic vision of how it may achieve power, expressed through Le Pen's emphasis on the Front's role as a 'last resort' and his exhortations to the party youth to 'prepare for revolution', the organisation's efforts to construct a network of affiliated structures should be seen not just as part of an attempt to extend its influence, but as part of an extra-parliamentary strategy, which it will attempt to activate when it decides that circumstances are sufficiently in its favour.

When all the features of the Front outlined in this book are taken together, the picture that emerges is of a modern fascist party. The National Front's political project is not just a shopping list of gut prejudices aimed at Arabs, Jews, gays or women who want a life outside the home, but a complete plan to remake society by any means at its disposal, which include, but are not restricted to, legal methods. To reduce, as Simmons does (1996, pp.265–6), the Front's project to the use of 'democratic means', in order to 'isolate and marginalise immigrants and Jews', is to see only half the picture. How could this characterisation of the Front's activities distinguish them from those of Pasqua, Debré or the Socialist Philippe Marchand, who have deliberately used their powers as interior ministers to demonstrate their toughness against immigrants? Or from those of Jacques Chirac, who sought to use his powers as Mayor of Paris to exclude immigrants from the city's income-support programme? How could it explain why one of the Front's regional councillors and three members of its security squad were convicted of impersonating policemen during the anti-Front demonstration in Strasbourg? (*Le Monde* 3 April 1997). Those who have written that the Front should not be regarded as fascist because it claims to favour the 'flowering of the individual' (Milza 1987, p.435) have to explain how this is compatible with the sacking of a cinema manager in Vitrolles on the grounds of 'promoting homosexuality' simply for organising a debate on the subject!

It is certainly true that, during the decade which followed the Front's initial electoral breakthrough, its relentless attacks on France's immigrant-origin population had a direct and deleterious effect both on public policy and on the atmosphere in which immigrant-origin children have to grow up. Certainly, for the first time since World War II, anti-semitism was openly displayed in the mass media; Le Pen, aside from numerous insinuations about a Jewish 'conspiracy', has publicly (in a television debate) baited a minister of the Republic for being a Jew, as we recounted in Chapter 3. In the southern towns gained by the Front since 1995, the four administrations targeted from the outset local immigrant populations and stopped school canteens serving kosher food. But they also set out to suppress the independence of all those engaged in cultural activities and to root out opposition. In Vitrolles it was claimed that a 'hit-list' of those to be sacked had been prepared before the Mégrets took office (*Nouvel Observateur* 31 July 1997); in Orange a systematic purge of the municipal libraries removed a range of material, including works on racism and rap, and even detective novels and a book on Montaigne written by authors who had previously taken up anti-Front positions (*Le Monde* 12 July 1996), all at a time when the Front was keen to stress its conventional 'managerial' qualities. Here, as on so many other occasions, the NF has exceeded the worst expectations of many observers. The Front will proclaim its fidelity to democratic rules for as long as the people it is addressing identify with them, but its ultimate purpose is to impose a totalitarian model of society, in which critical thought is suppressed and individuals' emotional and spiritual needs are satisfied by an enveloping, homogeneous 'culture', defined by a self-selecting elite and imposed by state power. As long as it is allowed to do so, the Front will use freedom of speech and freedom of the press in pursuit of its goal, which is the extinction of such freedoms.

Confronting the fascist revival

What strategy and tactics should be used to oppose the Front? During the 1980s and for much of the 1990s one influential argument held that the way to combat the NF was first to address the social causes of its emergence and expansion by improving housing and the quality of urban life and restoring job security. This emphasis on civic values and social reform was stressed in the late 1980s by SOS Racisme and in the 1990s by Pierre-André Taguieff, whose ideas had a major effect on the Manifesto against the National Front. This 'new anti-racism', argued Taguieff, would amount to an 'indirect' struggle against the National Front, seeking to combat racism not by verbally denouncing it but by relying on the traditional social mechanisms of republican integration. This led him to call for anti-racists to prioritise the fight against illegal immigration and defend the 'true' values of the nation (Taguieff 1995a, pp.226, 230). Thankfully, as we saw in Chapter 7, rather than wait for social reforms to be introduced and to take effect, activists towards the end of the 1990s not only began to take action themselves on a whole range of social questions, including the scapegoating of 'illegal' immigrants, but also took the fight to the National Front, the successive demonstrations of spring 1997 against the Debré laws and against the Front's congress in Strasbourg giving a glimpse of what a broad-based movement devoted to general anti-racist campaigning *plus* deliberate targeting of the Front might look like.

One of the central themes of our account of anti-racism in Chapter 6 was that its inconsistency has largely been due to a failure to create a movement that unites the mainstream left with immigrant-origin youth. A broad-based and vibrant movement can only be built if obstacles to unity are removed. Taguieff's entreaties to Beur youth, effectively telling them that they must exchange their 'ethno-religious' identity (Taguieff 1995, p.230) for another if they want to be part of the movement, reducing anti-racism to a club with a dress code, were typical of the narrow and pessimistic republican outlook which permeated the 'days of defeat' of the Front's rise (Tristan 1987, p.140). But just as pessimism has given way to confidence, however, another positive development of recent years has been the signs that the left's reliance on the limiting and complacent 'Republican model' is beginning to diminish, as we saw in Chapter 8, opening up the prospect that the historic long-term weaknesses of anti-racism in France may yet be overcome.

The second element of Taguieff's 'indirect' struggle stressed the necessity of an 'intellectual war' against the Front (Taguieff 1995, p.223), exposing the flaws in the party's programme in order to weaken its electoral credibility. While we would be the last to deprecate the need for intellectual struggle, we believe that this should parallel, not replace political struggle. For one thing, it is simply not true that proving by rational means the futility of the Front's formulas will automatically discredit them in the eyes of its supporters. Mobilisation behind Le Pen, like mobilisation behind Hitler, has a powerful irrational component, based on grievance (real or imagined), identity and emotion. There is little evidence that Front supporters can be swayed by rational argument. Secondly, ideas, as the Front's leadership has long been aware, do not just float in the air, or generate spontaneously, '... they are spread, they are effective only to the extent that people work for them, that men help them along' (Blot 1985, p.41). This being the case, like it or not, essential tactics in combating the power of malignant ideas are to discredit the person who is carrying those ideas, or to prevent them from being expressed. To advocate 'indirect' anti-racism is to turn the problem of the NF on its head. The NF exists because various problems in French society created the conditions for it to grow. Today, however, the tasks facing its opponents include not only tidying up the mess that allowed it to emerge, but also working out how to nullify its threat.

If it is accepted that the National Front is a fascist party which makes use of democratic institutions because it wants to destroy them and replace them with something else, then the central aim of its opponents must be systematically to exclude it from those institutions. This cannot be achieved by passing legislation to outlaw the NF, as the attempts to ban the PPF and the Croix de Feu in the 1930s and Occident in the 1960s illustrate. It can only be achieved by a wide-ranging campaign which incorporates a variety of different initiatives, including letter writing campaigns to the local press to protest at the staging of NF events; the picketing of party offices following 'outrages' committed by the organisation; the ostracising by colleagues of active National Front members in the workplace; the targeting of individual NF candidates, whether at national or local level, asking them to give an account of why they choose to stand for such a party; demonstrations, such as those organised during the spring of 1992, 1997 and 2002, involving anything from a few score to many thousands of individuals.

Protests of whatever scale which directly challenge the Front can have two important functions. Firstly, they demoralise those who sympathise with the NF by disrupting the party's activities and making the prospect of participation in them less attractive. Anne Tristan has described how the confidence of the Front's supporters in Marseilles surged when they found that they could march and hold meetings, losing their embarrassment in publicly identifying with the organisation (Tristan 1987, p.201). On another level, mobilisation against the Front provokes internal ructions, as the period leading up to the 1999 split clearly illustrates, with tensions between Le Pen and Mégret over the party's election strategy emerging in public for the first time following the impressive mobilisations which overshadowed its Strasbourg congress (*Le Monde* 21 May, 15–16 June 1997).

Naturally, those who seek to oppose the Front must also equip themselves with the arguments needed to challenge NF propaganda, and to this end debates, workshops and seminars, along with information bulletins and magazines, can form part of a campaign which needs above all to forge confidence. The example of SOS Racisme's 'Hands off my mate' badge, reportedly bought by a million people, is an example of how any act, no matter how apparently trivial, can play a part in countering the pessimism inevitably engendered by the rise of the far right.

Is the NF back from the dead?

The trajectory of the Front's development since its electoral breakthrough in the 1980s may be divided into three periods: its emergence between 1981 and 1988; its consolidation as a durable political player between 1988 and 1998; and the years covering its decline and renewal, 1999–2002. Until the mid-1990s the Front's rise was relatively uncomplicated: it won successively more votes at each election and recruited more and more members, fashioning in the process an increasingly sophisticated party apparatus. As the decade wore on this steady progression was upset. The convergence of all the mainstream parties around an orthodox neo-liberal world view, combined with their collective involvement in countless high-profile corruption scandals, increased the scope for the Front to grow at their expense. Between 1995 and 1997 the Front achieved record presidential and parliamentary votes, along with the control of four towns and its highest number of local elected representatives. But this time electoral success was not accompanied by a growth in membership and the Front found itself put on the defensive by a general change in attitudes to immigration-related issues and by a resurgent anti-racist movement. The events of 1997–99 proved that the party's dual strategy was subject to a number of problems. The emergence of grassroots opposition provoked the Front into displays of anti-democratic behaviour which frightened off potential 'respectable' recruits. The twin dilemmas of finding a way to profit from the crisis of mainstream politics and ensure organisational renewal brought the Front's leadership conflict to a head and caused the organisation to break up.

Le Pen's result in 2002 is a product of the same circumstances which accompanied the split. That a weakened Front could come second in a presidential election highlighted above all the collapse of official politics, the size of Le Pen's vote testifying to his organisation's resilience but not to the existence of a new and dramatic swing to the extreme right. If the unprecedented mobilisations between the two rounds of the election were an indication of the strength of the revived anti-racism of recent years, their abrupt end as soon as Chirac's victory was secure, and the lack of any mobilisations against the Front in the subsequent parliamentary elections, underlined the weaknesses of the movement. In the first chapter we argued that the emergence and consolidation of the Front was helped greatly by political traditions peculiar to France: the traditional weakness of the conservative mainstream and the attachment by part of the left to an ambiguous republican discourse which served as an alibi for the refusal to defend minorities. During the 1990s, while French social democracy foundered in its attempts to deal with neo-liberalism, not knowing whether to challenge it or to accept globalisation, a combative grassroots movement did emerge to confront both the neo-liberal consensus and the National Front. But the volatile nature of the movement indicates that these types of struggle, anti-racism included, may well follow a pattern previously illustrated in 1936 and 1968 by the labour movement, that of periodic outbursts of militancy which carry all before them only to subside for lack of durable organisation, allowing their opponents to return to the offensive and wipe out a large part of their gains. In the aftermath of the election the Front could still claim credibly to be the only viable opposition to a corrupt and discredited mainstream. The post-1995 social movement had not provided itself with a structured and representative political organisation that was either willing to run for election at local and national level or able to offer an alternative vision of society both to the existing state of affairs and the NF's desperate solutions. In the absence of such an alternative there was every reason to suppose that the National Front would continue to remain a major force.

Bibliography

Books and articles

Ageron, Charles-Robert (1964) *Histoire de l'Algérie Contemporaine* (Paris: PUF)

Algazy, Joseph (1984) *La tentation Néo-fasciste en France, 1944–1965* (Paris: Fayard)

Algazy, Joseph (1989) *L'Extrême Droite en France de 1965 à 1984* (Paris: L'Harmattan)

Amar, Cécile and Ariane Chemin (2002) *Jospin & Cie, histoire de la gauche plurielle 1993–2002* (Paris: Seuil)

Anderson, Malcolm (1974) *Conservative Politics in France* (London: George Allen and Unwin)

Angeli, Claude and Stéphanie Mesnier (2000) *Chirac père et fille* (Paris: Grasset)

Azéma, Jean-Pierre (1979) *De Munich à la Libération, 1938–1944* (Paris: Seuil)

Balladur, Edouard (1999) *L'avenir de la différence* (Paris: Plon)

Bardèche, Maurice (1961) *Qu'est-ce que le Fascisme?* (Paris: Les Sept Couleurs)

Bardèche, Maurice (1979) 'Les silences de la Nouvelle Droite', *Défense de l'Occident* (December)

Barets, Paul (1996) 'Journal de grève. Notes de terrain', *Actes de la recherche en sciences sociales*, no. 115

Barthélemy, Victor (1978) *Du Communisme au Fascisme, Histoire d'un Engagement Politique* (Paris: Albin Michel)

Bartolini, Stefano (1984) 'Institutional constraints and party competition in the French party system', *West European Politics* (October)

Bell, David S. (1993) 'French Communism's final struggle', in D.S. Bell (ed.) *Western European Communists and the Collapse of Communism* (Oxford: Berg)

Bensaïd, Daniel (1998) 'Les gauches européennes au pied du mur', *Le Monde Diplomatique* (December)

Bergeron, François and Philippe Vilgier (1985) *De Le Pen à Le Pen. Une Histoire des Nationaux et Nationalistes sous la Ve République* (Bouère: Dominique Martin Morin)

Berstein, Serge (1984) 'La France des années trente allergique au fascisme. A propos d'un livre de Zeev Sternhell', *Vingtième Siècle* (April)

Bettati, Caroline (1993) *Responsables et Coupables. Une Affaire de Sang* (Paris: Seuil)

Bihr, Alain (1986) *La Farce Tranquille, Normalisation à la Française* (Paris: Spartacus)

Bihr, Alain (1992) *Pour en finir avec le Front National* (Paris: Syros)

Birenbaum, Guy (1992) *Le Front National en Politique* (Paris: Balland)

Blot, Yvan (1985) *Les Racines de la Liberté* (Paris: Albin Michel)

Blot, Yvan (1992) *Baroque et Politique* (Paris: Editions Nationales)

Bocquet, Jacques (1994) *La Scolarisation des Enfants d'Immigrés, Rapport Présenté au Conseil Economique et Social* (Paris: CES)

Bon, F. and J-P. Cheylan (1988) *La France qui Vote* (Paris: Hachette)

Bouamama, Saïd (1994) *Dix ans de Marche des Beurs, Chronique d'un Mouvement Avorté* (Paris: Epi/Desclée de Brouwer)

Boubeker, Ahmed and Nicolas Beau (1986) *Chroniques Métissées* (Paris: Alain Moreau)

Bouzid (1984) *La Marche* (Paris: Sinbad)

Bréchon, Pierre (1991) 'Le Front National en France: une montée inquiétante', *Economie et Humanisme* (April–June)

Bréchon, Pierre (1993) *La France aux Urnes: Cinquante ans d'Histoire Electorale* (Paris: La Documentation Française)

Bresson, Gilles and Jean-Michel Thénard (1989) *Les 21 Jours qui Ebranlèrent la Droite* (Paris: Grasset)

Bromberger, Merry and Serge (1959) *Les 13 Complots du 13 Mai* (Paris: Fayard)

Burrin, Philippe (1984) 'La France dans le Champ Magnétique des Fascismes', *Le Débat* (November)

Burrin, Philippe (1986) *La Dérive Fasciste, Doriot, Déat, Bergery, 1933–1945* (Paris: Seuil)

Calvès, Gwénaële (2000) 'Les Politiques françaises de lutte contre le racisme, des politiques en mutation', *French Politics Culture and Society* 18/3 (Fall)

Camus, Jean-Yves (1997) *Le Front National: histoire et analyses* (Paris: Olivier Laurens)

Camus, Jean-Yves and René Monzat (1992) *Les Droites Nationales et Radicales en France* (Lyon: Presses Universitaires de Lyon)

Castel, Robert (1999) *Les métamorphoses de la question sociale* (Paris: Gallimard)

Cathala, Jérôme and Jean-Baptiste Prédali (2002) *Nous nous sommes tant haïs* (Paris: Seuil)

Cesari, Jocelyne (1993) 'Les leaders associatifs issus de l'immigration maghrébine: intermédiaires ou clientèle?', *Horizons maghrébins*

Chagnollaud, Dominique (ed.) (1991) *Bilan Politique de la France 1991* (Paris: Hachette)

Chalier, Yves (1991) *La République Corrompue* (Paris: Laffont)

Charlot, Monica (1986) 'L'émergence du Front National', *Revue Française de Science Politique* 36/1 (February)

Chebel d'Appollonia, Ariane (1987) *L'Extrême-Droite en France: de Maurras à Le Pen* (Brussels: Editions Complexe)

Colliard, Jean Claude (1982) 'The Giscardians', in Zig Layton-Henry (ed.) *Conservative Politics in Western Europe* (London: Macmillan)

Costa-Lascoux, Jacqueline (1994) 'Les lois "Pasqua": une nouvelle politique de l'immigration?', *Regards sur l'Actualité* (March)

Courtois, Stéphane, Denis Peschanski and Adam Rayski (1989) *Le Sang de l'Etranger, les Immigrés de la MOI dans la Résistance* (Paris: Fayard)

Coutrot, Thomas and Sylvie Mabile (1993) 'Le développement des politiques salariales incitatrices', in INSEE, *La Société Française, Données Sociales* (Paris: INSEE)

Danos, Jacques and Marcel Gibelin (1986) *June '36: Class Struggle and the Popular Front in France* (London: Bookmarks)

Darmon, Michaël and Romain Rosso (1998) *L'après Le Pen. Enquête dans les coulisses du FN* (Paris: Seuil)

David, Renée (1991) 'Nouvelles cultures, nouveaux droits', *Informations Sociales* 14 (October/November)

De Benoist, Alain (1980) 'Le totalitarisme raciste', *Eléments* (February/March)

De Benoist, Alain (1986) 'Racisme: remarques autour d'une définition', in André Béjin and Julien Freund (eds) *Racismes, Antiracismes* (Paris: Méridiens Klincksieck)

De Villiers, Philippe (1994) *La Société de Connivence* (Paris: Albin Michel)

Declair, Edward G. (1999) *Politics on the Fringe. The People, Politics and Organization of the French National Front* (Durham: Duke University Press)

Delorme, Christian (1985) *Par Amour et Par Colère* (Paris: Le Centurion)

Dély, Renaud (1999) *Histoire Secrète du Front National* (Paris: Grasset)

Désir, Harlem (1985) *Touche Pas à Mon Pote* (Paris: Grasset)

Désir, Harlem (1987) *SOS Désirs* (Paris: Calmann-Lévy)

Desplanques, Guy and Michel Isnard (1993) 'La fécondité des étrangères en France diminue', in INSEE, *La Société Française, Données Sociales* (Paris: INSEE)

Do Céu Cunha, Maria (1988) *Portugais de France* (Paris: L'Harmattan)

Dray, Julien (1987) *SOS Génération* (Paris: Ramsay)

Droz, Bernard and Evelyne Lever (1982) *Histoire de la Guerre d'Algérie, 1954–1962* (Paris: Seuil)

Dubois, Jean (1996) 'Décembre 1995: un mouvement polysémique', *Projet* 245 (Spring)

Duhamel, Olivier and Jérôme Jaffré (1989) *L'Etat de l'Opinion. Clés pour 1989* (Paris: Seuil)

Dupoirier, Elisabeth and Gérard Grunberg (eds) (1986) *Mars 1986: la Drôle de Défaite de la Gauche* (Paris: PUF)

Duprat, François (1968) *Histoire des SS* (Paris: Les Sept Couleurs)

Duprat, François (1972a) *L'Ascension du MSI* (Paris: Les Sept Couleurs)

Duprat, François (1972b) *Les Mouvements d'Extrême Droite en France depuis 1944* (Paris: Albatros)

Durand, Géraud (1996) *Enquête au Coeur du Front National* (Paris: Jacques Grancher)

Duranton-Crabol, Anne-Marie (1988) *Visages de la Nouvelle Droite: Le GRECE et son Histoire* (Paris: Presses de la Fondation Nationale des Sciences Politiques)

Duranton-Crabol, Anne-Marie (1991) *L'Europe de l'Extrême Droite. De 1945 à nos Jours* (Brussels: Editions Complexe)

Echardour, Annick and Eric Maurin (1993) 'La main d'oeuvre étrangère', in INSEE, *La Société Française, Données Sociales 1993* (Paris: INSEE)

Einaudi, Jean-Luc (1991) *La Bataille de Paris, 17 Octobre 1961* (Paris: Seuil)

Elgie, Robert (1991) 'La méthode Rocard existe-t-elle?', *Modern and Contemporary France* 44 (January)

Festy, Patrick (1993) 'Les populations issues de l'immigration étrangère', *Cahiers Français* 259 (January–February)

Filoche, Gérard (1999) *Le travail jetable non. Les 35 heures oui* (Paris: Ramsay)

Franceries, Franck (1993) 'Des votes aveugles, l'exemple des électeurs FN en milieu populaire', *Politix* 22

Frémeaux, Philippe (1994) 'Le bilan économique des années Mitterrand', *Alternatives économiques*, no. 118 (June)

Front National (1978) *Droite et Démocratie Economique* (reprint, supplement to *National Hebdo*, October 1984)

Front National (1988) *Nos Valeurs* (Paris: May 1988; authors' collection)

Front National (1991) *Militer au Front* (Paris: Editions Nationales)

Front National (1992) *Hommes et Femmes du Front, Annuaire Politique du Front National* (Paris: Editions Nationales)

Front National (1993) *300 Mesures Pour la Renaissance de la France* (Paris: Editions Nationales)

Front National (1996) *Pour un Nouveau Protectionnisme* (Paris: St Cloud)

Fysh, Peter (1987) 'Government policy and the challenge of the National Front – the first twelve months', *Modern and Contemporary France* 31 (October)

Fysh, Peter (1988) 'Defeat and reconstruction: the RPR in 1988', *Modern and Contemporary France* 35 (October)

Fysh, Peter (1990) 'Gaullism and the Liberal Challenge', unpublished PhD thesis, University of London

Fysh, Peter (1991) 'Political review of the year 1990: from Carpentras to Kuwait', *Modern and Contemporary France* 46 (July)

Fysh, Peter (1993) 'Gaullism today', *Parliamentary Affairs* 46/3 (July)

Fysh, Peter and Jim Wolfreys (1992) 'Le Pen, the National Front and the Extreme Right in France', *Parliamentary Affairs* 45/3 (July)

Gallissot, René, Nadir Boumaza and Ghislaine Clément (1994) *Ces Migrants qui Font le Prolétariat* (Paris: Meridiens Klincksieck)

Garaud, Philippe (1992) 'Le kaléidoscope des candidatures et des campagnes', in Philippe Habert, Pascal Perrineau and Colette Ysmal (eds) *Le Vote Eclaté* (Paris: Presses de la FNSP)

Gaspard, Françoise (1990) *Une Petite Ville en France* (Paris: Gallimard)

Gaspard, Françoise and Farhad Khosrokhavar (1995) *Le Foulard et la République* (Paris: La Découverte)

Gaspard, Françoise and Claude Servan-Schreiber (1985) *La Fin des Immigrés* (Paris: Seuil)

Gaucher, François (1961) *Le Fascisme est-il Actuel?* (Paris: Documents et Témoignages)

Gaudino, Antoine (1990) *L'Enquête Impossible* (Paris: Albin Michel)

Geisser, Vincent (1992) 'Les élites politiques issues de l'immigration maghrébine: l'impossible médiation', *Migrations Société* 4/22–3

Gildea, Robert (1996) *France Since 1945* (Oxford: Oxford University Press)

Ginesy-Galano, M (1984) *Les Immigrés hors la Cité: le Système d'Encadrement dans les Foyers 1973–1982* (Paris: L'Harmattan)

Girardet, Raoul (1955) 'Notes sur l'esprit d'un fascisme français 1934–1939', *Revue Française de Science Politique* (July/September)

Girardet, Raoul (1983) *Le Nationalisme Français, Anthologie, 1871–1914* (Paris: Seuil)

Gonzalez-Quijano, Yves (1987) 'Les "nouvelles" générations issues de l'immigration maghrébine et la question de l'Islam', *Revue Française de Science Politique* 37/6

Green, Nancy (1985) *Les Travailleurs Immigrés Juifs à la Belle Epoque* (Paris: Fayard)

Grillo, Ralph (1991) 'Les chargeurs sont dans la rue! racism and trade unions in Lyons', in Maxim Silverman (ed.) *Race, Discourse and Power in France* (Aldershot: Avebury)

Griotteray, Alain (1984) *Les Immigrés: le Choc* (Paris: Plon)

Grunberg, Gérard, Pierre Giacometti, Florence Haegel and Béatrice Roy (1988) 'Trois candidats, trois droites, trois électorats', in *L'Election Présidentielle, Supplément aux Dossiers et Documents du Monde* (Paris: Le Monde)

Guérin, Daniel (1963) *Front Populaire, Révolution Manquée* (Paris: Maspero)

Habert, Philippe, Pascal Perrineau and Colette Ysmal (1992) (eds) *Le Vote Eclaté* (Paris: Presses de la Fondation Nationale des Sciences Politiques)

Hainsworth, Paul (ed.) (1992) *The Extreme Right in Europe and the USA* (London: Pinter)

Halimi, Serge (1983) *Sisyphe est Fatigue. Les échecs de la gauche au pouvoir* (Paris: Robert Laffont)

Hamon, Hervé and Patrick Rotman (1979) *Les porteurs de valises, la résistance française à la guerre d'Algérie* (Paris: Albin Michel)

Hamoumou, Mohand (1993) *Et Ils Sont Devenus Harkis* (Paris: Fayard)

Hanley, David (1993) 'Socialism routed ? The French legislative elections of 1993', in *Modern and Contemporary France*, New Series 1/4

Hansson, Nelly (1991) 'France: the Carpentras syndrome and beyond', *Patterns of Prejudice* 25/1

Hargreaves, Alec (1987) (ed.) *Immigration in Post-war France, a Documentary Anthology* (London: Methuen)

Hargreaves, Alec (1988) 'Le Pen's paradoxes', *Modern and Contemporary France* 35 (October)

Hargreaves, Alec (1990) 'Algerians in France: the end of the line?', *Contemporary French Civilisation* 14/2

Hargreaves, Alec (1995) *Immigration, 'Race' and Ethnicity in Contemporary France* (London: Routledge)

Hargreaves, Alec G. (2000) 'Half-Measures, Antidiscrimination policy in France', *French Politics Culture and Society* 18/3 (Fall)

Hargreaves, Alec and Timothy Stenhouse (1991) 'Islamic beliefs among youths of north African origin in France', *Modern and Contemporary France* 45 (April)

Harman, Chris (1996) 'France's hot December', *International Socialism* (Spring)

Haroun, Ali (1986*) La 7e Wilaya, la Guerre du FLN en France 1954–1962* (Paris: Seuil)

Haudry, Jean (1992) 'Préhistoire du mondialisme', in Jacques Robichez (ed.) *Le Mondialisme, Mythe et Réalité* (Paris: Editions Nationales)

Hincker, François (1997) 'French socialists: Towards post-republican values?', in Donald Sassoon (ed.) *Looking Left. European Socialism after the Cold War* (London: I.B. Tauris)

Hennion, Blandine (1993) *Le Front National, l'Argent et l'Establishment, 1972–1993* (Paris: La Découverte)

Holmes, Peter (1987) 'Broken dreams: economic policy in Mitterrand's France', in Sonia Mazey and Mike Newman (eds) *Mitterrand's France* (London: Croom Helm)

Howorth, Jolyon (1982) 'The French Communist party and "Class Alliances": intellectuals, workers and the crisis of social ideology,' in David S. Bell (ed.) *Contemporary French Political Parties* (London: Croom Helm)

Husbands, Christopher (1991a) 'The mainstream right and the politics of immigration in France: major developments in the 1980s', *Ethnic and Racial Studies* 14/2 (April)

Husbands, Christopher (1991b) 'The support for the *Front National*: analyses and findings', *Ethnic and Racial Studies* 14/3 (July)

Hutton, Patrick H. (1976) 'Popular Boulangism and the advent of mass politics in France, 1886–90', *Journal of Contemporary History* (January)

INSEE (1993) *La Société Française, Données Sociales* (Paris: INSEE)

Irvine, William D. (1991) 'Fascism in France and the strange case of the Croix de Feu', *Journal of Modern History*, no. 63 (June)

Jackson, Julian (1988) *The Popular Front in France. Defending Democracy 1934–1938* (Cambridge: Cambridge University Press)

Jaffré, Jérôme (1985) 'Les fantassins de l'extrême droite', in SOFRES, *L'Opinion Publique* (Paris: Gallimard)

Jaffré, Jérôme (1986) 'Front national: la relève protestataire', in E. Dupoirier and G. Grunberg (eds) *Mars 1986: la Drôle de Défaite de la Gauche* (Paris: PUF)

Jaffré, Jérôme (1988) 'Le Pen ou le vote exutoire', *Le Monde*, 12 April

Jaffré, Jérôme (1992) 'Les courants politiques et les élections de mars 1992', in Philippe Habert, Pascal Perrineau and Colette Ysmal (eds) *Le Vote Eclaté* (Paris: Presses de la FNSP)

Jazouli, Adil (1986) *L'Action Collective des Jeunes Maghrébins de France* (Paris: l'Harmattan)

Jazouli, Adil (1992) *Les Années Banlieues* (Paris: Seuil)

Kepel, Gilles (1991) *Les Banlieues de l'Islam, Naissance d'une Religion en France* (Paris: Seuil)

Lapeyronnie, Didier (1987) 'Assimilation, mobilisation et action collective chez les jeunes de la seconde génération de l'immigration maghrébine', *Revue Française de Sociologie* 28

Lapeyronnie, Didier (1991) 'Actions collectives', *Informations Sociales* 14 (October)

Laurent, Frédéric (1978) *L'Orchestre Noir* (Paris: Stock)

Le Bras, Hervé (1986) *Les Trois France* (Paris: Odile Jacob)

Lecomte, Patrick (1982) 'The political forces of French Conservatism', in Zig Layton-Henry (ed.), *Conservative Politics in Western Europe* (London: Macmillan)

Le Gall, Gérard (1984) 'Une élection sans enjeu, avec conséquences', *Revue Politique et Parlementaire* 910 (May–June)

Le Gallou, Jean-Yves (1984) *Les Racines du Futur* (Paris: Albatros)

Le Gallou, Jean-Yves (1985) *La Préférence Nationale: Réponse à l'Immigration* (Paris: Albin Michel)

Le Gallou, Jean-Yves (1991) 'Préserver notre identité', *Identité* 13 (June/July/August)

Le Gallou, Jean-Yves and Philippe Olivier (n.d.) *Immigration* (Paris: Editions Nationales)

Lepage, Henri (1980) *Demain le Libéralisme* (Paris: Livre de Poche)

Le Pen, Jean-Marie (1984) *Les Français d'Abord* (Paris: Carrère/Laffon)

Le Pen, Jean-Marie (1985a) *Pour la France, Programme du Front National* (Paris: Albatros)

Le Pen, Jean-Marie (1985b) *La France est de Retour* (Paris: Carrère/Laffon)

Le Pen, Jean-Marie (1996) 'Pour un protectionnisme de prospérité et d'indépendance', in Front National, *Pour un Nouveau Protectionnisme* (Paris: Editions Nationales)

Le Pen, Jean-Marie (1999) *Lettres Françaises Ouvertes* (Paris: Objectif France)

Leveau, Rémy (1994) 'Les associations ethniques en France', in Bernard Falga, Cathérine Wihtol de Wenden and Claus Leggewie (eds) *Au Miroir de l'Autre, de l'Immigration à l'Intégration en France et en Allemagne* (Paris: Cerf)

Livian, Marcel (1982) *Le Parti Socialiste et l'Immigration* (Paris: Anthropos)

Llaumett, Maria (1984) *Les Jeunes d'Origine Etrangère, de la Marginalisation à la Participation* (Paris: L'Harmattan)

Lorien, Joseph, Karl Criton and Serge Dumont (1985) *Le Système Le Pen* (Brussels: Editions EPO)

Lovecy, Jill (1991) '"Une majorité à géométrie variable". Government, Parliament and the Parties, June 1988–June 1990', *Modern and Contemporary France* 46 (July)

MacEwen, Martin (1995) *Tackling Racism in Europe* (Oxford: Berg)

Machin, Howard (1990) 'Changing patterns of party competition', in Peter Hall, Jack Hayward and Howard Machin (eds) *Developments in French Politics* (London: Macmillan)

MacMaster, Neil (1991) 'The "seuil de tolérance": the uses of a "scientific" racist concept', in Maxim Silverman (ed.) *Race, Discourse and Power in France* (Aldershot: Avebury)

McMillan, James (1992) *Twentieth Century France* (London: Edward Arnold)

Magraw, Roger (1992) *A History of the French Working-Class vol. 2 Workers and the Bourgeois Republic, 1871–1939* (Oxford: Blackwell)

Malik, Serge (1990) *Histoire Secrète de SOS Racisme* (Paris: Albin Michel)

Marcilly, Jean (1984) *Le Pen sans Bandeau* (Paris: Jacques Grancher)

Marcus, Jonathon (1995) *The National Front in French Politics, the Resistible Rise of Jean-Marie Le Pen* (Basingstoke: Macmillan)

Marie, Romain (1985) *Romain Marie sans Concession, Entretiens avec Yves Daoudal* (Bouère: Dominique Martin Morin)

Martin, Virginie (1996) *Toulon la Noire* (Paris: Denoël)

Mayer, Nonna (1987) 'De Passy à Barbès: Deux Visages du Vote Le Pen à Paris', *Revue Française de Science Politique* (December)

Mayer, Nonna (1991) 'Le Front National', in D. Chagnollaud (ed.) *Bilan Politique de la France 1991* (Paris: Hachette)

Mayer, Nonna (1993) 'Ethnocentrism and the National Front Vote in the 1988 French presidential election', paper presented at the International Conference on Racism, Ethnicity and Politics in Contemporary Europe, European Research Centre, Loughborough University, 24–26 September

Mayer, Nonna (1999) *Ces Français qui votent FN* (Paris: Flammarion)

Mayer, Nonna and Pascal Perrineau (eds) (1989) *Le Front National à Découvert* (Paris: Presses de la Fondation Nationale des Sciences Politiques)

Mayer, Nonna and Pascal Perrineau (1990) 'Pourquoi votent-ils Front National?', *Pouvoirs* 55

Mayer, Nonna and Pascal Perrineau (1993) 'La puissance et le rejet ou le lepénisme dans l'opinion', in SOFRES, *L'Etat de l'Opinion* (Paris: Seuil)

Mégret, Bruno (1990) *La Flamme, les Voies de la Renaissance* (Paris: Robert Laffont)

Mégret, Bruno (1992) 'Réflexions sur le mondialisme', in Jacques Robichez (ed.) *Le Mondialisme, Mythe et Réalité* (Paris: Editions Nationales)

Mégret, Bruno (1996) *L'Alternative Nationale. Les priorités du Front National* (Saint-Cloud: Editions Nationales)

Méliani, Abd-el-Aziz (1993) *Le Drame des Harkis* (Paris: Perrin)

Menanteau, Jean (1994) *Les Banlieues* (Paris: Le Monde-Editions)

Miller, Mark J. (1981) *Foreign Workers in Western Europe, an Emerging Political Force* (New York: Praeger)

Miller, M.J. and Martin P.L. (1982) *Administering Foreign Worker Programmes* (Toronto: Lexington Books)

Milloz, Pierre (1992) 'Un mot qui cache une réalité', in Jacques Robichez (ed.) *Le Mondialisme, Mythe et Réalité* (Paris: Editions Nationales)

Milloz, Pierre (n.d.) *Rapport Milloz: Le Coût de l'Immigration* (Paris: Editions Nationales)

Milza, Olivier (1988) *Les Français Devant l'Immigration* (Paris: Editions Complexe)

Milza, Pierre (1987) *Fascisme Français* (Paris: Flammarion)

Milza, Pierre (1992) 'Le Front National: droite extrême ... ou national-populisme?', in Jean-François Sirinelli (ed.) *Histoire des Droites en France* (Paris: Gallimard)

Monzat, René (1996) 'Un zeste de "social" sur la "préférence nationale"', *Les idées en mouvement* 37 (March)

Morris, Peter (1988) 'Raymond Barre and the presidential election', *Modern and Contemporary France* 35 (October)

Morris, Peter (1994) *French Politics Today* (Manchester: Manchester University Press)

Mouriaux, René and Françoise Subileau (1996) 'Les grèves françaises de l'automne 1995: défense des acquis ou mouvement social?', *Modern and Contemporary France* NS4(3)

Mouriaux, René and Cathérine Wihtol de Wenden (1988) 'Syndicalisme français et Islam', in R. Leveau and G. Kepel (eds) *Les Musulmans dans la Société Française* (Paris: Presses de la Fondation Nationale des Sciences Politiques)

Nadaud, Christophe (1996) 'Le vote Front National à Venissieux: les méchanismes d'un enracinement', in SOFRES, *L'Etat de l'Opinion 1996* (Paris: Seuil)

National Hebdo (1990) 'Le guide du militant', *Les Dossiers Tricolores de National Hebdo* 3 (Winter 1990–91)

Noiriel, Gérard (1984) *Longwy, Immigrés et Prolétaires 1880–1980* (Paris: PUF)

Noiriel, Gérard (1988) *Le Creuset Français* (Paris: Seuil)

Noiriel, Gérard (1990) *Workers in French Society in the 19th and 20th Centuries* (Leamington Spa: Berg) (Original Edition, 1986 Paris: Seuil, translated by Helen McPhail)

Noiriel, Gérard (1992) *Population, Immigration et Identité Nationale en France, 19e–20e siècle* (Paris: Hachette)

Nord, Philip G. (1986) *Paris Shopkeepers and the Politics of Resentment* (Princeton, New Jersey: Princeton University Press)

Pasqua, Charles (1985) *Une Ardeur Nouvelle* (Paris: Albin Michel)

Pasqua, Charles (1992) *Que Demande le Peuple* (Paris: Albin Michel)

Paxton, Robert O. (1972) *Vichy France: Old Guard and New Order 1940–1944* (London: Barrie and Jenkins)

Perrineau, Pascal (1985) 'Le Front national: un électorat autoritaire', *Revue Politique et Parlementaire* (August)

Perrineau, Pascal (1988) 'Front national: l'écho politique de l'anomie urbaine', *Esprit* (April)

Perrineau, Pascal (1989) 'Les étapes d'une implantation électorale', in Nonna Mayer and Pascal Perrineau (eds) *Le Front National à Découvert* (Paris: Presses de la Fondation Nationale des Sciences Politiques)

Perrineau, Pascal (1990) 'Le Front National d'une élection l'autre', *Regards sur l'actualité* 161 (May)

Perrineau, Pascal (1993) 'Le Front National: 1972–1992', in Michel Winock (ed.) *Histoire de l'Extrême Droite en France* (Paris: Seuil)

Perrineau, Pascal (1995a) 'La dynamique du vote Le Pen, le poids du "gaucho-Lepénisme"', in Pascal Perrineau and Colette Ysmal (eds) *Le Vote de Crise, L'Élection Présidentielle de 1995* (Paris: Presses de la Fondation Nationale de Sciences Politiques)

Perrineau, Pascal (1995b) 'L'electorat à reconquérir', in David Martin-Castelnau (ed.) *Combattre Le Front National* (Paris: Editions Vinci)

Perrineau, Pascal (1997) *Le symptôme Le Pen: radiographie des électeurs du Front National* (Paris: Fayard)

Perrineau, Pascal (1999) 'Le FN saisi par la "debauche democratique"', *Le Monde des Débats* (March)

Perrineau, Pascal and Colette Ysmal (eds) (1995) *Le Vote de Crise, L'Election Présidentielle de 1995* (Paris: Presses de la Fondation Nationale de Sciences Politiques)

Piat, Yann (1991) *Seule, Tout en Haut à Droite* (Paris: Fixot)

Plenel, Edwy and Alain Rollat (1984) *L'Effet Le Pen* (Paris: La Découverte/Le Monde)

Plenel, Edwy and Alain Rollat (1992) *La République Menacée, Dix Ans de l'Effet Le Pen* (Paris: Le Monde-Editions)

Plumyène, Jean and Raymond Lasierra (1963) *Les Fascismes Français, 1923–1963* (Paris: Seuil)

Poinsot, Marie (1993) 'Competition for political legitimacy at local and national level among young North Africans in France', *New Community* 20/1 (October)

Ponthieux, Philippe (1998) 'Le développement de l'emploi à bas salaire', *L'Etat de la France 98–99* (Paris)

Ponty, Janine (1990) *Polonais Méconnus, histoire des travailleurs immigrés en France dans l'entre-deux-guerres* (Paris: Publications de la Sorbonne)

Ponty, Janine (1995) *Les Polonais du Nord ou la Mémoire des Corons* (original edition, 1988) (Paris: Autrement)

Portelli, Hugues 'Les élections législatives de mars 1993', *Regards sur l'Actualité*, no. 190 (April)

Prost, Antoine (1992) *Education, Société et Politiques* (Paris: Seuil)

Rachedi, Nadia (1994) 'Elites of Maghreb extraction in France', in Bernard Lewis and Dominique Schnapper (eds) *Muslims in Europe* (London: Pinter)

Ranger, Jean (1989) 'Le cercle des sympathisants', in Nonna Mayev and Pascal Perrineau (eds) *Le Front National à Découvert* (Paris: Presses de la Fondation Nationale des Sciences Politiques)

Raymond, Gino (1990) 'The Party of the Masses and its Marginalisation', in Alastair Cole (ed.) *French Political Parties in Transition* (Aldershot: Dartmouth)

Raymond, Gino (ed.) (1994) *France During the Socialist Years* (Aldershot: Dartmouth)

Rémond, René (1982) *Les Droites en France* (Paris: Aubier Montaigne)

Robichez, Jacques (ed.) (1992) *Le Mondialisme. Mythe et Réalité* (Paris: Editions Nationales)

Rollat, Alain (1985) *Les Hommes de l'Extrême-droite. Le Pen, Marie, Ortiz et les Autres* (Paris: Calmann-Lévy)

Ross, George and Jane Jenson (1989) '*Quel joli consensus!* Strikes and politics in autumn 1988', *French Politics and Society* 7/1 (Winter)

Roy, Olivier (1994) 'Islam in France: Religion, ethnic community or social ghetto?', in Bernard Lewis and Dominique Schnapper (eds) *Muslims in Europe* (London: Pinter)

Rutkoff, Peter M. (1981) *Revanche and Revision. The Ligue des Patriotes and the Origins of the Radical Right in France, 1882–1900* (Athens: Athens University Press)

Schain, Martin (1985) 'Immigrants and Politics in France', in John S. Ambler (ed.) *The French Socialist Experiment* (Philadelphia: Institute for the Study of Human Issues)

Schain, Martin (1987) 'The National Front in France and the construction of political legitimacy', *West European Politics* 10/2 (April)

Schain, Martin (1993) 'Policy-making and defining ethnic minorities: the case of immigration in France', *New Community* 20/1 (October)

Schlegel, Jean-Louis (1985) 'Le Pen dans sa presse', *Projet* 191 (February)

Schor, Ralph (1985) *L'Opinion Française et les Étrangers, 1919–1939* (Paris: Publications de la Sorbonne)

Seager, F.H. (1969) *The Boulanger Affair. Political Crossroad of France, 1886–1889* (Ithaca: Cornell University Press)

Seidel, Gillian (1981) 'Le fascisme dans les textes de la nouvelle droite', *Mots* (March)

Servent, Pierre (1988) 'La "préférence nationale" et la restauration des valeurs morales', *Le Monde, Supplément aux Dossiers et Documents de Monde, l'Élection Présidentielle.*

Shields, James G. (1990) 'A new chapter in the history of the French extreme right: the National Front', in Alistair Cole (ed.) *French Political Parties in Transition* (Aldershot: Dartmouth)

Shields, James G. (1994) 'Immigration politics in Mitterrand's France', in Gino Raymond (ed.) *France During the Socialist Years* (Aldershot: Dartmouth)

Shields, James G. (1995) 'Le Pen and the progression of the far-right vote in France', *French Politics and Society* 13/2 (Spring)

Simmons, Harvey G. (1996) *The French National Front, the Extremist Challenge to Democracy* (Boulder: Westview Press)

SOFRES (1986) *Opinion Publique* (Paris: Gallimard)

Soucy, Robert (1986) *French Fascism: The First Wave, 1924–1933* (New Haven: Yale University Press)

Soucy, Robert (1995) *French Fascism: The Second Wave, 1933–1939* (New Haven: Yale University Press)

Soudais, Michel (1996) *Le Front National en Face* (Paris: Flammarion)

Sternhell, Zeev (1978) *La Droite Révolutionnaire, 1885–1914. Les Origines Françaises du Fascisme* (Paris: Seuil)

Stora, Benjamin (1992a) *Ils Venaient d'Algérie, l'Immigration Algérienne en France, 1912–1992* (Paris: Fayard)

Stora, Benjamin (1992b) *Aide-Mémoire de l'Immigration Algérienne, Chronologie Bibliographique* (Paris: CIEMI l'Harmattan)

Taguieff, Pierre-André (1984) 'La rhétorique du national-populisme', *Mots* (October)

Taguieff, Pierre-André (1986) 'La doctrine du national-populisme en France', *Etudes* 364/1 (January)

Taguieff, Pierre-André (1989a) 'La métaphysique de Jean-Marie Le Pen', in Nonna Mayer and Pascal Perrineau (eds) (1989) *Le Front National a Découvert* (Paris: Presses de la Fondation Nationale des Sciences Politiques)

Taguieff, Pierre-André (1989b) 'Un programme révolutionnaire?' in Nonna Mayer and Pascal Perrineau (eds) *Le Front National a Découvert* (Paris: Presses de la Fondation Nationale des Sciences Politiques)

Taguieff, Pierre-André (1991) 'Les métamorphoses idéologiques du racisme et la crise de l'antiracisme', in Pierre-André Taguieff (ed.) *Face au Racisme*, vol. 2 (Paris: La Découverte)

Taguieff, Pierre-André (1994) *Sur la Nouvelle Droite* (Paris: Descartes et Cie)

Taguieff, Pierre-André (1995a) 'Antilepénisme: Les erreurs à ne plus commettre', in David Martin-Castelneau (ed.) *Combattre le Front National* (Paris: Editions Vinci)

Taguieff, Pierre-André (1995b) *Les Fins de l'Anti-racisme* (Paris: Editions Michalon)

Taguieff, Pierre-André (1996) 'De l'anti-racisme médiatique au civisme républicain', *Hommes et Migrations* 1197 (April)

Thomson, David (1968) *France: Empire and Republic, 1850–1940* (New York: Walker)

Tribalat, Michèle (1991) 'Esquisse en chiffres', *Informations Sociales* 14 (October–November)

Tribalat, Michèle (1995) *Faire France: une enquête sur immigrés et leurs enfants* (Paris: La Découverte)

Tripier, Maryse (1990) *L'Immigration dans la Classe Ouvrière en France* (Paris: CIEMI l'Harmattan)

Tristan, Anne (1987) *Au Front* (Paris: Gallimard)

Vaughan, Michalina (1982) 'Nouvelle Droite: cultural power and political influence', in David S. Bell (ed.) *Contemporary Political Parties* (Croom Helm: London)

Vaughan, Michalina (1991) 'The extreme right in France: "Lepenisme", or the politics of fear', in Luciano Cheles, Ronnie Ferguson and M. Vaughan (eds) *Neofascism in Europe* (London: Longman)

Vichniac, Judith E (1991) 'French Socialists and *Droit à la Différence*, a changing dynamic', *French Politics and Society* 9/1 (Winter)

Vilgier, Philippe (1981) *La Droite en Mouvements, 1962/1981* (Paris: Vastra)

Wayland, Sarah (1993) 'Mobilising to defend nationality law in France', *New Community* 20/1 (October)

Weber, Eugen (1962) *Action Française. Royalism and Reaction in Twentieth-Century France* (Stanford, California: Stanford University Press)

Weil, Patrick (1995) *La France et ses Etrangers* (Paris: Gallimard; original edition, Calmann-Lévy 1991)

Weil, Patrick (1996) 'The lessons of the French experience for Germany and Europe', in D. Cesarani and M. Fulbrook (eds) *Citizenship, Nationality and Migration in Europe* (London: Routledge)

Wieviorka, Michel (1992) *La France Raciste* (Paris: Seuil)

Wihtol de Wenden, Cathérine (1988) *Les Immigrés et la Politique* (Paris: Presses de la Fondation Nationale des Sciences Politiques)

Wihtol de Wenden, Cathérine (1994) 'Changes in the Franco-Maghrebian association movement', in John Rex and Beatrice Drury (eds) *Ethnic Mobilisation in a Multicultural Europe* (Aldershot: Avebury)

Wilson, Stephen (1982) *Ideology and Experience. Antisemitism in France at the Time of the Dreyfus Affair* (London: Associated University Press)

Winock, Michel (1990) *Nationalisme, Antisémitisme et Fascisme en France* (Paris: Seuil)

Winock, Michel (ed.) (1993) *Histoire de l'Extrême Droite en France* (Paris: Seuil)

Wolfreys, Jim (1993) 'An iron hand in a velvet glove: the programme of the French Front National', *Parliamentary Affairs* 46/3 (July)

Wolfreys, Jim (1997) 'Neither right nor left? Towards an integrated analysis of the Front National', in Nicholas Atkin and Frank Tallet, *The Right in France 1789–1997* (London: I.B. Tauris)

Wolfreys, Jim (1999) 'Class struggles in France', *International Socialism* 84 (Autumn)

Wolfreys, Jim (2000a) 'In perspective: Pierre Bourdieu', *International Socialism* 87 (Summer)

Wolfreys, Jim (2000b) 'Controlling State Crime in France', in Jeffrey Ian Ross (ed.) *Varieties of State Crime and its Control* (New York: Criminal Justice Press)

Wolfreys, Jim (2001) 'Shoes, lies and videotape: corruption and the French state', *Modern and Contemporary France* 9/4

Wolfreys, Jim (2002) '"The centre cannot hold": fascism, the left and the crisis of French politics', *International Socialism* 95 (Summer)

Yague, Pascal (1973) 'Immigration et révolution', *Défense de l'Occident* (December)

Ysmal, Colette (1998) '*L'eclatement du système des partis politiques'*, *L'Etat de la France 98–99* (Paris: La Découverte/Syros)

Zylberstein, Jean-Claude (1993) *L'Intégration à la Française* (Paris: Union Générale d'Editions)

Interviews

Jean-Claude Bardet; editor, *Identité*; 12 May 1993
Areski Dahmani; president, *France-Plus*; 19 April 1995
Françoise Gaspard; former PS mayor of Dreux; 16 April 1996
Roland Gaucher; former editor, *National Hebdo*; 21 May 1993
Véronique Lambert; SOS Racisme; 20 April 1995
Carl Lang; former NF general secretary; 28 May 1993
Jean-Yves Le Gallou; NF politbureau; 19 May 1993, 26 May 1993
Anicet Le Pors; Conseil d'Etat; 17 April 1996
Danièle Lochack; GISTI; 10 April 1996
Bruno Mégret; NF chairman; 28 May 1993
Paul Mercieca; Mayor of Vitry; 10 April 1996
Eric Osmond; Manifeste Contre le Front National; 9 April 1996, 15 April 1996
Christian Picquet; Ras l'Front; 17 April 1996
Alain Sanders; *Présent*; 14 September 1992

All interviews were conducted in Paris.

Index